# Doctrines of Shiʿi Islam

*A Compendium of Imami Beliefs and Practices*

Ayatollah Jaʿfar Sobhani

Translated and Edited by

Reza Shah-Kazemi

BP 211.5 .S2M8

Sobhani, Ja`far, 1929-

Doctrines of Shii islam/ Ja'far Sobhani: Translated and Edited by

Reza Shah Kazemi.- Qom: Imam Sadeq Institute,2003.

240 p.

ISBN:964-357-088-6

Offset from The institue of Ismaili Studies, London

1.Doctrines - - Shiah. I . Shah - Kazemi, Reza, Translated and Edited. I I. Title.

Author: Ayatollah Ja'far Sobhani

Translated and Edited: Reza Shah-Kazemi

Title: Doctrines of Shii islam

Publisher: IRAN.Qom. Imam Sadeq Institute

Circulation: 3000

E-mail: office@imamsadeq.org

http://www.imamsadeq.org

# DOCTRINES OF SHIʿI ISLAM

This book is a result of collaboration between
The Imam Sadiq Institute, Qom
and
The Institute of Ismaili Studies, London

# Table of Contents

# The Institute of Ismaili Studies

The Institute of Ismaili Studies was established in 1977 with the object of promoting scholarship and learning on Islam, in the historical as well as contemporary contexts, and a better understanding of its relationship with other societies and faiths.

The Institute's programmes encourage a perspective which is not confined to the theological and religious heritage of Islam, but seeks to explore the relationship of religious ideas to broader dimensions of society and culture. The programmes thus encourage an interdisciplinary approach to the materials of Islamic history and thought. Particular attention is also given to issues of modernity that arise as Muslims seek to relate their heritage to the contemporary situation.

Within the Islamic tradition, the Institute's programmes seek to promote research on those areas which have, to date, received relatively little attention from scholars. These include the intellectual and literary expressions of Shiʿism in general, and Ismailism in particular.

In the context of Islamic societies, the Institute's programmes are informed by the full range and diversity of cultures in which Islam is practised today, from the Middle East, South and Central Asia and Africa to the industrialized societies of the West, thus taking into consideration the variety of contexts which shape the ideals, beliefs and practices of the faith.

These objectives are realized through concrete programmes and activities organised and implemented by various departments of the Institute. The Institute also collaborates periodically, on a programme-specific basis, with other institutions of learning in the United Kingdom and abroad.

The Institute's academic publications fall into several interrelated categories:

1. Occasional papers or essays addressing broad themes of the relationship between religion and society, with special reference to Islam.
2. Monographs exploring specific aspects of Islamic faith and culture, or the contributions of individual Muslim figures or writers.
3. Editions or translations of significant primary or secondary texts.
4. Translations of poetic or literary texts which illustrate the rich heritage of spiritual, devotional and symbolic expressions in Muslim history.
5. Works on Ismaili history and thought, and the relationship of the Ismailis to other traditions, communities and schools of thought in Islam.
6. Proceedings of conferences and seminars sponsored by the Institute.
7. Bibliographical works and catalogues which document manuscripts, printed texts and other source materials.

This book falls into category two listed above.

In facilitating these and other publications, the Institute's sole aim is to encourage original research and analysis of relevant issues. While every effort is made to ensure that the publications are of a high academic standard, there is naturally bound to be a diversity of views, ideas and interpretations. As such, the opinions expressed in these publications are to be understood as belonging to their authors alone.

philosophical discussion of the nature of being, the relationship between substance and accidents, and other technical issues; this kind of discussion is absent from the present book. But Sobhani's presentation conforms to Ṭūsī's paradigm in that, as regards 'theology in the specific sense', it discusses the five classical principles of Shiʿi theology: Divine Unity, Divine Justice, Prophecy, Imamate, and Eschatology. In addition, moving outside the framework of the traditional theological paradigm, the author offers, in the final part of the book, interesting explanations of controversial religious issues, going into concrete details pertaining to the practicalities of religious life and legal rulings in the light of contemporary exigencies.

The book is not, however, intended to be exhaustive either as a theological or a jurisprudential treatise; hence the author's repeated reference to more 'detailed' works specializing in the areas he touches upon. It is, therefore, the range of themes covered, and the means by which they are presented and substantiated, that gives this synthetic exposition a certain originality.

Throughout his presentation, the author upholds the validity of Shiʿi perspectives by rational argument on the basis, principally, of the Qur'an and the Sunna of the Prophet; and he does so in a manner that, refreshingly, steers clear of polemics. Doubtless, some of the positions upheld will be contested, but the author himself welcomes debate over differences, and pleads for an end to intra-Muslim diatribes and ill-considered anathematization by one school or group of the other. 'No Muslim school,' he writes, 'should accuse another of being *kāfir* ['unbeliever'] solely on account of differences over certain secondary religious duties.' Then, in an ecumenical affirmation of what constitutes the essential principles of Islam, implying open-minded tolerance of diversity on the plane of secondary applications, he asserts, 'the only basis upon which one can legitimately accuse someone of being a *kāfir* is if he denies one of the three fundamental principles of Islam: attestation of the oneness of God; belief in the message of the final Prophet; and belief in the Resurrection in the hereafter.' (Article 121)

Where differences of opinion on matters of secondary importance do exist, Sobhani calls for Muslims to resort to 'reasoned debate, based on scholarly research'. It ought to be said here that the author himself does precisely this whenever he touches on sensitive or contested issues, but especially in regard to that most vigorously debated issue, the question of legitimate authority after the death of the Prophet.[8] The traditional Shiʿi position is upheld by the author: that ʿAlī b. Abī Ṭālib was nominated by the Prophet as his successor, but this designation was not recognised by other leading companions of the Prophet, as a result of which ʿAlī was prevented from assuming the caliphate until after the rule of the third caliph. Sobhani presents an impressive array of logical arguments, buttressed by sayings of the Prophet that are corroborated by both Shiʿi and Sunni sources, in support of ʿAlī's right to the caliphate. But what is particularly noteworthy here is the non-polemical way in which the author marshalls his arguments: the Shiʿi point of view is articulated with precision, while avoiding the kind of gratuitous denigration of the first three caliphs that is all too often the corollary of championing the cause of ʿAlī. Veneration of ʿAlī, in other words, does not require vituperation of the other 'rightly-guided' caliphs. The whole question of the caliphate, although important on its own plane, is accorded a significance strictly proportioned to that plane: it does not encroach upon the domain of the three fundamental, universally acknowledged principles of Islam, as these have been defined by Ayatollah Sobhani, as noted above. From the author's point of view, any differences of opinion on the issue of the caliphate should be a cause of constructive debate rather than destructive polemics, giving rise to intellectual inquiry rather than mutual ostracism.

The book also has the merit of focusing attention not only upon the most fundamental elements of Shiʿi belief and practice, but also upon those aspects of Shiʿism that have been particularly misunderstood or misrepresented. The explanations offered in this area, and the clarification of the foundations on which particular concepts and practices are based, will be of value to those who are keen to build bridges between the different schools of Islam, and

# Translator's Foreword

The present work is an edited translation of the book, *Manshūr-i ʿaqāyid-i Imāmiyya* (literally, *A Charter of Imami Beliefs*) by Ayatollah Jaʿfar Sobhani, written in Persian with the intention of presenting to a non-specialist audience a concise but wide-ranging overview of the principal tenets of Twelver-Shiʿi Islam. Sobhani is a well-known and highly respected contemporary religious scholar in Iran, with a significant literary output to his credit. He is the author of two impressive on-going commentaries on the Qurʾan (a seven-volume commentary in Arabic and a fourteen-volume commentary in Persian); a major biography of the Prophet Muḥammad; one of the most comprehensive biographies ever written of the first Shiʿi Imam, ʿAlī b. Abī Ṭālib;[1] and several other works dealing with theology and jurisprudence. Here Sobhani brings together in a single volume many of the themes that are addressed in greater detail in his other works, themes which are rooted in the classical Shiʿi tradition of scholarship.

The manner in which these themes are expounded offers a useful insight into what one might call 'mainstream' religious thinking in the official religious establishment in Iran today; given the diversity of views and opinions within 'official' religious circles, however, it would probably be more circumspect to say that it is at least broadly representative of significant elements within the religious establishment. As such, it is useful not only as an introductory text on Shiʿi thought and practice—for students of

Islam in general and Shiʿism in particular—but also as a contemporary expression, from within, of the Shiʿi tradition in present-day Iran, the country with which this branch of Islam has been principally associated for the past five hundred years.[2]

Although the main angles from which the author approaches the subject are theological, juridical and ethical, the book is not entirely devoid of traces of the other dimensions that have entered into the articulation of the Shiʿi tradition, namely the philosophical, gnostic and metaphysical. In his discussion of certain subjects—such as the nature of being, the problem of evil and the question of theodicy—he confronts the atheistic and sceptical worldview with arguments that, to a certain extent, reveal the influence of traditional philosophy or *ḥikmat* in Iran: philosophy expressed through logic, guided by revelation and nourished by inward faith, spiritual certainty, and at its highest by mystical illumination.[3]

Despite its comprehensive scope, *Doctrines of Shiʿi Islam* is nonetheless a concise work composed of 150 short 'articles', some consisting of no more than a paragraph, others a few pages in length. It is thus useful as an overall sketch of the essential elements of Shiʿi Islam, giving the reader a 'taste' of the tradition as a whole, a certain feel for what makes up the worldview of this branch of Islam that has received scant, but now rapidly increasing, attention in the West. Although there are now outstanding studies in European languages of specific aspects of Shiʿism,[4] there are still relatively few works that deal with the tradition as a whole,[5] and still fewer that do so from within the tradition itself.[6]

The book is divided into three chapters, the first dealing with universal themes, the second with theology in the specific sense, and the third with a number of religious questions, practical rulings and contemporary issues. The first two chapters broadly mirror the paradigm of theological treatises in Twelver Shiʿism as it was established by Naṣīr al-Dīn Ṭūsī in his celebrated work *Tajrīd al-iʿtiqād*.[7] That is, it begins with what has been called 'theology in the general sense' (*al-ilāhiyyāt bi maʿnā'l-ʿāmm*) and then proceeds to 'theology in the specific sense' (*al-ilāhiyyāt bi maʿnā'l-khāṣṣ*). This 'general' dimension of theology led Ṭūsī to a detailed quently used in the text or have become part of the English lexicon. Also, wherever possible, the dates of the Islamic calendar are accompanied by corresponding ones of the Common Era.

Finally, the reader should be aware that, in accordance with Muslim practice, after every mention of the name of the Prophet of Islam, the author invokes the blessing 'God bless him and his family and give them peace' (*Ṣalla'llāhu ʿalayhi wa ālihi wa sallam*); likewise, after the mention of every Prophet other than Muḥammad, as well as the names of the Imams of the *ahl al-bayt*, and Fāṭima, the daughter of the Prophet, he invokes the blessing 'Peace be with him/her' (*ʿAlayhi/ʿAlayhā al-salām*).

Reza Shah-Kazemi
London, 2001

# Author's Preface

The contemporary era is characterized, as a whole, in industrial and technical terms, as a result of the recent remarkable advances made by mankind in these two domains. It is therefore altogether natural to accept these terms as particularly indicative of the nature of our times. But, alongside these material advances, another great cultural phenomenon has emerged: a re-orientation of contemporary man towards religion and spirituality.

Of all human needs, that for religion is one of the most fundamental and primordial; man's religious quest has been, and will continue to be, recorded as a major theme of human history. There is a wealth of reliable historical data that corroborates the fact that there has been no period of human history when man has lived without religious belief or spiritual sensibility. Nevertheless, the Renaissance, the transformation in scientific method, and the resulting domination of nature by mankind, dovetailed with certain political and cultural factors to bring about a major dilution of religious commitment; and a kind of spiritual heedlessness subsequently spread throughout Western society. This malaise spread like a contagious wave, little by little, to countries of the East, where it began to afflict many traditional peoples; so much so that it came to be widely believed that modern science could not only provide all the material necessities of life, but also satisfy all those basic human needs which religion alone can fulfil.

to stem the rising tide of sectarianism within contemporary Muslim societies.

Sobhani does not shy away from various sensitive issues such as *taqiyya* (dissimulation), *mutʿa* (temporary marriage), pilgrimage to tombs of the saints, or the distinctively Shiʿi aspects of the ritual prayer—from the particular form of the call to prayer to the way of making the ablution; from the joining of certain prayers to the insistence of prostration upon the earth or a stone. Hence, whilst beginning with the most universal Islamic themes—relating to knowledge, being, the nature of man—he finishes with the most specific, and often controversial, issues pertaining to practical religious life. In one fell swoop, then, he takes in the most abstract and the most concrete aspects of the religious worldview of Shiʿi Islam.

It would be appropriate here to mention that in respect of the most universal dimensions of the perspectives he deals with, the religious worldview sketched out by the author shares many essential features with those of the other faith communities worldwide. There is also much in this book that speaks a language and unfolds a vision which will be common to both branches of the Islamic faith, Sunni and Shiʿi. Naturally, there are many aspects that are distinctly Ithnāʿasharī, pertaining to Twelver-Shiʿism, but there is much too that is common to the other communities of the Shiʿi world. It is for this reason that the author uses the term 'Imāmī' in the title, a designation which stems from the 3rd/9th century and refers to all those Muslims who uphold the principle of Imamate, on account of which they are called the Imāmiyya.

It is the principle of Imamate, precisely, that at once unites and differentiates the three main sub-divisions within Shiʿism: the Ithnāʿashariyya, Ismāʿīliyya and Zaydiyya. This is not the place to go into the doctrinal and historical relationships between these communities,[9] but it is important to make a few points. All three come together on the question of the necessity of following a supreme leader, an Imam from the progeny of the Prophet, who is vested with authority at once temporal and spiritual. There was no distinction, historically, within the nascent Shiʿi movement—comprising all those who upheld the rights of the *ahl al-bayt*—over the identity of the Imam for the first few generations down to the fourth Imam, ʿAlī b. al-Ḥusayn (Zayn al-ʿĀbidīn), the great-grandson of the Prophet. It was over the succession of Imams after him that the Shiʿa became divided into a number of groups, from which later emerged the three major Shiʿi communities of today, each with their own line of Imams.[10]

The smallest of these communities, the Zaydīs, assert that following the martyrdom of Ḥusayn b. ʿAli in 61/680, the Imamate is the preserve not of any particular line of descent, but of the ʿAlids as a whole, and that it can be claimed by any member of the family of the Prophet who is able to establish his temporal authority, by force of arms if necessary.[11] The Ithnāʿasharīs or Twelvers, who constitute the majority of the Shiʿa today, believe that the Imamate continued among the direct descendants of Ḥusayn b. ʿAlī to the twelfth Imam, Muḥammad b. al-Ḥasan, who disappeared in 260/873–4 and is currently deemed to be in a state of occultation, remaining hidden until his re-appearance in the Last Days as the Mahdī, the 'Guided', under hose leadership the hopes and aspirations of the Muslim community will be realized, and the original ideals of Islam will be re-established. The Ismāʿīlīs, for their part, acknowledge the same Imams as the Twelver Shiʿis to Jaʿfar al-Ṣādiq, the sixth Imam, and then continue the line of Imamate through his eldest son, Ismāʿīl, in successive generations to their present 49th Imam, Shāh Karīm al-Ḥusaynī, also known as the Aga Khan, who is revered by them as the direct lineal descendant of the Prophet.[12]

Regarding this translation of Sobhani's work, it should be noted that all Qur'anic verses cited in the Persian text have been rendered directly from the Arabic, using the translation of M. Pickthall, which has been modified where appropriate and necessary. The sayings of the Prophet and of the Imams are, on the whole, also translated directly from the Arabic. We have added certain clarifications in the main body of the text, which appear between square brackets, and inserted a few additional points in the footnotes, preceded by the words 'Translator's note'. As a rule, all transliterations from Arabic or Persian carry diacritics, except for terms such as Shiʿa, Sunni, Qur'an and Shariʿa, which are fre-

But the advent of a series of devastating phenomena gave the lie to this vain supposition, and proved that human beings have never been able to live without religion and the guidance it affords; it proved in addition that nothing can possibly supersede or replace religion as the essential defining element of human life.

From amongst this series of destructive phenomena, we shall mention here the following three:

1. The occurrence of world wars in the twentieth century. The First and Second World Wars, which resulted in the deaths of millions of human beings, were guided and implemented by science cut off from religion: the science that was supposed to bring to fruition the most noble ideals of mankind instead dealt it a devastating blow.
2. The collapse of the family unit through the spread of immorality. In most parts of the Western world, the principle of the family as the basic building block of society is breaking down. A transient, unstable form of social organization is taking the place of the traditional family-based society.
3. The invidious power of modern science and its accompanying modes of thought. Needless to say, what we mean here is unenlightened science, conducted contrary to religious values. We do not mean to imply that modern science and technology are necessarily negative or destructive phenomena *per se*. However, we do assert that science and technology—deprived of religious and spiritual guidance—have been the principal material source of the suffering and damage wreaked in our times.

These and similar factors have caused modern man to turn back towards his primordial human nature, and re-direct his attention to religion and its spiritual doctrines. In fact, after an intermission during which modern man deprived himself of the noble virtues of religion, he started searching, like a thirsty man, for the clear and refreshing water of faith. This return to religion is so obvious that it does not need to be proved or demonstrated. This resurgent spiritual inclination is so strong that once again religion has become a serious subject for discussion in the most distinguished centres of learning; hardly does a month or even a week go by without dozens of scholarly articles and books being published on the subject of religion.

Despite the palpable alarm felt by certain circles in the West in the face of this evident resurgence of interest in religious and spiritual values, we regard this phenomenon as a good omen; we cannot but be gratified at the prospect of large numbers of people returning to the compassionate fold of religion. However, a note of caution must be sounded. If this thirst for truth is not quenched in the right way, and is instead fed with crude and erroneous doctrines parading in the guise of true religion, contemporary man might be led even further away from what constitutes authentic religion. Therefore, it is incumbent upon sympathetic writers, aware of the problem and knowledgeable in religion, to provide the correct response to this appeal for guidance, an appeal that has arisen from the primordial nature of man; and to explain with clarity the true principles of religion, so that seekers after truth might be brought within reach of the flowing stream of divine grace. We are faced, then, with a pressing obligation—we who believe that the religion of Islam is the final and most complete heavenly dispensation, and that this religion provides all the necessities of life, individual and collective, until the Day of Judgement; it behoves us to assist others in their search by making the exalted principles of this religion as clear and accessible as possible.

From a somewhat different point of view, it is our belief that the school of the *ahl al-bayt*[13] represents the true and authentic form of Islam, reaching us by means of the Qurʾan, the Holy Prophet and his purified progeny. The essential principles of this school have exerted a powerful attraction throughout history, and continue to do so today, drawing to itself those enamoured of the truth, and causing its devoted adherents to offer up their lives in the service of this sacred heritage. Given the many false accusations that have been levelled against the Shiʿa, not to mention the innumerable exaggerations and distortions that are presented as 'Shiʿi' positions, we hope that the present work might help to bring about a better understanding of what the school of the *ahl al-bayt* actually teaches, both in respect of doctrine and practice.

Calling upon the divine bounty, we undertake the writing of this short work with the intention of clarifying the fundamental principles of Islam according to the school of the *ahl al-bayt.* We offer below a series of concise articles articulating the most essential aspects of these principles which relate to man, religion and the nature of existence. The scope of the work in hand is wide but, mindful of the need to curtail our exposition of such a vast subject as this, we shall endeavour to express ourselves as succinctly as possible. For deeper insight into this perspective, and more comprehensive explanations of the points made here, the books referred to in the bibliography should be consulted.

Finally, I must offer heartfelt gratitude to Hojjatul-Islam Rabbani Golpaygani for all the time and effort he spent in helping me to write this book. And all praise and thanks be to God for His most gracious assistance.

Ja'far Sobhani
14 Ramaḍān 1418
23 Dey 1376/12 January 1998

Ibn ʿAbbās reported that a man went to the Holy Prophet and asked him: 'O Prophet of God, what is the summit of knowledge?' The Holy Prophet replied: 'To know God—as He ought to be known.'

Shaykh Ṣadūq (Ibn Bābūya),
*Kitāb al-tawḥīd*, ch.40, hadith no.5.

Imam Jaʿfar al-Ṣādiq said: 'Truly the most excellent and the most necessary obligation incumbent upon man is knowledge of the Lord, and acknowledgement of one's servitude to Him.'

Muḥammad Bāqir al-Majlisī,
*Biḥār al-anwār*, vol. 4, p. 55.

ONE

# The Worldview of Islam

## I. WAYS OF ACQUIRING KNOWLEDGE IN ISLAM

### Article 1

Islam makes use of three principal means of acquiring knowledge of the world and of the truths of religion, recognizing the validity of each of them within their respective spheres. These three means are: (a) the senses, the most important of which are hearing and seeing; (b) intellect and reason, which arrive at truths in a manner at once definitive and certain—albeit within a delimited realm, on the basis of particular principles and in accordance with certain conditions; (c) revelation, the means by which specially selected, exalted individuals receive knowledge from the unseen domain.

The first two means are common to all people, helping them to gain an understanding of the world, and are the effective supports for the comprehension of the Shariʿa. The third way concerns those individuals who have received a special blessing from the Almighty, the most evident examples of whom are the Messengers of God.[1] The senses can be used as cognitive means only in the sensible realm; intelligence is useful as regards finite domains; while the realm of revelation is infinitely more vast, casting light on diverse areas, including religious beliefs and practical obligations.

The Holy Qur'an has several verses relating to these means, of which we shall cite here two examples. Regarding the senses and the intellect, it states:

*And God brought you forth from the wombs of your mothers while ye knew nothing, and He gave you hearing and sight and hearts* (*af'ida*), *that ye may give thanks.* (Sūra al-Naḥl, XVI:78)

The word *af'ida* in Arabic is the plural of *fu'ād*; it denotes the inner sphere within which the human faculties of hearing, seeing and intelligence are articulated. At the end of this verse, God commands gratitude; this shows that man must benefit from all three faculties, which are to be seen as blessings: the true meaning of gratitude is to be grateful for every blessing, in a manner appropriate to the blessing.

As regards revelation, it states:

*And We sent not before thee but men* [as Our Messengers] *whom We inspired; so ask the people of the remembrance if ye know not.* (Sūra al-Naḥl, XVI:43)

The religious man, in acquiring knowledge of the world and of religion, benefits from the senses. But sensible perceptions only constitute the empirical foundations of intellectual judgement; he benefits from his intellect by acquiring knowledge of God, His attributes and His acts. The proper utilization of each of these three means, within their respective fields, proves their efficacy in the disclosure of the truth, at different degrees.[2]

### Article 2

The substance of the message delivered by God's Prophets can be summarized under two headings, belief and action. As regards the realm of belief, there is first faith in the reality of God, in His attributes of Beauty (*jamāl*) and Majesty (*jalāl*), and in His divine acts.[3] Likewise, as regards action, there are duties and commands, so ordained that man might conduct both his individual and social life according to the divine norm.

The aim of right belief is knowledge and certainty; naturally, it is only decisive self-evidence (*ḥujja*) that can lead the way to this certainty. Thus, it is incumbent on every Muslim to attain certainty in his beliefs on his own account—he cannot simply resort to the imitation (*taqlīd*) of others in this realm. As regards duties and commands with respect to actions, their goal is to make our lives conform with our beliefs. In addition to certainty, one must have recourse to ways of acting that are confirmed by the Shariʿa; this, in turn, means that one must have recourse to a *mujtahid*, an expert on the Shariʿa. This is a subject which will be further considered below.

## Article 3

We benefit from all valid modes of cognition in our comprehension of beliefs and religious commands, but the chief means of affirming these principles are the intellect and revelation. By the word 'revelation' we mean the heavenly book, that is, the Holy Qur'an, along with the sayings of the Prophet that reach us through verified chains of transmission. The sayings of the Imams of the *ahl al-bayt*, which will be considered below, are also classified under the heading of 'Sunna', as they, too, form part of the divine proofs.

Intellect and revelation are mutually corroborative proofs: if on the one hand, decisive intellectual judgement confirms the veracity of revelation, on the other hand revelation confirms the validity of the intellect in its proper domain. In many places, the Holy Qur'an calls upon us to use our intellectual discernment; it invites man to reflect upon and contemplate the marvels of creation, and even goes so far as to enlist the support of the intellect in order to substantiate the content of its own call to accept the truth of God and of Islam. No other revealed book bestows so much value upon the intelligible demonstration of beliefs and doctrines; such reasoned demonstrations abound in the Qur'an.

The Imams of the *ahl al-bayt* have also stressed the importance of the evidence provided by the intellect in those domains where the intellect is competent to judge; the seventh Imam, Mūsā al-

Kāẓim, referred to revelation as outward evidence and intelligence as inward evidence.[4]

**Article 4**

Insofar as revelation is a definitive guide, and the intellect is an inner light, placed within every individual by God, there should never be any incompatibility between these two divinely ordained sources of evidence. If any opposition does arise between them, however, we must deduce from this opposition either a lack of comprehension on our part as regards the religious point in question, or an error in the premises of our logical reasoning. For God, in His infinite wisdom, could never call upon man to follow two contradictory paths.

Just as there is no real contradiction between intellect and revelation, so between science and revelation there should be no contradiction; if there be an apparent incompatibility between them in certain areas, it again has to be said that either our understanding of religion in those areas is deficient, or else that science has not attained definitive certainty in those same areas. In large part, it is this latter case that causes the divergence between science and religion—scientific hypotheses and assumptions being rashly accepted as verified science, and then posited as refutations of certain religious principles.

**Article 5**

In respect of laws which govern the order of existence—laws which are objective and independent of our thought and imagination—they are definitive and permanent realities. This means that if mankind comes to discover, by means of one of the paths of cognition, a given aspect of reality as being absolutely true, then we must say that it is true in an unconditional and permanent way. If, in the process of discovering some aspect of reality, a part of the knowledge resulting therefrom conforms to the truth, while another part does not, that part which is true is always going to be true; for a change in the environmental conditions does not effect a change in universal reality. In other words, the real import of the concept of 'relativity' as regards existence is that a truth that is valid in one period of time and invalid in another period, cannot be regarded as truth at all. If two times two equals four, it will always and unconditionally be so, and if it does not, then it will never do so, in an equally absolute manner. Knowledge cannot be at one with the truth in one domain and in another be erroneous.

'Relativity' in respect of knowledge, is [conventionally] understood to mean that reality has no existence independent of human thought and ratification. For example [applying this concept to the political domain], those societies which are not inspired by divine revelation as regards government have the right to decide upon policies with unrestricted freedom. If they agree on a particular policy one day, for as long as they maintain agreement, this policy will be regarded as right and true; but if they agree later to oppose that policy, then 'truth' will appear in the form of the second policy. In fact, each of these two contradictory policies will have been assimilated as 'true' according to the intellectual capacity of the individual. On the other hand, as regards those principles that are considered as independent of one's mind, possessing specific, objective qualities and definite boundaries—once they are correctly grasped and situated within one's cognitive horizons, they will always and unconditionally be correct, valid and reliable; just as, conversely, opposition to them will always, and necessarily, be false and unfounded.

## II. EXISTENCE FROM THE ISLAMIC VIEWPOINT

### Article 6

The cosmos—meaning by this all that which is other than God—is the creation of God, and it has not been nor ever will be independent of God, even for a single instant. In saying that the world is the creation of God, we mean that the world has been brought into being by His will. However, the relation between the world and God is not a generative relationship of the father-son type, as it is said:

*He begetteth not, nor is He begotten.* (Sūra al-Ikhlāṣ, CXII:3)

**Article 7**

The present order of our universe is not eternal and everlasting. Rather, after a period of time, the extent of which is known only to God, this order will collapse and another order will arise, an order that pertains to the Resurrection in the Hereafter. As God says:

*On the day when the earth will be transformed into another earth, and the heavens* [also will be transformed], *and* [all] *will come forth unto God, the One, the Almighty.* (Sūra Ibrāhīm, XIV:48)

Elsewhere it is said, in allusion to this same hidden reality:

*Truly we belong to God and truly unto Him we are returning.* (Sūra al-Baqara, II:156)

**Article 8**

The order of the world is based on cause and effect, all existential phenomena being established according to this relationship. The effect of one phenomenon upon another is contingent, however, upon the authority of the divine will. The wisdom of God's will manifests itself through this order, such that the effusion of His grace shines through the very nature of things, being manifested by the observable relationships between cause and effect.

The Holy Qur'an has expressed these two points, that natural phenomena are governed by causal relationships; and that the effective influence of each cause in the world is derived from the authority of the universal divine will. As regards the first point, it is sufficient to refer to this verse from the Holy Qur'an:

*He hath appointed the sky as a canopy, and sent down rain from the sky causing therewith fruits to arise* [from the earth] *as sustenance for you.* (Sūra al-Baqara, II:22)

Regarding the second point, the following verse suffices:

*As for the good land, its vegetation comes forth, with the permission of its Lord.* (Sūra al-Aʿrāf, VII:58)[5]

**Article 9**

Existence is not equivalent to material nature; rather, what we call 'nature' is but the formal expression of a dimension of the created order, an order of things which goes infinitely beyond the realm of nature; the Qur'an gives this infinite 'beyond' the name 'the world of the unseen' (*ʿālam al-ghayb*). As all material phenomena mutually affect each other, according to the will of God, just so do the things of the unseen world influence the world of nature. To put this differently, they are means by which the grace of God is manifested. The Holy Qur'an has mentioned the effective influence of God's angels upon events in the natural world, where it says, for example:

... *and those who implement the Command.* (Sūra al-Nāziʿāt, LXXIX:5)

*He is the Omnipotent over His slaves; He sendeth guardians over you.* (Sūra al-Anʿām, VI:61)

From these clear verses we can conclude that the created order—whether natural or supernatural—by virtue of being governed by the law of cause and effect, subsists by the will of God, upon which it depends absolutely.

**Article 10**

The world is a guided reality; all its particles, at whatever degree of existence, benefit from the light of divine guidance according to the measure of their receptivity. The degrees of this universal guidance are found as follows: natural guidance, instinctive guidance and creative guidance.

The Holy Qur'an mentions in different verses this creative, universal guidance; for example:

*Our Lord is He Who gave unto everything its nature and then guided it aright.* (Sūra Ṭā Hā, XX:50)

### Article 11

The order of creation is complete and possesses innate excellence. The structure of existence has been fashioned to the highest level of perfection, such that a better or more complete order is inconceivable. The Holy Qur'an states:

*... the Knower of the invisible and the visible, the Mighty, the Merciful, Who made excellent all things which He created.* (Sūra al-Sajda, XXXII:6–7)

And also:

*Blessed be God, the best of Creators!* (Sūra al-Mu'minūn, XXIII:14)

It is self-evident that the excellence of the Creator has as its concomitant the excellence of the creature. The intellectual argument that arises from this principle is that the action of any agent is proportioned to the qualities and the perfection of the agent; thus, if the agent is devoid of any ontological imperfection, it follows naturally that his actions will, likewise, be free from any imperfection or deficiency. Insofar as God Most High is the possessor of ontological perfection, in infinite modes, it follows that His act must be the most perfect and complete of all acts.

This having been said, the necessity of God's being wise is proven by the fact that, despite the [apparently negative] possibilities inherent in the creation of an excellent world, nothing other than excellence was in fact brought about by God. It is worth mentioning here that nothing in the realm of nature that is referred to as 'evil' contradicts in the least the excellence of the order of nature; further explanation of this point will be given below, in the discussion entitled 'unity in divine creatorship'.

### Article 12

Insofar as the world is the creation and the act of God, and He is the absolute Truth, the world itself is true and wisely ordered, devoid of futility and vanity. The Holy Qur'an refers to this principle in numerous verses, of which the following may be cited:

*We created not the heaven and earth and all that is between them save with truth, and for a term appointed.* (Sūra al-Aḥqāf, XLVI:3)

The ultimate end of man and the world alike is consummated in the Resurrection. Thus, Imam ʿAlī states: 'Verily, the end (*al-ghāya*) is the Resurrection.'[6]

## III. MAN FROM THE PERSPECTIVE OF ISLAM

### Article 13

A human being is an entity compounded of spirit and matter. After death, the body becomes a decomposing corpse, whereas the spirit continues to live. The death of a human being does not mean his obliteration. Rather, he continues to live in the domain of the Barzakh until the Resurrection takes place. In regard to the degrees of the creation of man, the Qurʾan refers to the final stage of existentiation, when the spirit is cast into the body, in the following words:

*Then We produced it as another creation.* (Sūra al-Mu'minūn, XXIII:14)

Several verses allude to life in the world of the Barzakh; for example:

*Behind them is a barrier* (barzakh) *until the day when they are raised up.* (Sūra al-Mu'minūn, XXIII:100)

There are many more such verses that testify to the reality of life in the Barzakh.

### Article 14

Each person is created with a pure primordial nature (*fiṭra*) and with the consciousness of the Divine Oneness, such that were he continuously to develop this intrinsic nature, avoiding all tendencies that militate against it, he would inevitably find his way to the ultimate Truth.

No one has been born sinful, wicked or with malicious intentions. All impurity and indecency arise from contingent factors, being the result of extraneous elements combined with the exercise of free will. Moreover, even negative tendencies acquired through heredity can be overcome by the power of the human will together with the right motivation. Thus, the Christian conception of 'original sin' in respect of the children of Adam is utterly alien to Islam.

The Holy Qur'an states in this respect:

*So set thou thy purpose for religion as a man by nature upright* (ḥanīfan)*—the nature of God* (fiṭrat Allāh)*, in which He created mankind. There is no altering God's creation.* (Sūra al-Rūm, XXX:30)

And the Holy Prophet also states: 'Every child is born in conformity with the primordial nature (*al-fiṭra*).'[7]

## Article 15

Man is endowed with free will; he is capable of exercising independent choice—this means that, when deciding whether or not to undertake a particular action, he takes account of its various dimensions in the light of his intellectual faculty. The Holy Qur'an states:

*Verily, We have shown him the way, whether he be grateful or disbelieving.* (Sūra al-Insān, LXXVI:3)

It also says:

*Say:* [It is] *the Truth from your Lord. Then whosoever will, let him believe, and whosoever will, let him disbelieve.* (Sūra al-Kahf, XVIII: 29)

## Article 16

Insofar as an individual benefits from his wholesome, innate nature, from his capacity to discriminate between good and evil, and from his ability to exercise his free will—on these foundations his ethical and spiritual development becomes a real possibility. The gateway to the transcendent path of right guidance leading back to God is always open to man; it is only at the moment of death that it closes, that is, when repentance is no longer accepted.

Thus, the call of the Prophets is universal; it is to all peoples, even to those such as Pharaoh. Moses is told by God:

*And say* [to him], *Hast thou* [the will] *to purify thyself* [from sin], *and that I guide thee to thy Lord, so that thou might fear him?* (Sūra al-Nāziʿāt, LXXIX:18–19)

Therefore, man must never despair of the mercy and forgiveness of God; as the Qur'an says:

*Despair not of the mercy of God; truly, God forgiveth all sins. Lo! He is the Forgiving, the Merciful.* (Sūra al-Zumar, XXXIX:53)

## Article 17

Insofar as man benefits from the light of wisdom and the gift of his free will, he is a being endowed with responsibility. He has a responsibility towards God, His Messenger and towards divinely inspired guides. He also has a responsibility towards the substance of his own humanity, towards other human beings and towards the world. The Qur'an has many verses clarifying the nature of human responsibility:

*Lo! Of the covenant it will be asked.* (Sūra Banī Isrā'īl, XVII:34)

*Truly, the hearing and the sight and the heart—of each of these it will be asked.* (Sūra Banī Isrā'īl, XVII:36)

*Thinketh man that he is to be left aimless?* (Sūra al-Qiyāma, LXXV:36)

The Holy Prophet also asked: 'Are not all of you shepherds [in respect of those over whom you have authority]? All of you are indeed responsible for your flocks.'[8]

## Article 18

No person has superiority or preference over others, except by virtue of a greater degree of realization of his spiritual gifts. The most exalted kind of superiority is based upon piety and virtue, which must be manifest in all walks of life. As the Qur'an says:

*O mankind! Truly We have created you male and female, and have made you nations and tribes that ye may know one another. Truly the noblest of you, in the sight of God, is the most pious amongst you.* (Sūra al-Ḥujurāt, XLIX:13)

Therefore, racial or geographical factors cannot be used in Islam as the basis of any claim to superiority or the source of any pride.

**Article 19**

Ethical values, which pertain to the very principle of humanity, and which are thus rooted in the *fiṭra*, are permanent and immutable; neither the passage of time nor transformations in society can alter them. For example, the propriety of fulfilling promises, or reciprocating goodness with goodness—such ethical imperatives are constant, having been established at the very dawn of creation and will continue thus for as long as man exists. These moral norms are not subject to change. The converse is no less true: the ugliness of, for example, treachery, or of breaking promises, will always be so. Therefore, from a properly intellectual perspective, one understands that there is a range of immutable and deeply-rooted principles woven into the very texture of man's character, determining his moral and social life. On the margins of these ethical principles there can arise certain customs and manners which do undergo the influence of time and place, and are thus subject to change; these, however, cannot impinge upon or significantly modify the immutable principles of morality.

The Holy Qur'an alludes to some of these intelligible and immutable moral principles; for example:

*Is the reward of goodness anything other than goodness?* (Sūra al-Raḥmān, LV:60)

*Against those who are good there is no way* [of blame]. (Sūra al-Tawba, IX:91)

*Truly, God will not cause the reward of those who do good to be lost.* (Sūra Yūsuf, XII:90)

*Truly God enjoineth justice and kindness and giving to kinsfolk, and forbiddeth lewdness and abomination and wickedness. He exhorteth you in order that ye may take heed.* (Sūra al-Naḥl, XVI:90)

**Article 20**

The actions of man, apart from entailing an appropriate reward or punishment in the Hereafter, are not without their consequences in the herebelow either. Indeed, some events in the world are direct results of human actions; this pertains to a subtle reality, one which the Revelation has alluded to, and of which man has an inkling. There are many verses in this respect; two examples may suffice:

*And if the people of the townships had believed and kept from evil, surely We should have opened for them blessings from the sky and from the earth. But they gave the lie* [to the Messengers of God], *and so We seized them because of their* [evil] *deeds.* (Sūra al-Aʿrāf, VII:96)

The Prophet Noah reminded his people of the relationship between the avoidance of sin by man and the opening up of the gates of mercy by God:

*And I have said: Seek pardon of your Lord. Lo! He is Ever-forgiving. He will let loose the sky for you in plenteous rain, and will help you with wealth and sons, and will assign unto you rivers.* (Sūra Nūḥ, LXXI:10–12)

**Article 21**

The advance or decline of peoples is bound up with a complex series of causes, which—leaving aside the influence of external factors—is rooted chiefly in the way in which religious beliefs and moral principles are assimilated by the people in question. This principle does not contradict that of divine predestination (*qaḍāʾ wa qadar*).[9] This is because the principle of causality is itself an expression of the universal will of God. In other words, the will of God manifests itself such that societies chalk out their own destiny by means of their beliefs and actions. A society that bases itself upon justice and rectitude will be prosperous and stable;

inversely, one that bases itself upon elements contrary to such principles will find an unpleasant fate in store for it. This principle is referred to in the Qur'an as the *sunnat Allāh*, 'the way of God':

*When a warner came unto them, it aroused in them naught save repugnance,* [shown in their] *behaving arrogantly in the land and plotting evil; and the evil plot encloseth but the men who make it. Then, can they expect aught save the treatment of the folk of old? Thou wilt not find for God's way* (sunnat Allāh) [of dealing with people] *any substitute, nor wilt thou find for God's way* [of dealing with people] *aught of power to change.* (Sūra al-Fāṭir, XXXV:42–43)

*Faint not, nor grieve, for ye will overcome them if ye are* [indeed] *believers ... These are only the vicissitudes which We cause to follow one another for mankind...*(Sūra Āl ʿImrān, III:139–140)

**Article 22**

The destiny of man holds out a bright future. It is true that human life is in large part accompanied by inequality and hardship, but this will not always be the case. Human history is moving towards a better future, one in which a comprehensive system of justice will prevail. According to the Qur'an, the pious will rule over the earth:

*And verily We have written in the Psalms, after the Reminder: My righteous slaves shall inherit the earth.* (Sūra al-Anbiyā', XXI:105)

And also:

*God hath promised such of you as believe and do good works that He will surely make them to succeed* [the present rulers] *in the earth, even as He caused those who were before them to succeed* [others]. (Sūra al-Nūr, XXIV:55)

Therefore, after a protracted battle between truth and falsehood, the future will behold the ultimate victory of the truth, however long it may take. As the Qur'an says:

*Nay, but We hurl the Truth against falsehood, and it doth break its head and lo! it vanisheth.* (Sūra al-Anbiyāʾ, XXI:18)

**Article 23**

From the Qurʾanic point of view, man benefits from special favours; this, to such an extent that even the angels bow down to him. The Qurʾan tells us:

*Verily We have honoured the children of Adam. We carry them on the land and the sea, and have made provision of good things for them, and have preferred them above many of those whom We created, with a marked preferment.* (Sūra Banī Isrāʾīl, XVII:70)

Taking full note of the fact that the foundation of man's life is the safeguarding of his spiritual dignity, it follows naturally that any action which detracts from human dignity and all the other God-given qualities is forbidden in Islam. To be more specific, every kind of tyrannical authority—both in respect of those exercising it and those subjected to it—is strictly prohibited. As Imam ʿAlī says: 'Do not be the slave of others, for truly, God created you free.'[10] He also said: 'God has granted unto the believer every right, except that of self-degradation.'[11]

**Article 24**

From the viewpoint of Islam, the intellectual life of man is accorded a special dignity; for the superiority of man—the basis of his pre-eminence among all creatures—consists in his capacity to reflect and to think, using the full scope of his intelligence. In this connection, many verses of the Qurʾan call upon man to exercise his faculties of intellectual reflection, so much so that the cultivation of thought, and reflection upon the phenomena of creation are given as the distinguishing features of the wise. As the Qurʾan says, in one of the many places where the importance of reflection and contemplation upon God's signs and marvels of creation is stressed:

*Such as remember God standing, sitting and reclining, and reflect upon the creation of the Heavens and the earth,* [and say:] *Our Lord, Thou didst not create this in vain.*(Sūra Āl ʿImrān, III:192)

One concomitant of this perspective is the prohibition in the Qur'an against the thoughtless imitation or blind following of one's predecessors.

**Article 25**

The freedom granted to the individual in such areas as economics and politics is, in Islam, conditioned by the following principle: that such freedom does not conflict with man's spiritual imperatives, nor undermine the foundations of public welfare. In fact, the philosophy of obligation in Islam is rooted in the need to make man aware of the extent of his responsibility, so that he properly safeguards his essential dignity, while at the same time upholding public welfare. The prohibition of idolatry, alcohol and other vices is founded, precisely, upon the need to safeguard the dignity and sanctity of the human state; in this light one can better appreciate the wisdom of the law of reprisal in Islam.

The Qur'an considers the law of proportionate retaliation to be a source of preserving human life:

*And there is life for you in retaliation, O men of understanding ...*(Sūra al-Baqara, II:179)

The Holy Prophet said: 'If somebody commits a sin in secret, he harms only himself. But if he commits it openly, and is not stopped, the whole society is harmed.'[12]

Imam Ṣādiq, after narrating some hadiths, said: 'The one who openly and actively displays his sins violates the sanctity of God's rulings, and the enemies of God become his followers.'[13]

**Article 26**

One of the expressions of the principle of the freedom of the individual in Islam is that there is no obligation in respect of which religion one chooses to follow:

*There is no compulsion in religion. The right way is distinct from error.* (Sūra al-Baqara, II:256)

In Islam, religion is sought after only as a result of inner conviction and heartfelt faith, and such things cannot be forced upon the soul from without; rather, they flow from the prior realization of a whole series of factors, the most important of which is the ability to discern the true from the false, the real from the unreal. Once such discernment is attained, the individual—under normal circumstances—will choose to follow the truth.

It is true that Jihād is an obligation for all Muslims; but this does not in any way mean forcing others to accept Islam. The aim of Jihād is, rather, the removal of barriers that prevent the divine message from being [peacefully] conveyed to people throughout the world, so that the 'right way' can indeed be clarified and presented to all. It is to be expected that if the liberating message of Islam is prevented from being spread peacefully, then Jihād must be undertaken, [but only] in order to remove these obstacles and establish the conditions necessary for the peaceful propagation of the message among all peoples.

As we have tried to show, the Islamic perspective illuminates the nature of man and the universe. There are, of course, many other principles and points to be considered in this vast subject; some of them will be addressed, implicitly, in what follows.

TWO

# General Beliefs

## I. THE ONENESS OF GOD (TAWḤĪD)

### Article 27

Belief in the reality of God is a principle held in common by all heavenly religions: herein lies the decisive distinction between a religious person (no matter what religion is followed) and a materialist.

The Holy Qur'an asserts that the reality of God is a self-evident fact, one that does not stand in need of proof; doubt and obscurity on this question should not, as a rule, enter into this axiomatic principle. As the Qur'an says:

*Can there be doubt concerning God, the Creator of the heavens and the earth?* (Sūra Ibrāhīm, XIV:10)

This dazzling self-evidence of divine reality notwithstanding, the Qur'an also opens up ways of removing contingent doubts from the minds of those who seek to arrive at belief in God by means of rational reflection and argument. To begin with, the individual normally has the sense of being connected to, and dependent upon, some entity that transcends the domain revealed by his own particular consciousness; this sense is as an echo of that call from the primordial human nature referred to earlier. It is this call that leads man to the source and origin of creation. The Qur'an says:

*So set thy purpose for religion as a man by nature upright—the nature of God* (fiṭrat Allāh) *in which He hath created man.* (Sūra al-Rūm, xxx: 30)

It also says:

*And when they board the ships they pray to God, making their faith pure, for Him only; but when He bringeth them safe to land, behold! they ascribe partners to Him.* (Sūra al-ʿAnkabūt, xxix:65)

Man is continuously invited to study the natural world and meditate upon its marvels, all of which clearly point to the existence of God. These wondrous signs indicate and, in principle, prove the existence of a Being possessed of transcendent knowledge and supreme power, Who establishes and determines all things in harmony and perfection within the realm of existence:

*Lo! In the creation of the heavens and the earth, and* [in] *the alternation of night and day, are signs for men of understanding.* (Sūra Āl ʿImrān, iii:190)

There are many other verses regarding this point, but we shall confine ourselves to this one alone as being altogether representative of the Qur'anic exhortation to meditate on the creation. It is clear that the ways of acquiring knowledge are not confined to what we have briefly alluded to; there are many ways of proving the existence of God, and these can be studied in detail in theological treatises.

## Article 28

### Degrees of *Tawḥīd*

All divinely revealed religions are based on *Tawḥīd*, that is, the Oneness of God, and on the worship of this one and only God. The most evident of the principles held in common by all true religions is belief in *Tawḥīd*, however much some religious believers may have deviated from this universally held belief. In what follows, we intend to clarify the degrees of *Tawḥīd*, with reference to the Holy Qurʾan and the hadiths, and with the application of intellectual reasoning.

**Oneness of the Essence**

The first degree of *Tawḥīd* pertains to the Essence (*dhāt*) of God. We might explain this 'essential' *Tawḥīd* by saying that the Essence of God is absolutely one and peerless; nothing analogous or similar to Him is conceivable. God's nature is absolutely simple, non-compound, without any plurality.

Imam ʿAlī states, in accordance with these two principles: 'He is One (*wāḥid*) and there is nothing similar to Him among the [existent] things (*al-ashyāʾ*),' and 'He—Glorified and Exalted be He!—is one in meaning [or: spiritual substance] (*maʿnā*); He is not divided into parts by outward existence, by the imagination or by the intellect.'[1]

The Sūra of *Tawḥīd* (al-Ikhlāṣ), the veritable cornerstone of Muslim belief in Divine Unity, alludes to both aspects of this 'essential' *Tawḥīd*; as regards the first, in the verse: '*There is none like unto Him*,' and as regards the second, in the verse: '*Say: He is God, the One.*'[2]

In the light of what has been said above, it will be clear that the Christian doctrine of the Trinity—God the Father, the Son and the Holy Spirit—is unacceptable from the point of view of Islamic logic. The inadmissibility of this doctrine has been exposed in certain verses of the Qurʾan, which have been amply commented upon in theological treatises; here, we shall limit ourselves to the following, altogether sufficient, argument.

The Trinity, in the sense of three gods, must mean one of two things: (a) either it means that each of the three gods possesses a distinct ontological personality, along with all attributes of divinity—in which case 'essential' *Tawḥīd* is contradicted in respect of its first meaning, that is, He has no peer or like; (b) or else it means that these three gods partake of a single ontological personality, such that each is a part of the whole—in which case such an entity would perforce be compound, thus contradicting the second meaning of 'essential' *Tawḥīd*, namely, that God is absolutely simple and not composed of 'parts'.

## Article 29

**Oneness of the Attributes**

The second degree of *Tawḥīd* pertains to the oneness of the divine attributes. We know that God is the possessor of all attributes of perfection; both intellect and revelation indicate the reality of the attributes within the Essence of the Creator. Therefore we know that God is Knowing, Powerful, Living, Hearing, Seeing, and so on. These attributes are distinguished one from the other as regards meaning: that which we understand by the word 'Knowing' is distinct from that which we understand by the word 'Powerful'. But the question is this: If these attributes are distinct in terms of meaning, are they also distinct in terms of objective reality, that is, within the divine nature, or are they united at this level?

In response to this question, we would say that if such distinctions are found within the Essence of God, then there will be multiplicity and compounded-ness within the Divine Essence. It must therefore be understood with the utmost clarity that while these attributes are distinct from each other as regards their respective meanings, they are at one as regards their inmost reality. In other words, the Essence of God comprises, within its absolutely undifferentiated nature, all of these perfections; it is not the case that one part of the Essence consists of knowledge, another part of power, and yet another of life. As the sages say: 'Nay, He is Knowledge, all of Him; He is Power, all of Him; He is Life, all of Him.'[3]

Therefore, the essential attributes of God are in reality eternal and everlasting, partaking of the absolute unity of the Divine Essence. The view of those who regard the attributes of God as eternal and everlasting, but somehow added to the Essence, is erroneous. This is an opinion derived from a false analogy between the attributes of God and those of man: just as man's attributes are distinct from, and added to, the essence of man, so, it is believed, the same holds true for God.

Imam Ṣādiq explains: 'God—Glorified and Exalted be He!—shall never cease to be our Lord. And knowledge is His Essence—and it cannot be known; hearing is His Essence—and it cannot be heard; seeing is His Essence—and it cannot be seen; power is His Essence—and it cannot be dominated.'[4]

Imam ʿAlī has said, in regard to the oneness of the divine attributes with the Divine Essence: 'Perfect sincerity in *Tawḥīd* is that we negate all attributes from Him; for every attribute testifies to its being other than the object to which it is attributed, and every such object in turn testifies to its being other than the attribute.'[5]

## Article 30

### Oneness of Creatorship

The third degree of *Tawḥīd* pertains to the oneness of the source of creatorship (*khāliqiyya*). This means that there is no creator but God, and that whoever or whatever dons the robe of existence is of necessity His creature. The Qur'an mentions this aspect of *Tawḥīd* thus:

*Say: God is the Creator of all things, and He is the One, the Almighty.* (Sūra al Raʿd, XIII:16)

And again:

*Such is God, your Lord, the Creator of all things. There is no God save Him.* (Sūra al-Ghāfir, XL:62)

In addition to revelation, the intelligence also bears witness to the oneness of creatorship. For all that which is other than God is a possibility, as opposed to a necessity, and thus stands in need of something other than itself, in order that it be translated from possibility into actuality. Naturally this need for existence can only be fulfilled by God, and only through God can all the subsequent aspirations of the creature, once it exists, be realized.

Needless to say, this affirmation of the oneness of creatorship does not imply the negation of secondary causality in the order of existence, for the principle by which contingent phenomena have reciprocal effects upon each other is itself derived from the authority of God. The reality of the cause and the very principle by which causality inheres in existent things—both should be grasped as manifestations of His will. It is He who bestows upon the sun and the moon their heat and light; and if He so desires, He can withdraw from them their capacity to influence phenomena. From these points it should be clear that He is indeed the sole Creator, without peer.

As mentioned in Article 8 above, the Qur'an has confirmed the principle of causality; for example:

*God is He Who sendeth the winds so that they raise clouds, and spreadeth them along the sky as He will ...* (Sūra al-Rūm, xxx:48)

Despite the fact that all phenomena are connected with the all-inclusive sphere of divine creatorship, it does not follow that the evil acts of God's creatures are also to be linked to God. It is true that every single phenomenon, insofar as it is a contingent entity, cannot enter into existence without the support of the universal power and will of God. However, it must clearly be stated that in the case of man—since he is a being endowed by divine providence with free will[6] and the capacity for independent decision-making as regards his actions—the quality of his actions will depend upon his own decisions. From a somewhat different point of view, it can be said that since God is indeed the bestower of existence—such that existence, in the absolute and universal sense, comes from Him and depends upon Him—evil does not really enter into existence.[7] As the Qur'an says:

*... Who made all things good which He created.* (Sūra al-Sajda, xxxii:7)

But the capacity to make rational decisions, proper to man alone, determines the extent to which man's actions will conform to the standards established by the intelligence and the divine law alike. Let us consider two actions such as eating and drinking. Insofar as these actions partake of existence, they are grounded in the divine reality. But from another angle we must note, firstly that 'existence', within these two actions, manifests in the form of 'eating' and 'drinking'; then, since it is man's free actions that result in these particular forms of existence, the actions must be seen as pertaining to the agent, man. These two actions, in their particular forms and qualities, cannot in any respect pertain to God. Thus, God must be understood as the bestower of existence, while man is the agent of the acts within existence, the actual eater and drinker.

## Article 31

**Oneness of Lordship**

The fourth degree of *Tawḥīd* pertains to the oneness of lordship and of the governance of the world and man. This oneness of lordship has two aspects: (a) creative governance (*tadbīr takwīnī*), and (b) religious governance (*tadbīr tashrīʿī*).

As regards the second aspect, religious governance, this will be addressed in a separate Article below; for now we shall focus on the first aspect. What we mean by creative governance is the means by which the created universe is ordered. The arrangement of the domain of existence, including its origination and creation, pertains to God's act alone. It is true that as regards human activities, one is able to separate the aspect of governance from that of origination; for example, one person might construct a factory and another might manage it. But in the domain of creation, the 'originator' and 'manager' are one and the same. The point here is that the governance of the universe is inseparable from the source of its creation.

The history of the Prophets reveals that this principle of the oneness of creatorship has never been in dispute within their respective communities. If polytheism (*shirk*) entered into the picture, it generally did so in regard to the question of governance and maintenance of the created order, resulting in the worship of, and servitude to, the agents through which these functions were effected. The polytheists in the time of the Prophet Abraham believed in one Creator, but erroneously conceived of the stars, the sun and the moon as the lords and governors of the universe. The dispute between Abraham and his people was over this question, precisely.[8]

Likewise, in the time of the Prophet Joseph, long after that of Abraham, polytheism asserted itself in respect of this aspect of governance, it being supposed that God, having created the universe, entrusted its governance to others; this subject comes up in the discourse of Joseph addressed to his fellow prisoners. He asked them:

*Are diverse lords better or God, the One, the Almighty?* (Sūra Yūsuf, XII:39)

There are also verses in the Qur'an which show that the polytheists of the time of the Prophet [Muḥammad] believed that a part of their destiny was determined by their gods. For example:

*And they have chosen gods beside God that they may be a power for them.* (Sūra Maryam, XIX:81)

Likewise it is mentioned:

*And they have taken gods beside God in order that they may be helped. It is not in their power to help them; but they* [the worshippers] *are unto them a host in arms.* (Sūra Yā Sīn, XXXVI:74–75)

In many verses, the Qur'an warns the polytheists that the gods they worship have no power to benefit or harm either those who worship them or their own selves. These verses indicate that the polytheists of the time of the Prophet believed that their gods could produce benefit or harm for them.[9] It was this belief that motivated their idol-worship. The verses show also that the polytheists associated partners with God, violating thereby the principle of the oneness of creatorship, in respect of the lordship and governance of the Creator over the creation, believing that in these domains their gods wielded effective power. In order to make them cease their idolatry, the Qur'an affirms the falsity of the aforesaid motive, saying, in effect: the gods which you worship are in no way capable of performing such tasks as you expect of them.

In some verses the polytheists are upbraided for conceiving

equals and peers of God, and loving them as they ought to love God:

*And of mankind are some who take unto themselves rivals to God, loving them with a love like that* [which is the due only] *of God.* (Sūra al-Baqara, II:165)

This condemnation of associating rivals (*nidd*, pl. *andād*) with God is expressed in other verses,[10] the polytheists attributing to their own creations the prerogatives of God, and thus bestowing upon these false gods the love and worship that should be directed solely to transcendent spiritual authority. In other words, it was because they supposed God to have rivals, peers and similitudes, that they engaged in the worship of these imaginary beings.

The Qur'an tells us, in the words spoken by the polytheists on the Day of Resurrection, that they upbraid both themselves and their idols thus:

*By God, we were truly in error manifest, when we made you equal with the Lord of the worlds.* (Sūra al-Shuʿarāʾ, XXVI:97–98)

The sphere of the lordship of God is indeed all-encompassing. In this respect, the polytheists of the Prophet's time agreed with him; that is, they acknowledged God's lordship in such domains as the provision of sustenance, the giving and taking away of life and the overall governance of the universe:

*Say: Who provideth for you from the sky and the earth, or Who owneth hearing and sight; and Who bringeth forth the living from the dead, and bringeth forth the dead from the living; and Who governs over the affair* [of creation] *? They will say: God. Then say: Will ye not then keep your duty to Him?* (Sūra Yūnus, X:31)

*Say: Unto Whom belongeth the earth and whosoever is therein, if you have knowledge? Then they will say: Unto God. Say: Will ye not then remember? Say: Who is Lord of the seven heavens and Lord of the tremendous Throne? They will say: Unto God* [all that belongeth]. *Say: Will ye not then keep your duty to Him?* (Sūra al-Mu'minūn, XXIII:84–87)

But these very people, according to the verses cited from Sūra

Maryam and Sūra Yā Sīn above, believed their gods to have effective power as regards such matters as victory in war, protection against dangers whilst on journeys, and so on; and, clearer still, they believed their gods to have the right to intercede, supposing them capable of intercession without needing the permission of God, and that such intercession would be effective.

Therefore, it is not contradictory to say that, on the one hand, some of the people, in certain matters, recognize that governance pertains to God—and in this respect being, therefore, monotheistic (*muwaḥḥid*)—and, on the other hand, that they attribute the power of governance and supervision to their gods, believing in their effective authority as regards such matters as making intercession, bestowing profit or causing loss, dispensing of might and granting of forgiveness.

Indeed, the polytheists occasionally said, by way of accounting for their practice of polytheism and idolatry: 'We perform this worship only in order to attain nearness unto God thereby; we do not believe in their effective authority over our lives.' The Qur'an relays this [attempted] justification thus:

*We worship them only that they may bring us near unto God.* (Sūra al-Zumar, XXXIX:3)

But the end of the same verse asserts that such claims are but lies:

*Lo! God guideth not him who is a liar and ungrateful.*

However, the affirmation of the oneness of lordship consists in the total rejection of all types of belief in any kind of governance—whether on the universal or particular planes—which is independent of God's command, and is carried out by any being other than God, in relation to man and the universe. The unitive logic of the Qur'an dictates not only the rejection of the idea of any kind of independent governance, but also of any kind of worship of what is other than God.

The rationale for the oneness of lordship is clear: in respect of the universe and man, the continuous operation of the 'tools' of creation cannot be separated from the initial 'act' of creation; and if the creator of man and the universe is one, their governor can only be one. Because of this clear link between creating and governing the universe, one finds that God, in the course of describing the creation of the heavens, makes Himself known as the governor over all creation, saying:

*God it is Who raised up the heavens without visible supports, then mounted the Throne, and compelled the sun and the moon to be of service. Each runneth unto an appointed term; He governs over the affair* [of creation]. (Sūra al-Raʿd, XIII:2)

In another verse, the harmony of the order ruling over creation is given as evidence of the unity of the governor of the universe:

*If there had been therein gods other than God, then verily both* [the heavens and the earth] *would have been disordered.* (Sūra al-Anbiyāʾ, XXI:22)

The principle of the oneness of governance, however, does not preclude the validity of belief in other 'governors' who, with the permission of God, carry out their respective duties. In truth, they do but constitute one aspect of the various means by which the lordship of God is outwardly deployed. Thus, the Qurʾan, in the very midst of stressing the oneness of lordship, clearly establishes the reality of other 'governors'.

... *And those who govern the event.* (Sūra al-Nāziʿāt, LXXIX:5)[11]

**Article 32**

The meaning of governance (*tadbīr*) is the ordering and administering of the universe and man at every level and in every respect, both in this life and in the Hereafter, from the point of view of both the engendering of existence (*takwīnī*) and the establishment of religion (*tashrīʿī*). Therefore, the governance of human affairs, in all respects, is the exclusive preserve of the one-and-only God.

Now we shall consider the second aspect of the oneness of lordship, that is, governance as regards religion. Just as God alone governs over the domain of engendered existence, so all matters concerning religion are likewise His prerogative alone—whether in respect of the imposition of rules and commands, the framing of religious laws, defining obedience and submission to such laws, establishing the principles of intercession and the forgiving of sins. Nobody has the right to change any religious prescriptions without His authority.

Thus, oneness in rulership, oneness in the establishment of religious law, oneness in obedience—all of these are counted as so many dimensions of oneness of governance. Therefore, if the Prophet is given the title of 'ruler' over the Muslims, this is because he was chosen to be so by God, and such rulership is in accordance with divine authority. It is for this reason that obedience to him, like obedience to God, is incumbent upon all Muslims; indeed, obedience to him is at one with obedience to God. As the Qur'an says:

*Whoso obeyeth the Messenger hath obeyed God.* (Sūra al-Nisā', IV:80)

And also:

*We sent no Messenger but that he should be obeyed by God's leave.* (Sūra al Nisā', IV:64)

However, without the permission and command of God, the Prophet would neither be a ruler nor one to whom obedience is due; and, in truth, his rulership and his right to be obeyed are but loci for the manifestation of these properties which, in reality, pertain to God alone. Since the specification of religious obligations forms part of the preserve of lordship, nobody has the right to judge that which God has commanded:

*Whoso judgeth not according to that which God hath revealed: such are disbelievers.* (Sūra al-Mā'ida, V:44)

Likewise, the right to make intercession, and to forgive sins, are the exclusive prerogatives of God; none has the right to intercede without His permission, as the Qur'an says:

*Who is he that intercedeth with Him save by His permission?* (Sūra al-Baqara, II:255)

And also:

*And they cannot intercede except him whom He accepteth.* (Sūra al-Anbiyā', XXI:28)

Therefore, from the Islamic perspective, the buying and selling of 'title deeds' to forgiveness, on the assumption that a person—someone who, by definition, is distinct from the rank of divine lordship—can 'sell' heaven to another, or who can prevent the punishment of the Hereafter from afflicting him, such practices, which once prevailed in Christianity,[12] are utterly futile; as the Qur'an says:

... *then implore forgiveness for their sins—Who forgiveth sins save God only?* (Sūra Āl 'Imrān, III:135)

Taking into consideration what has been said, a believer in the Oneness of God must recognize that God alone is the source of authority, and the sole governor in respect of all matters concerning religion, unless God Himself appoints someone to enforce and explain the religious obligations laid down by Him.

## Article 33

### Oneness of Worship

Oneness in worship is a principle that is held in common by all the divinely-revealed religions. A key reason why Messengers were sent by God to mankind was that they might remind people of this principle. As the Qur'an says:

*And verily We have raised in every nation a Messenger* [proclaiming]: *Worship God and shun false gods.* (Sūra al-Naḥl, XVI:36)

All Muslims, in the course of performing their five daily prayers, testify to this principle of oneness in worship when they utter the words of the Sūra al-Fātiḥa: '*Thee alone do we worship.*' Therefore, there is no doubting the fact that God alone is to be worshipped and that the worship of anything else is prohibited; nobody opposes this fundamental principle of religion. Insofar as there is debate on this subject, it concerns the status of other acts: namely, whether the performance of these acts be considered as evidence of worship of what is other than God. In order to arrive at a definitive judgement as regards this question, we must provide, first, a logical definition of worship, and then clearly separate those acts which can properly be subsumed within this definition, from those acts which pertain, on the contrary, to veneration (*taʿẓīm*) and revering (*takrīm*).

There is no doubt that the worshipping of one's parents, of the Prophets and of the saints is polytheism (*shirk*) and thus forbidden; on the other hand, bestowing veneration and respect upon them is necessary, and indeed forms part of integral *Tawḥīd*:

*Thy Lord hath decreed that ye worship none save Him, and* [that ye show] *kindness to parents.* (Sūra Banī Isrāʾīl, XVII:23)

Now we must focus on the element that distinguishes 'worship' from 'veneration', and ask the question: How can a given act in certain circumstances—such as the prostration of the angels before Adam, and the prostration of the sons of Jacob before Joseph—be at one with *Tawḥīd*, while the same act, in different circumstances—such as prostration before idols—be an expression of *shirk* and idol-worship? An answer to this question emerges clearly from the discussion above, on the issue of oneness in governance. The type of worship which is directed to what is other than God, and which is therefore rejected and forbidden, is that whereby a person humbles himself before a relative, engendered being, in the belief that this being possesses some independent power to change the destiny of man and the universe, wholly or in part; in other words, in the belief that such a being is the lord or master of the world and of men.

On the other hand, if humility is manifested before a person who is himself a righteous slave of God, one who is blessed with virtue and nobility, and is, moreover, a model of piety and righteousness for mankind, then such humility is an aspect of proper respect and reverence for that person and not worship of him.

If the prostration of the angels, and that of the sons of Jacob, did not take on the taint of idolatrous worship, this is because such prostration is based upon a belief in our slavehood and servitude to God; but, accompanying this belief, there is the knowledge of the nobility of Adam and of Joseph, a nobility and a majesty that derive from their being honoured in the spiritual realm. In other words, the act of prostration is in no sense based upon a belief in their divinity or omnipotence.

Taking full cognisance of this principle, one is in a better position to evaluate the respect and veneration accorded by Muslims, in holy places, to the saints (*awlīyāʾ*), those brought close to God. It is obvious that the kissing of the holy tomb of the Prophet, or expressing joy on the anniversary of his birth, or on the anniversary of the advent of his mission (*biʿtha*)—all are aspects of the reverence and love which are due to the Prophet; they are not in the least derived from any belief in his divinity. In like manner, such acts as the chanting of poems praising the exemplary lives or lamenting the death of the saints, the preserving of all monuments left as traces of the prophetic mission, the building of mausoleums above the graves of holy personages—none of these acts can be called *shirk* (associating partners with God), nor can they be called *bidʿa* (innovation). They are not to be equated with *shirk* because their source is love and affection for the saints of God, and not a belief in their divinity; neither can they be regarded as *bidʿa*, since these actions are rooted in a principle enshrined in the Qur'an and Hadith, that is, the necessity of loving and honouring the Prophet and his family. Our acts of reverence towards the Prophet on the occasion of his birthday and the onset of his mission (*biʿtha*) are but the expression of the outpouring of our love for him (we shall return to this issue below, in Article 123 on *bidʿa*).

In stark contrast to this is the prostration of the polytheists before their idols, which is rejected and forbidden precisely because it springs from a belief in the divinity and authority of the idols, and from the false supposition that they exercise control over part of man's destiny; for the idolators believe that their idols have, at the very least, the power to glorify or abase, to forgive and to grant intercession.

## Article 34

**The Divine Attributes (*Ṣifāt*)**

Given the fact that the Essence of God is an infinite reality, having thus no like or equal, man has no way of grasping the depth of this Essence; he can only come to know God by way of an appreciation of God's attributes of Beauty (*jamāl*) and Majesty (*jalāl*).

The attributes of Beauty are those which display the perfection of God's nature, such as Knowledge, Power, Life, Will, and the like. As for the attributes of Majesty, they refer, on the contrary, to His being too exalted to be described by any attribute; they therefore refer [in the first instance] to a lack, an absence or inability. Now God is absolutely self-sufficient, utterly transcending all imperfection or deficiency. Possessing a material body, occupying a particular space, being established in a particular time, being a composite entity, and so on—all of these qualities fall into this type of attribute. Sometimes these two types of attribute are referred to as *thubūtī* (affirmative) and *salbī* (negative), while the object to which both ultimately refer is one and the same. [13]

## Article 35

In our discussion [in Chapter One] on the means of acquiring knowledge, we stated that the principal paths leading to the knowledge of objective truths are those opened up by the senses, the intellect and revelation. In order to acquire knowledge of the attributes of God, both of Beauty and Majesty, we can benefit from two of these paths: (a) the way of intellect, and (b) the way of revelation.

**The Way of Intellect**

Careful study of the created universe—along with meditation upon its secrets and its mysteries, all of which are part of God's creation—leads us to a discovery of the perfections of God's Being. Can one conceive of the raising up of the magnificent edifice of creation without the active involvement of some transcendent Knowledge, Power and Will? The Glorious Qur'an calls attention to this capacity of the intellect to arrive at the natural conclusion of such reflection, by inviting man to ponder deeply the signs of creation, both the external signs outside himself and the internal ones within his own soul:

*Say: Behold what is in the heavens and the earth.* (Sūra Yūnus, X:101)[14]

In such reflection upon the natural world, intellectual discernment operates with the assistance of the senses: it is the senses that first register the impressions of wonder and marvel upon beholding a particular, tangible phenomenon, and then the intellect discerns the glory and beauty of the Creator through this marvel of His creation.

**The Way of Revelation**

Once prophecy and revelation have been clearly upheld by decisive evidence, so that it is clear that both the Qurʾan and the Hadith of the Prophet are inspired by God, it will naturally follow that the verses of the Scripture and the sayings of the Prophet will lead one to an understanding of the attributes of God. Within these two sources, God has described Himself with the best of attributes; suffice to note here that the Qurʾan mentions 135 names and attributes of God. The following verses contain several of these names:

*He is God, other than Whom there is no god, the Sovereign Lord, the Holy One, Peace, the Keeper of Faith, the Guardian, the Majestic, the Compeller, the Superb. Glorified be God from all that they ascribe as partner* (unto Him).

*He is God, the Creator, the Shaper, the Fashioner. His are the most beautiful names. All that is in the heavens and the earth glorifieth Him, and He is the Mighty, the Wise.* (Sūra al-Ḥashr, LIX:23–24)

Here, we should recall that those who subscribe to the *muʿaṭṭila* position—stripping God of all qualities—would deprive man of the lofty, sacred sciences made possible by the intellect and revelation on the question of the attributes of God. We would reply to this by asserting that if discussion and investigation of these sciences pertaining to the divine Names and Qualities were to be forbidden, the mentioning of all these attributes in the Qur'an, along with the command to meditate upon them, would have been utterly redundant.

## Article 36

From another point of view, the attributes of God can be divided thus: (a) attributes of the Essence (*ṣifāt al-dhāt*), and (b) attributes of Activity (*ṣifāt al-fiʿl*).

The attributes of the Essence are those which describe God in a manner that adequately enables us to form some kind of conception of His essential nature. These attributes are, so to speak, derived from the station of the Essence; attributes such as Knowledge, Power and Life.

As for the attributes of Activity, these pertain to the various kinds of action that emanate from God, actions by which He becomes described, such as creating, sustaining, forgiving, and the like. In other words, it is only in the measure that God *actually* creates and sustains that He can be called Creator and Sustainer, however much His Essence may contain *principially* the power to create, sustain, forgive, and so on.

To conclude this discussion, let us recall that all the active attributes of God spring from His Essence, and, in particular, from the perfections of His Essence; that is to say, God is the possessor of absolute perfection, which is the source of all the differentiated active perfections which He displays.

## Article 37

### Attributes of the Divine Essence

Having noted the distinctions, within the realm of divine attributes, between the affirmative and the negative, and between the essential and the active attributes, it is appropriate to elaborate somewhat upon the most important questions relating to these attributes.

**Knowledge**

The knowledge of God, since it partakes of His very Essence, is eternal and infinite. In addition to possessing absolute knowledge of His own Essence, God is aware of all that is other than Him—whether universal or particular realities, before or after creation. The Qur'an lays much stress upon this truth; for example:

*Verily, God is aware of all things.* (Sūra al-ʿAnkabūt, XXIX:62)

And again:

*Should He not know what He created? And He is the Subtle, the Aware.* (Sūra al-Mulk, LXVII:14)

In the sayings of the Imams of the *ahl al-bayt,* there is also great emphasis on the eternity and totality of God's knowledge. Imam Ṣādiq says, for example: 'His knowledge of a place before its creation is like the knowledge of it after its creation; and His knowledge is thus as regards all things.'[15]

**Power**

The power of god, like His Knowledge, is eternal; and insofar as it, too, partakes of His very Essence, it is infinite. The Qur'an emphasizes the comprehensiveness of God's power thus:

*And God is ever able to do all things.* (Sūra al-Aḥzāb, XXXIII:27)

And again:

*God has power to do all things.* (Sūra al-Kahf, XVIII:45)

Imam Ṣādiq stated: 'All things are equal before Him in respect of [His] knowledge, power, authority, dominion and all-comprehensiveness.'[16]

Now, if the engendering of impossible things—those entities which cannot be—fall outside the domain of God's power and control, this is not due to the inadequacy of divine power; rather, it is due to the inadequacy inherent in the impossible: the impossible lacks receptivity to being, that is, it lacks the capacity to actualize itself. When asked about the engendering of impossible things, Imam 'Alī replied: 'God has no connection with incapacity, so that about which you ask cannot be.'[17]

**Life**

A knowing and powerful God is obviously a living God, as the two former qualities are distinctive features of life; they furnish evidence, indeed, for the reality of His life. The divine attribute of Life, as with all the other attributes, is devoid of imperfection, and transcends the particular features of this attribute insofar as it pertains to man and other creatures—features such as being subject to the contingency of death. For, inasmuch as He is living, by His essential nature, death cannot affect Him. In other words, since the Being of God is absolute perfection, death, which is but a form of imperfection, cannot find a way into His Essence. Thus it is said:

*And trust in the Living One, Who dieth not*... (Sūra al-Furqān, xxv:58)

**Will**

An agent who is conscious of his activities is more complete than one who is not. A free agent, endowed with a will to perform his acts—such that he can choose to accomplish or not accomplish a given act—is more complete than an agent constrained and compelled [by some other agent] to do or not to do something, being helpless, and unable to choose for himself. Taking into account this point, and seeing that God is the most perfect agent in existence, it is altogether natural to assert that the Divine Essence is, by nature, an absolutely free agent, neither constrained from without nor imposed upon by anything other than Himself; and if it is said that God is 'one who wills' (*murīd*), the meaning is that He has perfect liberty to will whatever He desires.

Will, in the conventional sense of a human faculty that is originated in time and is actualized gradually thereafter, does not figure in the Divine Essence. Hence we have the sayings from the *ahl al-bayt*, intended to prevent error and deviation, to the effect that the will of God [with regard to a given act] is identical to the accomplishment and realization of the act, as it is said: 'Will, in regard to man, is an inner state, which man strives to realize in outward action, but the will of God itself constitutes the consummation of the action, without this involving temporal origination.'[18]

This explanation makes it clear that will, in the sense of liberty, is one of the attributes of the Essence, while in its aspect of existentiation, it is one of the attributes of Divine Activity.

## Article 38

### Attributes of Divine Activity

Now that we have dealt with the principal themes related to the attributes of the Essence, it is appropriate to turn our attention to some of the attributes of Divine Activity. Here we shall consider the following three attributes: speech (*takallum*), veracity (*ṣidq*) and wisdom (*ḥikma*).

### Speech

The Qur'an has described God as one who 'speaks':

*And God spoke directly with Moses.* (Sūra al-Nisā', IV:164)

And again:

*And it was not vouchsafed to any mortal that God should speak to him unless* [it be] *by revelation or from behind a veil, or* [that] *He sendeth a Messenger*...(Sūra al-Shūrā, XLII:51)

There is thus no doubt that speech is one of the attributes of God. There is, however, debate over the question of the ultimate nature of this attribute: is it an attribute of the Essence of God or of His Activity? It is clear, to begin with, that speech in the form in which it appears in man, cannot conceivably apply to God. Since the attribute of speech is given in the Qur'an, we ought to refer to the Scripture itself in order to understand the reality of this attribute.

As we have seen in the verse cited above, the Qur'an establishes the fact that God speaks to His slaves according to three modes of self-disclosure. It is impossible for the speech of God to reach man except by the following three modes: (a) '*unless* [it be] *by revelation*'—in other words, by divine inspiration; (b)'*or from behind a veil*'—in other words, that man can hear God's speech, but cannot see Him (God's speech to Moses took this form); (c) '*or* [that] *He sendeth a Messenger*'—in other words, an angel is sent by God to man to convey the inspiration.

In this verse, the speech of God has been explained as having been brought into being by God, either directly without intermediary, or indirectly through the intermediary of an angel. According to the first mode—divine inspiration—God sometimes casts His words directly into the heart of the Prophet, and sometimes He causes His words to enter the heart after having first been heard by the ear. In all three modes of speech, however, the words of God are brought into being. The speech of God is therefore to be considered as one of the attributes of Divine Activity.

This is one explanation of the speech of God, derived from the guidance given by the Qur'an. Another explanation is as follows: God has called all existent entities of the universe His 'words'. As the Qur'an says:

*Say: Were the sea to be ink for the words of my Lord, verily the sea would be used up before the words of my Lord were exhausted, even if We were to bring the like thereof to help.* (Sūra al-Kahf, XVIII:109)

In this verse, what is meant by 'words' is all of the creatures of God, which none but He can count. In the following verse, we find evidence of this [assimilation of all creatures as 'words' of God]. Jesus is explicitly referred to as the 'Word of God' (*kalimat-Allāh*):

*The Messiah, Jesus son of Mary, was only a Messenger of God, and His Word which He cast unto Mary.* (Sūra al-Nisā', IV:171)

Imam 'Alī, in one of his discourses, interprets the speech of God in terms of His creative activity: 'When God wishes to bring something into being, He says unto it "Be!", and it is; but [He does so] not with a voice that is sounded, nor with a call that can be heard. For the speech of God is one of His actions whereby a thing is endowed with existence.'[19]

### Article 39

From the discussion above regarding the reality of God's speech it should have become evident that the speech of God is originated in time (*ḥādith*), and is not eternal (*qadīm*). For His speech constitutes His act, and, as the act of God takes place in time, it follows naturally that His speech possesses, likewise, a temporal condition.

Nonetheless, in order to uphold correct spiritual courtesy (*adab*), and in order to forestall any misconceptions, we cannot call the speech of God 'created', because of the many for whom the idea of being created connotes being artificial or constructed. But leaving aside this point of view, we can regard all that is other than God as His creature.

Sulaymān al-Jaʿfarī related thus: 'I asked the seventh Imam, Mūsā Ibn Jaʿfar, "Is the Qur'an created?" The Imam replied, "I say that the Qur'an is the speech of God".'[20]

At this point the following should be noted: At the beginning of the 3rd/9th century, the question of whether the Qur'an was created or uncreated was being hotly debated by the Muslims, and was a source of acute acrimony and divisiveness. Those who advocated the eternity of the Qur'an did not support their position with sound reasoning, with the result that some Muslims viewed the Qur'an as temporally originated, while others regarded it as eternal. If the purpose of the Qur'an and its words is that these words be read, and if they are words which the angel Gabriel was charged by God to reveal to the heart of the Prophet, it is obvious that all of these words are temporally originated. Also, if the purpose of the Qur'anic verses is to impart knowledge and meaning, and some of these verses relate the historical tales of the Prophets, and also relate the wars fought by the Prophet [of Islam], then these verses cannot be regarded as eternal.

To conclude, if the aim is to acquire knowledge of God through the Qur'an, by means of both words and underlying meanings, the knowledge of God is, evidently, eternal, being one of the attributes of His Essence—but knowledge is one thing and speech, another.

## Article 40

### Veracity

One of the attributes of Divine Activity is veracity (*ṣidq*), that is to say, whatever He says is true; the blemish of falsehood does not tarnish His speech. The reason for this is clear: lying is the way of the ignorant, those in need, the afflicted and the frightened—and God is utterly beyond all such conditions. In other words, lying is an abomination and God cannot be tainted by any evil.

## Article 41

### Wisdom

Another of the divine attributes of perfection is wisdom (*ḥikma*), 'The Wise' (*al-Ḥakīm*) being one of His names. The meaning of God being wise is, first, that His actions are brought to ultimate fruition in a perfect, complete and definitive consummation. Secondly, God is utterly beyond performing any actions that are deficient or vain.

Evidence of the first fact is furnished by the marvellous order of the world of creation and by the beautiful way in which the awesome edifice of creation is raised up. As the Qur'an says:

... *the fashioning of God, Who perfecteth all things.* (Sūra al-Naml, XXVII:88)

Evidence of the second fact is provided by the following verse:

*And We created not the heaven and the earth, and all that is between them, in vain.* (Sūra Ṣād, XXXVIII:27)

God is absolute perfection; therefore, His actions must also partake of perfection and be devoid of all defect and futility.

## Article 42

### Negative (*Salbī*) Attributes

We recalled above that the attributes of God can be divided into two categories, those of Beauty (*jamāl*) and those of Majesty (*jalāl*). Those that pertain to perfection (*kamāl*) are referred to as attributes of Beauty or positive (*thubūtī*) attributes; while those that refer indirectly to God [by negating what He is not] and which relate to imperfection or deficiency, are referred to as attributes of Majesty or as negative (*salbī*) attributes.

The intention behind the formulation of negative attributes is to negate from the Divine Reality any possible susceptibility to imperfection, deficiency or inadequacy. Insofar as the Divine Essence is utterly self-sufficient and constitutes in Itself absolute perfection, It is necessarily devoid of any attributes that derive from imperfection and dependency. From this point of view, Muslim theologians argue that God does not have a body, nor is He material; He is not a locus for any other entity, nor is He incarnate in any other entity—such features presuppose the imperfection and dependency proper to contingent, existent entities.

Among the other attributes deriving from imperfection is the capacity of being seen; for, in order to be seen, an object must fulfil the conditions of visual sense-perception, such as: being in a particular place; being illuminated by some source (that is, not being in darkness); and being separate, in essence, from the perceiving subject.

It is clear that such conditions are but the traces of an entirely corporeal and material frame of existential reference; they are utterly inapplicable to God, exalted as He is above all things. In addition, we can say that a 'god' that can be seen cannot escape from the following two conditions: either the totality of its being would be visible or else a part of its being; in the first case, the all-encompassing divine reality would be encompassed and delimited, and in the second, it would consist of parts—both of which conditions are far removed from the divine reality, elevated in sublimity as It is.

The foregoing discussion has considered corporeal, sensible vision, but as regards the vision of the heart, that is, inward spiritual perception which sees by the light of perfected faith, this is of an entirely different order; there is no doubt as regards its possibility, or rather, of its reality, for the saints of God.

Imam ʿAlī was asked by one of his companions, Dhiʿlib al-Yamānī, 'Have you seen your Lord?' The Imam replied, 'I would not worship a lord whom I have not seen.' He was then asked, 'How did you see Him?' The Imam replied, 'The eyes cannot see Him according to outward vision; rather, it is the hearts that perceive Him, through the verities of faith.'[21]

Apart from the refutation of the possibility of corporeal perception of God by intellectual arguments, the possibility of this type of outward vision is also explicitly denied by the Qurʾan. When the Prophet Moses, at the insistence of the Children of Israel, asked to see God, he is given a negative reply:

*My Lord, show me* [Thy Self] *that I may gaze upon Thee. He said: Thou wilt not see Me.* (Sūra al-Aʿrāf, VII:143)

It might be asked: if seeing God is impossible, why does the Qurʾan tell us that on the Day of Resurrection those of His slaves who are worthy will behold Him?

*That Day will faces be radiant, looking at their Lord.* (Sūra al-Qiyāma, LXXV:22–23)

The reply to this question is that the meaning of '*looking*' in this verse is the expectation of the mercy of God, the verses themselves providing evidence supporting this interpretation. First, the looking in question is connected to 'faces', that is, to happy faces that are looking toward Him. If the meaning here were the actual vision of God, then it would have been necessary to connect this vision with the eyes and not with faces. Secondly, the discourse of the Sūra in question refers to two groups: one with bright and radiant faces, whose [anticipated] reward is made clear by the verse '*looking at their Lord*'; and the other group with grim and anguished faces, whose [anticipated] punishment is alluded to by the verse '*knowing that some great disaster is about to befall them*' (verse

25). The meaning of the second phrase is clear: they know that some painful punishment will soon befall them, and they are dreading its imminent advent.

As a parallel to the comparison between the two groups, we can make use of another aspect of the meaning of the first verse. In regard to those with radiant faces, the phrase '*looking at their Lord*' can be understood as a metaphor for their expectation of mercy. There are many examples of this metaphor in Arabic and Persian. To take one example from the Persian language, it is said that such-and-such is looking at another person's hand; this means that he is expecting help from him. Moreover, in commenting upon the meaning of Qur'anic verses, one must not in principle confine oneself to one verse alone; rather, one must locate verses which shed light on the subject in question, and then derive the true meanings of a given verse from a whole series of verses of similar import. On the question of seeing God, if we gather together those verses and prophetic sayings pertaining to this question, it is clear that, from the Islamic perspective, there can be no possibility of seeing God [in terms of visual sense-perception].

It also becomes clear from the above arguments that Moses's request for a vision of God was at the insistence of the Children of Israel who said: 'Just as you hear the voice of God and transmit that to us, so look upon God and describe Him to us.'

*...and when ye said: O Moses, we will not believe in thee till we see God plainly.* (Sūra al-Baqara, II:55)

It is also said:

*And when Moses came to Our appointed tryst and His Lord had spoken unto him, he said: My Lord, show me* [Thy Self], *that I may look upon Thee. He said: Thou wilt not see Me.* (Sūra al-Aʿrāf, VII:143)

## Article 43

### Informative (*khabarī*) Attributes

What has thus far been addressed in regard to the divine attributes (except for that of speech) pertains to the type of attribute that can be evaluated by means of intellectual affirmation or negation in regard to God. But there is another group of attributes mentioned in the Qur'an and Hadith that cannot be understood any other way than by means of traditional, transmitted knowledge (*naql*).[22] For example:

1. The Hand of God:

   *Truly, those who swear allegiance unto thee* [O Prophet], *swear allegiance only unto God. The Hand of God is above their hands.* (Sūra al-Fatḥ, XLVIII:10)

2. The Face of God:

   *Unto God belong the east and the west, and wherever ye turn, there is the Face of God.* (Sūra al-Baqara, II:115)

3. The Eye of God:

   *Build the ship under Our Eyes and by Our inspiration.* (Sūra Hūd, XI:37)

4. God being 'established' (*istiwā'*) on the Throne:

   *The Beneficent One, Who is established on the Throne.* (Sūra Ṭā Hā, XX:5)

The reason for calling these attributes *khabarī* (pertaining to information) is that it is only traditional, transmitted knowledge that can provide us with information regarding these attributes. It is important to remind ourselves that the intellect, or human wisdom, cannot interpret these attributes according to their conventional meanings, for this would lead to conceiving of God as 'embodied' (*tajsīm*), and therefore similar to us (*tashbīh*); intellectual and transmitted knowledge alike warn us against these misconceptions. Thus, we must keep firmly in mind all of the Qur'anic verses on this subject if we are to obtain a true explanation of these attributes. We must also remember that the Arabic language, like many others, is rich in metaphors and symbolic allusions, and the Holy Qur'an, which employs the language of the Arabs, makes ample use of this mode of discourse. This having been understood, we can proceed with an explanation of these attributes.

In the first verse quoted above, it is said that those who pledge allegiance to the Prophet—by taking his hand into theirs—are in fact making their pledge to God, since allegiance given to the one sent is *ipso facto* allegiance to the One who sent him. So it is said that the Hand of God is above their hands: this means that the power of God is greater than their power—not that he possesses a bodily 'Hand' and that His 'Hands' are literally above their 'hands'. In support of this interpretation we might adduce the remainder of the verse:

*So whoever breaketh his oath, breaketh it only to his soul's detriment; while whoever keepeth his covenant with God, on him will He bestow an immense reward.* (Sūra al-Fatḥ, XLVIII:10)

The content of this discourse—threatening those who break their promise and giving glad tidings to those who keep their promise—clearly reveals that the meaning of the 'Hand' of God is His power and authority. Also, the word 'hand' appears in many dictionaries as a metaphor for power, as it is said in Persian: 'There are many whose "hands" are higher than yours' [meaning: there are many who are more powerful than you.]

[In the second verse quoted above], the meaning of the 'Face' of God is His Essence; it is not to be compared with the human face or any other creature's face. When the Qur'an speaks of the annihilation (*fanāʾ*) and non-existence of human beings, it says, '*Everyone that is thereon will perish,*' following this with an affirmation of the subsistence (*baqāʾ*) and permanence of the Being of God, there being no possibility of annihilation in regard to Him:

*Everyone that is thereon will perish; and there subsists the Face of thy Lord, Possessor of Might and Glory.* (Sūra al-Raḥmān, LV:26–27)

The meaning of the 'Face' of God being everywhere is clarified by these verses. God is not to be located at a particular point; rather, His Being encompasses all things, such that wherever we look, we are facing Him. Further affirmation of this interpretation is given by reflecting upon the following two attributes [mentioned at the end of the verse partially cited above, al-Baqara, II:115]: the All-encompassing (*al-Wasīʿ*), the Being of God is infinite; and the Knowing (*al-ʿAlīm*), He knows all things.

In the third of the verses quoted above, the Prophet Noah is commanded to construct the ark. The building of such a vessel, far from the sea, led to Noah being mocked by his ignorant folk. In such circumstances, it is as if God said to him: 'Build the ark, you are under Our supervision; We have inspired you to do this.' The meaning here is that Noah was acting under divine guidance, hence he would be protected by God, and would not be disturbed by the mockery to which he was being subjected.

[In the fourth verse], the word *ʿarsh* in Arabic means 'throne'; and *istiwāʾ*, when used in conjunction with *ʿalā*, means 'being established' and 'having ascendancy over'. Those in power normally dispose of the affairs of state when they are firmly established in the seat of state authority; hence, we can interpret this verse as a metaphor for the divine authority, which holds sway over the disposition of all things. Apart from the evidence given by the intellect and traditionally received sources, which alike affirm that God is not spatially restricted, one can uphold the validity of our metaphorical interpretation of God 'being established on the Throne' by considering the following two points: (a) in many verses preceding this one there are descriptions of the creation of the heavens and the earth, and how God raised up the edifice of the universe without recourse to visible pillars; (b) in many verses following this one, mention is made of the governance of the affairs of the world.

The significance of the phrase '*established on the Throne*' becomes clearer when we see that this verse comes between the theme of creation, on the one hand, and that of governance, on the other. The Qur'an wishes to remind us that the creation of the universe, despite its awesome dimensions, does not require us to exclude God from being in absolute control of its affairs. On the contrary, in addition to being responsible for the initial act of creation, God has a firm grip on the reins of supreme power over all the affairs of the universe. Suffice to cite the following as one of the many verses demonstrating this point:

*Verily, your Lord is God Who created the heaven and the earth in six days, then He established Himself upon the Throne, directing all things. There is no intercessor* [with Him] *save after His permission...* (Sūra Yūnus, X:3)[23]

II. DIVINE JUSTICE (ʿADL)

**Article 44**

All Muslims believe that God is just and that justice is one of the divine attributes of Beauty (*jamāl*). The basis of this belief is the Qur'anic negation of any possibility of injustice on the part of God, referring to Him as being '*upright in justice*'. As it is said:

*Verily, God wrongeth not even the weight of an atom.* (Sūra al-Nisā', IV:40)

And again:

*Verily, God wrongeth not mankind in anything...* (Sūra Yūnus, X:44)

Also:

*God bears witness,* [as do also] *the angels and the men of knowledge, upright in justice, that there is no God save Him.* (Sūra Āl ʿImrān, III:18)

In addition to the evidence provided by these verses, the intellect can discern the justice of God with utmost clarity. For justice is an attribute of perfection (*kamāl*), while injustice is an attribute of imperfection; and the human intellect perceives that God possesses all possible perfections, and that He is exalted beyond any possibility of imperfection or deficiency, both as regards His Essence and His actions.

In principle, injustice and oppression are always consequences of one of the following factors: (a) ignorance—the one who acts unjustly is unaware of the ugliness of injustice; (b) incapacity and need—either the agent of injustice is aware of the ugliness of injustice, but is unable to enact justice, or else he is in need of the fruits of his injustice; (c) unscrupulousness through foolishness—the agent is both aware of the ugliness of injustice, and he is able to enact justice, but since he lacks wisdom, he has no scruples about committing unjust acts.

It is clear that none of these factors can have anything to do with the divine nature, all of God's actions being just and wise. The following hadith corroborates this: Shaykh Ṣadūq relates[24] that a Jew came to the Prophet [Muḥammad] asking various questions, some of which related to the question of divine justice. In explaining why God does not commit injustice, the Prophet said: '[It is] because God knows the ugliness of injustice and is not in any need of it.' Theologians of the *ʿadliyya* school[25] have seized upon this key hadith in the debate over the question of divine justice.

Given the verses cited above, and many others of similar import in the Qur'an, all Muslims are at one over the issue of divine justice; but there is a certain difference of opinion regarding the question of what the justice of God actually means. Muslims have opted for one of the two following positions:

1. The human intellect distinguishes between evil and good actions, understanding the latter to indicate the perfection of the agent, and the former the imperfection of the agent. Since God, by nature, possesses all ontological perfections, it follows that His acts must be perfect and pleasing, His most holy nature being devoid of all kind of evil. It is necessary to mention here that the intellect can never, as it were, issue an 'order' as regards God, saying that God 'must' be just; rather, the task of the intellect is to disclose the true reality of God's actions. In other words, taking due account of the absolute perfection of the divine Essence, devoid as It is of any possibility of imperfection, the intellect discloses the fact that His actions also partake of ultimate perfection, and are likewise devoid of any deficiency. Consequently, God deals justly in His relations with mankind. Verses from the Qur'an are adduced as evidence corroborating and stressing that which man can perceive, and in Islamic

theology this approach goes by the name of 'the intelligibility of good and evil' (*ḥusn wa qubḥ ʿaqlī*); the adherents of this approach are referred to as the *ʿadliyya,* the forerunners of whom were the scholars of the Imami school.

2. There is another perspective, contrasting with this one, according to which the human intellect is incapable of discriminating between good and evil actions, even in a general way. It is asserted that the distinction between good and evil can only be made on the basis of divine revelation: that it is God who commands us to do good and God who forbids us from doing evil. According to this perspective, if God were to consign sinless souls to Hell and sinners to Paradise, this would constitute perfect goodness and justice! If God is described as 'Just', it is only because He has been given this attribute by revelation.[26]

## Article 45

Since the principle of 'the intelligibility of good and evil' is the foundation of many Shiʿi beliefs, we ought to mention, albeit briefly, two of the many arguments from which its validity can be derived.

1. Every individual, whatever be his religious path or creed and wherever he be on this planet, is capable of grasping the beauty of justice and the ugliness of injustice, the beauty of keeping one's word and the ugliness of breaking it, the virtue of repaying goodness with goodness and the vice of repaying goodness with evil. History shows ample evidence of this truth, and hitherto the wise have never denied it.
2. If we were to suppose that the intellect were incapable—in a universal fashion—of grasping the distinction between good and evil acts, and that all people must refer to religion to enable them to perceive the goodness or evil of a given act, then we would be forced to accept the concomitant argument that even the validity of the religiously sanctioned distinction between good and evil could not be proven. For, assuming that the Lawgiver informs us about the goodness of one action and the evil of another, we could not truly benefit from this

information for as long as there were any possibility in our minds that the Lawgiver may not be speaking the truth. However, the case would be entirely different if it were already self-evident to us that the Lawgiver is utterly beyond the ugliness of lying—and this evidence only comes to us by means of the intellect.[27]

In addition to these two points, there are also verses from the Qur'an which uphold the principle that the intellect is indeed inherently capable of discriminating between good and evil:

*Shall We then treat those who have submitted* (al-Muslimūn) *as We treat the guilty? What aileth you? How foolishly ye judge!* (Sūra al-Qalam, LXVIII:35–36)

In this verse, a question is posed, and we are able to provide the answer:

*Is the reward of goodness other than goodness?* (Sūra al-Raḥmān, LV:60)

In the following verse, God says:

*He will not be questioned as to that which He doeth, but they will be questioned.* (Sūra al-Anbiyā', XXI:23)

Now the question might arise: God knows that He is too exalted to be accountable to anyone, therefore no action of His can be called to account; but if we operate on the basis of an intellectually posited distinction between good and evil, then, supposing that God were to commit [what may appear to us as] an 'evil' act, we would have to ask: why has this act been committed? The response to this is as follows: the reason why God is not called to account is, precisely, because He is Wise, and a wise agent cannot commit any type of unjust action, for wisdom is always inseparable from good action, so there can be no possible action that one might call into question on the part of God.[28]

## Article 46

There are various ways in which Divine Justice is expressed as regards the three domains of (a) creation, (b) religious dispensation, and (c) heavenly recompense. We shall explain some of these below, taking each of these domains in turn.

**Justice in creation**

God bestows upon each existent entity that which is appropriate to it, never depriving it of the receptivity inherent in its nature; this receptivity being determined at the plane of effusion of Being, and in the invisible dimension in which the act of bestowing existence occurs. As the Qur'an says:

*Our Lord is He Who gave unto everything its nature, then guided it aright.* (Sūra Ṭā Hā, xx:50)

**Justice in religious dispensation**

God guides man—endowed as he is with the capacity to acquire spiritual perfection—by sending Messengers to establish religious laws. He does not impose upon man obligations that go beyond his capacity. As the Qur'an says:

*Verily God enjoineth justice and kindness and generosity to kinsfolk, and forbiddeth lewdness and abomination and wickedness. He exhorteth you in order that ye may take heed.* (Sūra al-Naḥl, xvi:90)

Since justice, kindness and generosity contribute to human perfection, while the other three elements mentioned contribute to man's downfall, the first three qualities have been made obligatory, and the second three are prohibited. Likewise, as regards man not being charged with religious obligations that are beyond his capacity, the Qur'an says:

*And We task not any soul beyond its scope ...* (Sūra al-Mu'minūn, xxiii:62)

**Justice in recompense**

When it comes to apportioning reward and punishment, God never treats the believer in the same way as the disbeliever, the good in the same way as the bad; rather, He gives each person an appropriate, fitting recompense. Accordingly, God will never punish a people whose religious obligations have not been revealed by means of divinely-guided Messengers, and who have not, consequently, received the full force of the divine proof.[29] As the Qur'an says:

*We never punish until We have sent a Messenger.* (Sūra Banī Isrā'īl, XVII:15)

And also:

*And We set a just balance for the Day of Resurrection so that no soul is wronged in aught.* (Sūra al-Anbiyā', XXI:47)

## Article 47

God created man, and this creation has a purpose. This purpose is that man attain the plenitude of all that the human soul can aspire to, doing so by means of the graces realized through devotion to God. Whenever man is guided to the point where he becomes aware of this purpose, and pledges himself to undertake the first steps leading to its realization, God Himself sees to it that they are indeed accomplished. Without this divine help, the creation of man would be lacking any means of realizing the purpose of creation. It is for this reason that Messengers were sent to mankind, providing them with both explanations and miraculous acts. Thus, God proclaims messages containing promises and threats, with a view to inspiring His slaves with earnest desire (*targhīb*) for obedience, and with fearful anxiety (*taḥdhīr*) to avoid disobedience.

What has been expressed above is a summary of the principle of loving-kindness (*luṭf*) in the *ʿadliyya* theology, which in fact constitutes one of the branches of the principle of discernment between good and evil, the foundation of many theological concepts.

## Article 48

**Divine Decree (*Qaḍā*ʾ) and Measure (*Qadar*)**

Belief in the principles of *qaḍā*ʾ and *qadar* is of extreme importance in Islam, figuring prominently in the divine Scripture and in the hadiths of the Prophet; it is a belief that is strengthened also by intellectual arguments. There are many verses in the Qurʾan concerning these two principles; we quote a few of these below. First, in relation to measure (*qadar*):

*Verily, We have created everything by measure.* (Sūra al-Qamar, LIV:49)
*And there is not a thing but with Us are the treasuries thereof, and We send it not down save in appointed measure.* (Sūra al-Ḥijr, XV:21)

As regards the divine decree (*qaḍā*ʾ):

*When He decreeth a thing, He saith unto it only: Be! And it is.* (Sūra al-Baqara, II:117)

*He it is Who hath created you from clay, and hath decreed a term for you.* (Sūra al-Anʿām, VI:2)

Taking these verses, along with a large number of hadiths of similar import, no Muslim can deny the reality of divine predestination. However, an analytical knowledge of all the minute details of this complex question is not necessary; and, in principle, for those who lack the conceptual dexterity to assimilate this type of subtle reality, it would be better to avoid entering into discussions and deliberations upon it. For all too many are liable to open themselves up to erroneous doctrines or be thrown into doubt and lose their way. It is in regard to just such a type, one feels, that Imam ʿAlī said: 'This [doctrine of predestination] is a dark path—do not traverse it; a deep ocean—do not enter it; and a divine mystery—do not try and unveil it.'[30]

Needless to say, the Imam's warning here is directed to those who cannot comprehend such complex and subtle doctrines, considering the large number of people that would have become confused if they were to enter into debate on such questions. But elsewhere, the Imam has been quite forthcoming with regard to intellectual explanations of the doctrine.[31] Therefore we shall endeavour, within the limits imposed by our own knowledge, to explain this doctrine by highlighting certain Qur'anic verses and hadiths, and offering brief comments on them.

## Article 49

The term *qadar* in the Arabic language means 'measure' and 'portion'; and *qaḍā'* pertains to that which is definite and decided.[32] The eighth Imam, Imam Riḍā, said by way of commentary upon these two terms: '*Qadar* is to be understood as the measuring out of a thing in relation to its subsistence (*baqā'*) and its extinction (*fanā'*); and *qaḍā'* is the bestowal upon a given entity of its definitive capacity to actualize itself.'[33]

### Commentary on Qadar

Each creature, insofar as it is a contingent being (*mumkin al-wujūd*) has a particular existential limit and extent. All things other than God exist in a particular way, are limited in differing degrees, take on different modes of existence: minerals have a particular existential measure or 'cut', differing from that of plants and animals. Just as the very existence that is apportioned to all things is itself a creature of God, likewise, the initial measuring out (*taqdīr*) of all things comes from Him. Therefore, this measuring out of existence can be understood as an act of God: it is referred to as 'active determination and apportioning in act'. This, in turn, is to be understood in the light of the following: Before creating a thing, God already knows it in its unmanifest state of latency or potentiality; this being referred to as 'determination and apportioning in knowledge'.

Belief in *qadar* is tantamount to belief in the creatorship of God as regards the particular properties of all things, and His 'active determination' of things rests upon His pre-eternal knowledge; in consequence, belief in the divine knowledge of *qadar* is but a function of belief in the eternal knowledge of God.

**Commentary on *Qaḍāʾ***

As mentioned above, *qaḍāʾ* is to be understood as the bestowal of definitive existence upon an entity. Naturally, the process by which this definitive existence is attained rests upon the operation of the law of cause and effect. A thing receives its existence as a result of the complete actualization of the cause of its existence. Insofar as this law of causality derives ultimately from God, the reality of the definitive nature of each existing entity rests upon the power and will of God. There is an 'active' *qaḍāʾ* which operates at the level of creation, and an 'essential' *qaḍāʾ* which pertains to God's eternal knowledge of all things such as they are before they come into being.

What has been said so far has been in relation to creative *qaḍāʾ* and *qadar*—whether in essential or active mode. But both principles also apply to the realm of religious dispensation, in that the principle of religious obligation is also determined by divine *qaḍāʾ*; and the particular properties of these obligations—as regards what is necessary, forbidden, and so on—also derive from 'religious pre-determination' (*taqdīr tashrīʿī*). In reply to someone questioning the reality of *qaḍāʾ* and *qadar*, Imam ʿAlī referred to this ontological level and said: 'The meaning of *qaḍāʾ* and *qadar* pertains to commanding obedience and forbidding disobedience; the bestowing of power upon man to perform good works and renounce evil works; the provision of grace to increase nearness to God; delivering up the sinners to their own [inner] states; the making of promises and threats—all these relate to the *qaḍāʾ* and *qadar* of God in regard to our actions.'[34]

We can see from this reply that the Imam restricted himself to speaking about *qaḍāʾ* and *qadar* in relation to religious dispensation, possibly on account of his awareness of the need for the questioner—and those present at the gathering—to cultivate the particular attitude and state of soul that the questioner lacked. For, at that time, the issue of existential predestination, and its implications as regards human action, was leading towards an absolute pre-determinism (*jabr*), and therewith the negation of free will (*ikhtiyār*). Evidence for our interpretation is given by the fact that the hadith continues as follows: 'Do not speculate on anything other than this, for such speculation will nullify your actions.' The meaning here is that the value of man's actions is predicated upon his free will; and a belief in the absolute pre-determinism of action annuls this freedom, and hence the value of human action.

To conclude: *qaḍā'* and *qadar* are applicable both to creation and to religious dispensation, and each of these two realms comprises two modes: an 'essential' mode, related to divine knowledge; and an 'active' mode, related to manifestation.

### Article 50

Divine predestination is not in the least incompatible with human free will. For what God has ordained for man is, precisely, free will, the very feature which distinguishes him from the animals; man has been ordained a free agent, capable of choosing to perform or to abstain from his actions. The divine decree in regard to human action is that, once the will and desire to perform a given action are established, the action will follow decisively. In other words, the very creation of man inherently comprises freedom as regards human will, along with its capacity to evaluate and judge; in this respect, the divine decree is that whenever man decides upon an action, and possesses the necessary means to perform it, a divine power brings into effect the accomplishment of the action in question.

There are those who believe that their sinfulness is the product of divine predestination, and that it was never in fact possible for them to have chosen any path other than the one which they in fact followed; but both intellect and revelation alike repudiate such an opinion. From the intellectual point of view, man determines his destiny by means of his own decisions; from the religious point of view also, man is deemed to have the capacity to be either pious and grateful or impious and wicked, as the Qur'an says:

*Verily, We have shown him the way, whether he be grateful or disbelieving.* (Sūra al-Insān, LXXVI:3)

At the time of the Revelation, one party of idolators attributed their idol-worship to the will of God, arguing that were it not His will, they would not have worshipped idols. The Qur'an relates their fanciful notion thus:

*Those who are idolators will say: Had God only willed, we would not have ascribed* [unto Him] *partners, neither would our fathers, nor would we have forbidden anything.*

The response then follows:

*Thus did those who were before them give the lie, till they tasted of the fear of Us.* (Sūra al-An'ām, VI:148)

To conclude this discussion, let us remind ourselves that the universal pathways established by God in the created universe—some terminating in the ultimate felicity of man, others in his utter ruin—these pathways are but manifestations of divine predestination; and man, alone, has the freedom to choose either one of these paths.

## Article 51

**Man and Free Will**

Human free will is a self-evident reality which can be assimilated by man in various ways, some of which we shall discuss here.

1. The conscience of each person bears testimony to his ability to decide either to perform or to abstain from a given action; if this self-evident fact be denied, then no axiomatic truth whatsoever can ever be accepted.
2. Throughout human society—religiously governed or otherwise—one finds that widely differing persons are subject to praise or blame; this should be taken as a sign that the attribution of free will to the individual is a universally encountered fact.
3. If the free will of the individual were non-existent, the dictates of religion would be vain and futile. For if each individual were helpless in regard to his life, he would be compelled to continue to follow the course of life that had been established for him previously, and thus unable to deviate by even an inch

from that path; in such a case, the religious commands and prohibitions, promises and threats, rewards and punishments, would all be utterly meaningless.

4. Throughout the course of human history, one observes that the reform of the individual and of society has been an overriding concern, to which end many programmes and policies have been promulgated, yielding clear results. It is evident that such efforts are entirely incompatible with belief in determinism as regards human action, for if the individual were assumed to be devoid of free will, all such efforts would be a waste of time.

These four points decisively and irrefutably establish the reality of free will. However, the principle of free will does not allow us to conclude that man possesses absolute liberty, and that God exercises no influence over his actions. For such a belief, called *tafwīḍ*, contradicts the principle of man's eternal dependence upon God; it also restricts the sphere of power and creativity proper to God. This is an erroneous opinion, as will be made clearer in the following Article.

## Article 52

After the passing away of the Holy Prophet, one of the questions that engaged Muslim thinkers was that of the nature of human action. One group adopted the viewpoint of determinism (*jabr*), regarding man as an intrinsically constrained agent; another group took the diametrically opposite position, conceiving of man as an entity delivered up entirely to his own resources, his actions having no connection at all with God. Both groups upheld an exclusivist point of view: action either devolved entirely upon man or entirely upon God, it was either human power that was effective or divine power.

There is, however, a third perspective, the one upheld by the Holy Imams of the *ahl al-bayt*. Imam Ṣādiq stated: 'Neither compulsion (*jabr*) nor complete freedom (*tafwīḍ*): rather, something between the two.'[35]

In other words, although action devolves upon man, it is also dependent upon God; for the action proceeds from the human agent, but since in reality the agent, along with his power, is created by God, how can one consider the action of such an agent to be independent of God?

The way in which the *ahl al-bayt* clarify the reality of human action is nothing other than the way of the Qurʾan. This revealed Scripture occasionally refers action both to its immediate agent and to God, rendering one and the same action susceptible of dual attribution. As the following verse says:

... *And thou threwest not when thou didst throw* [a handful of dust], *but God threw.* (Sūra al-Anfāl, VIII:17)

The meaning here is that whenever the Holy Prophet undertook an action, he did not do so on the sole basis of his independent agency or power; rather, the action was accomplished through the power of God. Thus, the attribution of the action to two sources is sound and correct. Put differently, the power and might of God are present within every phenomenon; this touches upon a mystery which we might try and comprehend by means of the following simile: A current of electricity, generated by a power-station, is present in electric wires; however, it is we who switch the lights on and off. It is correct to say that we switch on the light, just as it is also correct to say that the light of the bulb is derived from the electric current.

## Article 53

An integral aspect of our belief in man's free will is our certainty of God's foreknowledge of all our actions from pre-eternity. There is no contradiction between these two beliefs. Whoever cannot in fact reconcile them should consider carefully that the eternal knowledge of God encompasses the principle by which actions proceed from the free will of man; naturally, there is no contradiction between such fore-knowledge, on the one hand, and human freedom, on the other.

## III. PROPHECY (NUBUWWA)

### Article 54

**Prophecy in General**

God, the All-Wise, has chosen certain exalted persons to guide mankind, entrusting them with His messages for all peoples. These are the Messengers and the Prophets, through whose mediation the current of grace and guidance flows down to earth from the divine empyrean. This grace has been flowing from His presence since the dawn of humanity, right up to the age of the Holy Prophet. It is necessary to understand that each of the particular religious dispensations brought by the Prophets was the most complete form of religion for the time and the people concerned. Were this flow of divine grace not perpetual, mankind would never be able to attain perfection.

**Reasons for the Necessity of Prophecy**

Since the creation of man is brought about by God, the Wise, it follows naturally that there is a goal and purpose for man's creation. Now, given the fact that what man, and man alone, possesses is intellect and wisdom, it follows that the goal and purpose of his creation must be intelligible.

From another angle, however much the intellect of man is useful and necessary to him in his quest for the path of perfection, it has not been sufficient. Were he to remain satisfied with his intellect alone, he would never be able to find an integral path, one that can really lead him to his own perfection. For example, one of the most compelling of all intellectual challenges is to comprehend the mystery of man's origin and his final destination. Man wishes to know from whence he came, why he came and whither he will go. But the intellect, acting alone, cannot clarify or resolve such issues.

The incapacity of the human intellect and its researches is not restricted to the domain of the origin and the end of humanity, but extends, rather, to many other questions of vital importance to life. The various and conflicting perspectives of man as regards economics, ethics, the family and other matters, all testify to the inability of the intellect to arrive at an infallible conclusion in these domains; and for this same reason, we observe the emergence of conflicting schools of thought. Considering these points carefully, the intelligence makes the sound judgement that divine wisdom has required that mankind be sent divinely guided leaders and teachers in order to establish clearly the path of right guidance.

Those who believe that the guidance offered by the intellect can replace the guidance bestowed by Heaven must address the following two questions:

1. Human intelligence and learning, as applied to the comprehension of man himself, of the mysteries of being, the past and the future of his existential journey, are inadequate; whilst the Creator of man, on the other hand—in accordance with the principle that every creator knows its creation—is completely aware of man, and all the dimensions and mysteries of his being. In the Qurʾan, we have this argument referred to thus:

   *Should He not know what He created? And He is the Subtle, the Aware.* (Sūra al-Mulk, LXVII:14)

2. Out of a compelling instinct of self-preservation, man consciously or unconsciously applies himself to the pursuit of his personal benefit, and in his planning he is unable to leave out of account the benefit accruing to his personal or group interests. However, he will never be able to take into account the totality of the human collectivity; he will always be, to some extent, prejudiced in favour of his own self-interest. The guidance given by the Prophets, on the other hand, because it derives from the divine reality, is devoid of such partiality and the deficiencies that flow therefrom.

Taking these points into consideration, one must conclude that mankind has always been in need of divine guidance and prophetic instruction, and always will be.

## Article 55

**The Qur'an and the Aims of Prophecy**

In the previous article we asserted, through intellectual argument, the necessity of divinely-guided Messengers. Now we ought to address the necessity of prophecy by focusing upon its aims, doing so from the point of view of the Qur'an and Hadith. It should be stressed, however, that the Qur'anic perspective on this question constitutes in itself a form of 'intellectual analysis', [that is, what the Qur'an teaches accords with what the intellect perceives].

The Qur'an relates the purpose of the raising up of Prophets to the following factors:

1. The consolidation of the foundation of *Tawḥīd*, and opposition to all forms of deviation therefrom. As it is said:

   *And verily We have raised in every nation a Messenger* [proclaiming]: *Serve God and shun false gods.* (Sūra al-Naḥl, XVI:36)

   Thus, the divinely-inspired Prophets were in constant conflict with the polytheists, having to undergo great tribulations as a result. Imam 'Alī said, in relation to the aims of the raising up of Prophets by God: the Prophets were appointed in order 'to teach [God's] slaves about their Lord that of which they were ignorant; to instruct them about His lordship after their denial [of it]; and to cause them to declare Him one in divinity after their deviation [from it].'[36]
2. To teach mankind the sciences of religion, the divine messages, and to show them the right path, and the way of purification. As the Qur'an says:

   *He it is Who hath sent among the unlettered ones a Messenger of their own, to recite unto them His revelations and to make them grow* [in purity], *and to teach them the Scripture and wisdom...* (Sūra al-Jum'a, LXII:2)
3. Establishing justice in human society. As the Qur'an says:

   *We verily sent Our Messengers with clear proofs, and revealed with them the Scripture and the Balance, that mankind might observe right measure...* (Sūra al-Ḥadīd, LVII:25)

Evidently, the establishment of justice requires that one know what justice calls for in a whole range of fields, and on different levels; and then that one bring it to fruition according to the dictates of divine governance.

4. Providing authoritative judgement in diverse matters. As it is said:

*Mankind were one community and God sent Prophets as bearers of good tidings and as warners and revealed therewith the Scripture with the truth that it might judge between mankind concerning that wherein they differed.* (Sūra al-Baqara, II:213)

It is clear that disputation amongst men is not confined to the domain of beliefs, but is found in diverse areas of human life.

5. To put an end to arguments against God by His slaves. As the Qur'an says:

*Messengers bearing good news and warning, in order that mankind might have no argument against God after the Messengers. God is ever Mighty, Wise.* (Sūra al-Nisā', IV:165)

It is obvious that God had a purpose in creating man, and this purpose was to be effected by means of the ordination of a perfect plan in all human affairs; and this plan had to be established by God for all people in such a manner that there could be no further possibility of arguing with Him, or proffering excuses by saying, for example, 'I did not know the right way to conduct my life.'

## Article 56

### Ways of Recognizing the Prophets

Primordial human nature compels man not to accept any claims without conclusive evidence; so whoever accepts as truthful one who makes claims without such evidence is acting contrary to his own innate nature. Making a claim to prophecy is the most awesome of all possible claims that a human being can make; and, naturally, such a claim can only be substantiated by presenting definitive and well-founded evidence. This evidence can come from one of the following three sources:

1. The previous Prophet—who, having conclusively proved his own prophethood, clearly stipulates the identity of the Prophet to come after him. Thus, the Prophet Jesus explicitly refers to the Seal of the Prophets [i.e. Muḥammad], giving good tidings of his advent.
2. Portents and signs, in different ways, bear testimony to the truth of the claim to be a Prophet. These proofs can come from the way of life of the Prophet, the content of the religious call he makes, the character of those who follow him, and the manner in which he issues his call. Today, in law-courts around the world, the same procedure is followed in order to distinguish the true from the false, the innocent from the guilty. At the time of the establishment of Islam, this very procedure was used in order to ascertain the truth of the claims made by the Holy Prophet.[37]
3. The performance of miracles. Accompanying his claim to prophethood, the Prophet performs extraordinary, miraculous feats, which convince others to accept his call, these miracles being in harmony with his claim.

The first two of the above ways are not universally applicable, whereas the third is, and throughout the course of the history of prophethood, people have made use of this way of recognizing true Prophets, and for their part, the Prophets have also substantiated their claims by the performance of miracles.

### Article 57

There is a logical relationship between the performance of miracles and the veracity of the claim to prophethood. For if the one who works miracles is truthful in his claims, the proof of the claim will be confirmed; and on the other hand, were the person lying in his claims, it would not be feasible to presume that God, the

All-Wise, who wishes right guidance for His slaves, would place such miraculous powers at his disposal. For people, upon witnessing such powers, would believe in the one possessing them, and would act upon what he said. Thus, whenever such a false prophet would lie, his followers would be led astray—and such a state of affairs is incompatible with the justice and wisdom of God. This position flows logically from the principle of discernment between good and evil that has been discussed earlier.

### Article 58

The performance of an act that transcends the boundaries of normal existence, and which accompanies and harmonizes with a claim to prophethood, is called a 'miracle' (*muʿjiza*); but if such an act is performed by a righteous slave of God who does not claim to be a Prophet, then it is called a 'charism' (*karāma*). Evidence of the fact that such righteous slaves of God, other than the Prophets, are also capable of performing extraordinary acts is given for example in the heavenly-sent food that was provided for the Virgin Mary; and in the transportation of the throne of the Queen of Sheba [Bilqīs] in a single moment from Yemen to Palestine, an act performed by one of Solomon's prominent companions, Āṣif b. Barkhiyā. The Qur'an relates both of these incidents. In regard to Mary:

*Whenever Zachariah went into the sanctuary where she was, he found that she had food* ...(Sūra Āl 'Imrān, III:37)

As for the incident concerning the throne of Queen Bilqīs:

*One who had knowledge of the Scripture said: I will bring it to thee before thy gaze returneth to thee.* (Sūra al-Naml, XXVII:40)

## Article 59

**The Miracles of Prophets**

The difference between a miracle and other extraordinary acts will be briefly explained below:

1. Unteachability. One who performs miracles does so without any prior training or teaching, while other extraordinary acts are the result of a whole series of methodical practices and instruction. For example, Moses, as a fully grown man, set out for Egypt; on his way, he received his call to prophethood when a voice called out to him:

   *O Moses! Lo! I am God, the Lord of the worlds, throw down your staff.* (Sūra al-Qaṣaṣ, XXVIII:30–31)

   Having done so, the staff suddenly took the form of a serpent, and Moses was terrified. The voice then commanded him to take his hand from his breast; it emerged luminous, glowing so much that it would have dazzled the sight of any onlooker. But the Qur'an also mentions the magicians of Solomon's time [the two angels in Babel, Hārūt and Mārūt] who teach mankind magic:

   *And from these two, people learn that by which they cause division between man and wife.* (Sūra al-Baqara, II:102)

2. Indisputability. As a miracle derives from the infinite power of God, it cannot be disputed, whereas magic and witchcraft, and such practices as are associated with ascetics, since they derive from the limited power of man, can be disputed.
3. Illimitability. The miracles of the Prophets are not limited to just one or two types, but are of such diverse character that they cannot be simplistically classified under a single heading. For example: how different are the throwing down of a staff that turns into a serpent, and the bringing forth of a luminous hand from one's breast; then, how different these two miracles are from the springing up of fountains of water as a result of striking a rock with a staff; and again, how different these three miracles are from the parting of the sea upon being struck by a

staff! As regards the Prophet Jesus, we read that he fashioned birds from clay, then breathed upon them and they came to life, by God's grace. In addition to this act, he told of things that were kept hidden within homes, he healed the blind man and the leper by passing his hand over their faces, and he even brought the dead to life.

4. Spirituality. In general, those who perform miracles or charisms are to be distinguished from other workers of extraordinary feats, such as magicians, both in respect of their aims, and in relation to spirituality generally. The first group have only the most noble aims in view, while the second have worldly aims; and, naturally, as regards spiritual temperament, the two groups differ markedly.

## Article 60

### Revelation and Prophecy

In the previous articles we have explained the ways by which true Prophets can be distinguished from false ones. Now we must address the manner in which communication takes place between the Prophets and the unseen world, that is, through revelation (*waḥy*).

Revelation is the most important means by which Prophets are in communion with the unseen. It is not the product of human instinct or intellect, but a special mode of awareness that God has bestowed upon the Prophets in order that they might convey divine messages to mankind. The Qur'an describes revelation thus:

*And truly, it is a revelation of the Lord of the worlds, which the faithful spirit hath brought down upon thy heart* ... (Sūra al-Shuʿarā', XXVI:192–194)

This verse shows that the Prophet's awareness of the divine message has nothing to do with the activities of the outward senses or the like; on the contrary, this awareness is cast by the angel of revelation into the heart of the Prophet.[38] Therefore, the complex reality of revelation cannot be explained by conventional means of analysis. In truth, the descent of revelation is one of the manifestations of the unseen which can only be properly assimilated by faith, however much its intrinsic reality may remain mysterious to us. As it is said:

*Those who believe in the unseen* ... (Sūra al-Baqara, II:3)

**Article 61**

Those who wish to measure all things according to material standards—using only empirical perception and thus confining the verities of the unseen within the limited framework of the senses—have explained divine revelation in various ways, all of which, in our opinion, are utterly false. We address below some of these attempts at explaining revelation.

One group of writers regard the Prophets as geniuses and suppose revelation to be the product of their meditations, the results of their own inward mental activity. According to this opinion, the reality of the *'faithful spirit'* is nothing other than the purified spirit and soul of these geniuses, and the 'revealed' scriptures are likewise nothing but the formal expression of the sublime ideas that crystallized in the minds of these geniuses.

This kind of explanation of revelation is a sign of the incapacity of modern empirical science, which relies exclusively upon material methods of verification. An important problem for this perspective is that it directly contradicts what the Prophets of God themselves actually say; for they have always declared that what they had brought to mankind was nothing but divine revelation; thus, a necessary corollary of the empirical explanation of revelation is that all Prophets are liars—a proposition which is completely at odds with their noble stature and with what history tells us regarding the sincerity and rectitude of their character.

Another group of writers, with the same motive as the group addressed above, consider revelation to be the consummation of the spiritual states of the Prophets. According to this view, the Prophet, because of the strength of his faith in God, and as a result of his intense devotions, attains a degree of realization whereby a series of profound truths are attained in his innermost being; he then imagines that these truths have been cast into his heart from the unseen, whereas in reality their source and origin are but his own soul. The adherents of this view claim that they do not doubt the sincerity of the Prophets, and they are certain that the Prophets really have witnessed these truths, as a result of their spiritual disciplines; but they will dispute the source of these truths. Whilst the Prophets claim that these truths are cast unto them from without, from an objective dimension in the unseen world, the proponents of this argument hold that the source of these truths is exclusively within the souls of the Prophets.[39]

This viewpoint is not something new, it is just an expression of one of the ideas held about revelation in the pre-Islamic [period of] *Jāhiliyya* ('ignorance'), an expression clothed in modern garb, however. The import of this perspective is that revelation is the outcome of the meditative reflections of the Prophets, their intense introspection, the frequency of their worship, their modes of contemplation upon God, their continuous meditation on ways of reforming humanity. Certain truths are suddenly perceived in embodied forms before them, truths which they believe have been bestowed upon them from the unseen. Such a view of revelation is at one with that of the Arabs of the *Jāhiliyya* period who said, '*Muddled dreams*' (Sūra al-Anbiyā', XXI:5).

In other verses, the Qur'an strongly refutes this view, saying that when the Prophets claim to have seen the angel of revelation, they spoke truthfully, neither their hearts nor their sights erred:

*The heart falsified not what it saw…*

And also:

*His sight never swerved, nor did it err.* (Sūra al-Najm, LIII, 11,17)

In other words, the Prophet truly beheld the angel of revelation, both with his outward and his inward perception.

## Article 62

### The Inerrancy (*ʿIṣma*) of the Prophets[40]

The term *ʿiṣma* is to be understood in the sense of inviolability and immunity. In the domain of prophecy it comprises the following aspects: (a) in respect of the station of receiving, preserving and conveying revelation; (b) in respect of being protected against all disobedience and sin; (c) in respect of being protected against error in both individual and social affairs.

As regards the first of these degrees, there is universal agreement; for were there to be any likelihood of error or mistake at this degree, the trust of the people in the Prophet would be shaken, and they would not be able to rely upon the other messages of the Prophet; in consequence, the whole purpose of revelation would be undermined. The Holy Qurʾan tells us that God has placed the Prophets under an all-encompassing supervision to ensure that the revelation is correctly conveyed unto mankind, as it is said:

> [He is the] *Knower of the unseen, and He revealeth unto none His secret, save unto every Messenger whom He hath chosen, and then He made a guard to go before him and a guard behind him, that He may know that they have indeed conveyed the messages of their Lord. He surroundeth all their doings, and He keepeth count of all things.* (Sūra al-Jinn, LXXII:26–28)

In these verses, two types of guardian are mentioned in regard to the function of protecting the integrity of the revelation: angels who guard the Prophet against every type of evil; and the Almighty Himself, who guards the Prophet and the angels. The reason for this comprehensive supervision is to ensure the realization of the purpose of prophecy, that is, that revelation be conveyed unto mankind.

## Article 63

The Messengers of God are rendered immune from all types of sin and error in their enactment of the rulings of the Shariʿa. For were they not absolutely in accord with the divine rulings which they themselves were propounding, nobody could rely upon the truth of their sayings, and in consequence the purpose of prophecy would not be fulfilled.

The sage Naṣīr al-Dīn Ṭūsī has given a concise explanation of this proof of the necessity of *'iṣma*: ''*Iṣma* is essential for the Messengers, in order that their sayings be trusted, and the purpose of prophecy be realized.'[41]

As for the Messengers being incapable of sin, many verses of the Qur'an stress this in different ways. We allude to some of these below.

1. The Qur'an refers to the Messengers as being guided and appointed by the Divine Reality:

   ... *and We chose them and guided them unto a straight path.* (Sūra al-An'ām, VI:87)

2. It reminds us that whomsoever God guides, none can lead astray:

   *And he whom God guideth, for him there can be no misleader.* (Sūra al-Zumar, XXXIX:37)

3. 'Sin' is understood in the sense of 'misguidance':

   *Yet he hath led astray of you a great multitude.* (Sūra Yā Sīn, XXXVI:62)

These verses, taken together, show that the Messengers are devoid of all kinds of error and sin.

The intellectual proof of the necessity of the *'iṣma* of the Messengers that was established above applies equally to the necessity of their *'iṣma* prior to their receiving their prophetic mission. For one who has spent part of his life in sin and error and then afterwards claims to offer authentic guidance cannot be relied upon. But as for one who, from the very beginning of his life, was devoid of every type of impurity, such a person would elicit the trust of all people. Also, those who denied the truth of the message would all too easily be able to point to the dark past of the Messenger, vilify his name and character, and thus undermine the message. In such an environment, only one who has lived a life of impeccable purity, such that he merits the title 'Muḥammad the Trustworthy' (*al-Amīn*), would be able, by the brilliance of his radiant personality, to cast aside the clouds of malicious propaganda generated by his enemies and, through an unwavering and noble rectitude, gradually illumine the murky ambience of the *Jāhiliyya* Arabs.

In addition to such considerations, it is clear that a man who was incapable of sin from the very beginning of his life is elevated above another who is only rendered such after having been appointed to a prophetic mission; and the scope of his guidance will, correspondingly, be much greater. Divine wisdom demands that only the best, most perfectly accomplished person be chosen as model and exemplar for humanity.

## Article 64

In addition to being incapable of sin, the Messengers are also immune from error in the following domains:

1. Judging disputes. The Messengers were charged by God to pass judgement according to the divinely-instituted scales of justice, and there could never be any question of the Messengers deviating in any way from the principles by which disputes and all other legal questions were to be ajudicated.
2. Specification of the boundaries of religious rulings: for example, ascertaining whether a given liquid is alcoholic or not.
3. The domain of social principles: for example, specifying what contributes to public welfare and what corrupts it.
4. The domain of conventional daily matters.

The reason for the *ʿiṣma* operating in the last three domains is this: In the minds of most people, error in these matters implies error in the domain of religious rulings also. Consequently, committing error in such matters undermines the certainty that people must have in the personality of the Messenger, and leads ultimately to the undermining of the purpose of prophecy. However, the necessity of *ʿiṣma* in the first two domains is more readily apparent than in the fourth.

## Article 65

One of the aspects of the *'iṣma* of the Messengers is that there can be no element within their being that might serve as a source of repulsion for mankind. We all know that certain diseases and certain character traits—such as crudity or baseness—give rise to aversion and repulsion. The Messengers must perforce be free from such bodily and psychic deformities, for the aversion of people from the Prophet is at odds with the purpose of prophecy, which is the transmission of the divine message to humanity by means of a Prophet.

Thus, let us note that intellectual judgement functions here in the form of a disclosure of a reality; a reality which is at one with the divine wisdom. Only those who are devoid of such faults can be chosen as Messengers.[42]

## Article 66

We have observed that both decisive intellectual judgement and explicit Qur'anic rulings alike establish the necessity of the *'iṣma* of the Messengers. But now we must take account of certain verses which, at first sight, appear to report the commission of sins by the Messengers (such as certain verses concerning Adam). What is to be said in this regard?

One must answer, first, by clarifying the following point: Evidently, despite the fact that there can be no contradiction in the Qur'an, one must take fully into account the actual context of the verses in order to arrive at their true meaning; in such matters, the immediately apparent meaning should not become the grounds for a rash judgement. Fortunately, the great Shi'i theologians and commentators of the Qur'an have explained such verses, some of them devoting entire treatises to them. A detailed explanation of each of these verses is beyond the scope of the present book; those who wish to investigate the matter further can consult the books referred to below.[43]

## Article 67

The sources and foundations of *ʿiṣma* can be summarized in the two following principles:

1. The Messengers (and certain saints) possess such a profound degree of gnosis, such a subtle mode of awareness of God, that they would not exchange their contentment with God for anything else. In other words, their perception of the divine grandeur, of His bounty and majesty, is such that they cannot see anything apart from His reality, and they can entertain no thought apart from that of seeking the satisfaction of God. This station of gnosis is referred to in the following saying of Imam ʿAlī: 'I have seen no thing without seeing God before it, after it, and along with it.' And Imam Ṣādiq said: 'I worship God out of love for Him; and this is the worship of the great ones.'[44]
2. The perfect awareness, on the part of the Messengers, of the beatific consequences of obedience, and the terrible retribution that follows disobedience—such an awareness gives rise to their immunity from disobedience to God. Of course, *ʿiṣma* in all its fullness is the exclusive preserve of the special saints of God, but in fact some pious believers are immune from the commission of sins in many spheres of their activity. For instance, a pious man would never commit suicide, at any price, nor would he kill innocent people.[45] There are also ordinary people who benefit from a kind of 'immunity' in some of their affairs. For instance, nobody would, at whatever price, touch a naked, live electrical wire. It is clear that immunity in such instances arises out of the individual's certain knowledge of the negative consequences of a given action: were such certain knowledge of the dangerous consequences of sin to be attained, it would be a potent source of rendering a person immune from sin.

## Article 68

It must be understood that there is no contradiction between *ʿiṣma* and the free will of the *maʿṣūm* (the inerrant). Rather, a *maʿṣūm*, despite having perfect consciousness of God, and of the effects of obedience and disobedience, does have the power to commit a sin, even if he would never avail himself of this power. It is akin to the case of a kind father, who has the power to kill his own child, but would never do so. A clearer instance of this principle is the non-existence of evil acts issuing from God. In His absolute omnipotence, God has the power to put pious souls in Hell and, inversely, disobedient souls in Heaven, but His justice and wisdom preclude such acts. From this point it should be clear that the renunciation of sin and the accomplishment of worship and obedience are considered a great honour by the *ma'ṣūm*; so, despite having the power to sin, the *ma'ṣūmīn* would never in fact commit one.

## Article 69

Despite our belief in the *'iṣma* of all the Prophets, we do not regard this *'iṣma* as being a property of the Prophets alone. For it is possible that a person be *ma'ṣūm* while not being a Prophet. The Holy Qur'an says about Mary:

*O Mary, Verily God hath chosen thee and made thee pure, and hath preferred thee above the women of creation.* (Sūra Āl 'Imrān, III:42)

Since the Qur'an uses the word *aṣṭafā* [lit. to choose, but also meaning 'to prefer'] in relation to Mary, it is clear that she was *ma'ṣūm*, for it is this word that is applied to the Prophets:

*Verily, God hath preferred Adam and Noah and the family of Abraham and the family of Imran above His creatures.* (Sūra Āl 'Imrān, III:33)

Apart from this point, it should be noted that in the verse cited above referring to Mary's purity, the meaning is that she was intrinsically uncontaminated by any kind of defilement, not that she was exonerated from the sin of which she was accused by the Jews in regard to her son. For her exoneration from this charge was in fact proven during the first days of the birth of Jesus, thanks to his miraculous speech;[46] there was no need for any further explanation.

This having been said, the verse relating to Mary's purity comes in the series of verses that pertain to the period when she was a devotee at the prayer-niche of the Temple in Jerusalem, and was not yet pregnant with Jesus. Thus, there was no accusation at this stage, so the purity in question could not simply mean that she was innocent of the charge against her.

## Article 70

### Specific Prophecy

In the previous sections we addressed the principle of prophecy in its general aspect; here we intend to address the specific prophecy pertaining to the Prophet of Islam, Muḥammad b. ʿAbd Allāh. We had noted that prophecy can be proved in three ways: (a) by miracles accompanying the prophetic call; (b) by the accumulated evidence from companions and witnesses in support of the truth of the call; and (c) by the verification provided by the previous Prophet. The prophecy of the Messenger of Islam can be confirmed by each of the above means, as we shall briefly show below.

### The Qur'an, the Eternal Miracle

History clearly shows that the Prophet of Islam performed diverse miracles in the course of his mission. But he laid stress above all else upon that miracle which is eternal, the Holy Qur'an itself. He declared his prophecy by means of the revealed Book and challenged anyone in the world to produce the like of it; but nobody at the time of the Revelation could respond to the challenge. Even to this day, after the passage of centuries, the Qur'an's inimitable uniqueness remains; as it says in the Book:

*Say: Though mankind and the jinn should assemble to produce the like of this Qur'an, they could not produce the like thereof, even if they were to help one another.* (Sūra Banī Isrā'īl, XVII:88)

Here, the Qur'an is saying, in effect, with regard to its own uniqueness: 'O Prophet, challenge the people to bring a book like this one'. Elsewhere, it challenges them to bring even less:

*Say: Then bring ten sūras the like thereof, invented* ... (Sūra Hūd, XI:13)

... *then produce a sūra the like thereof* ... (Sūra al-Baqara, II:23)

We know that the enemies of Islam have not spared any effort in their attempts, over the course of fourteen centuries, to harm Islam; they have not ceased accusing the Prophet of being a magician, a madman and other such things; but they have never been able to take up the challenge of producing anything comparable to the Qur'an. Today, despite all the different fields of contemporary thought and learning, and all the modern epistemological tools at their disposal, they are unable to refute or confound the limpid, inimitable uniqueness of the Qur'an; this, alone, bears witness to the fact that the Qur'an is something utterly beyond the speech of a human being.

**Article 71**

The Holy Prophet performed various miracles, the commentaries upon which are recorded in books of Hadith and history. But, as stated above, the eternal miracle which radiates throughout all the ages is the Holy Qur'an; and the secret as to why the Prophet of Islam, and not any other Prophet, should have been distinguished by this miracle resides in this: The religion brought by him is the last religion, and it is to last until the end of time. An everlasting religion needs an everlasting miracle, so that it be a decisive proof of prophecy in each age and for each succeeding generation; and so that mankind might, throughout the course of the centuries, have recourse directly to this miracle itself, rather than depend on the words of others.

The Qur'an is miraculous in several respects, extensive elaboration upon each of which would take us far beyond the scope of this book; so we shall confine ourselves to the following brief discussion.

From the time of the descent of the Holy Qur'an, the first thing that struck the Arabic-speaking world and those versed in oratory and rules of eloquence, was the beauty of the language, the elegance and originality of its composition, and the sublime meanings contained in the Scripture. This special feature of the Qur'an was clearly evident to the Arabs of that time, as it is for those of today; and because of this, the Prophet, through continuous recitation of its verses, and through repeated invitations to ponder the uniqueness of the Qur'an, cast the champions of oratory and the masters of eloquence into abasement and humiliation, causing them to gnaw at their fingers in bewildered rage at the majestic speech of the Qur'an, bitterly acknowledging its super-human quality.

Walīd b. Mughayra, a renowned poet and a master orator among the Quraysh, declared, after hearing the Prophet recite some verses: 'By God, I have just heard something from Muḥammad that is unlike the speech of man or the speech of *jinn*. It is a speech with its own unique sweetness and beauty. The branches of its words are laden with fruit, its roots are full of blessings; it is a surpassing discourse, than which no more distinguished speech exists. Indeed, nothing can begin to rival its excellence.'[47]

It was not just Walīd b. Mughayra who extolled the outward beauty and inward profundity of the Qur'an; other great orators also, such as 'Utba b. Rabī'a and Tufayl b. 'Umar, also expressed their utter incapacity to compete with the Qur'an and acknowledged it as a literary miracle.

Of course, the Arabs of the Jāhiliyya, because of their low level of culture, did not grasp anything but this aspect of the miraculous nature of the Qur'an. But when the sun of Islam illumined a quarter of the inhabited world, the great thinkers of the world reflected deeply upon the profound verses of the Qur'an, and were able to benefit not only from its miraculous literary aspects, but also from the evident connection that each of its other aspects had with the sacred and the miraculous; and in every age, new dimensions of its endless verities would be discovered, a process which continues to this day.

## Article 72

In the previous article, we briefly referred to the miraculous qualities of the Qur'an. Now, we shall summarize some other manifestations of its miraculous nature. If the literary miracle of the Qur'an can only be grasped by one who has some mastery in the Arabic language, the other miraculous qualities can, fortunately, be grasped by everyone.

The person who brought the Qur'an was unlettered and unlearned, not having been schooled; nor had he studied at the feet of a great master; nor had he read a single book, as it is stated:

*And thou wast not a reader of any scripture before it, nor didst thou write it with thy right hand, for then might those have doubted who follow falsehood.* (Sūra al-ʿAnkabūt, XXIX:48)

The Holy Prophet recited this verse to people who were well aware of his life-history. Naturally, had he studied previously, he would have been contradicted by those who knew of his past; so if he was accused by some of having had the Qur'an 'taught to him by a man', we know for sure that it is baseless, as are all the other accusations made against him. The Qur'an refutes this accusation, saying that the one who was supposed to have taught him was a non-Arab; while the Arabic of the Qur'an is classical, eloquent Arabic.[48]

The Qur'an was revealed in recitation to the Holy Prophet over the course of twenty-three years, under various conditions (peace and war, whilst journeying or residing at home, etc.). The nature of such an oral discourse normally imposes at least two or more different styles or modes upon the speaker. Even authors who compose their works under unvarying, stable conditions, and who attempt to maintain thematic consistency and stylistic harmony, are often unable to avoid discrepancies and disharmony in their works; such problems are even more likely to befall one who delivers a verbal discourse gradually, and under extremely variegated conditions and circumstances.

It would be appropriate here to recall that the Qur'an contains discourses on themes as diverse as theology, history, religious law and legislation, ethics, the natural world and other matters; but despite this immense variety of subject-matter, it maintains, from beginning to end, the most supreme harmony, its style of discourse flowing marvellously through its diverse contents. The Qur'an itself mentions this aspect of its own miraculous nature:

*Will they not then ponder the Qur'an? If it had been from other than God, they would have found therein much incongruity.* (Sūra al-Nisā', IV:82)

The Qur'an recognizes the capacity of human nature for far-sightedness, and on that basis establishes laws. Given this fundamental capacity for insight, all aspects of the spiritual and material life of man are encompassed by the Qur'an; universally applicable principles—ones which will never fade or become outmoded—are also given in this Scripture. One of the special features of the universal laws of Islam is that they are valid in the most diverse conditions and environments. When Muslims had conquered vast parts of the world, they were able to rule with authority and dignity over generations of different human collectivities by virtue of these laws. Imam Bāqir said: 'Everything of which mankind has need and has asked for is given by God in this Holy Book, and has been explained by Him to His Prophet; and He has established for everything a limit, and for each limit, a rationale has been given.'[49]

## Article 73

In different verses, the Qur'an explains the intricate relationships between the mysteries of the created universe, relationships and connections of which the people of the time had no inkling. The disclosure of these mysteries, by an unlettered individual, living in the midst of people ignorant of all such things, could only have come about by means of divine revelation. Many examples of this can be given, but we shall restrict ourselves here to one alone: The discovery of the law of universal polarity is a major finding of modern science; the Qur'an, at a time when there was not even the slightest information on such matters, refers to this law as follows:

*And all things We have created by pairs, that haply ye may reflect.* (Sūra al-Dhāriyāt, LI:49)

The Qur'an has prophesied events, giving precise and definite information about them before they unfolded, exactly as predicted. There are several examples of this, but we shall refer to just one. When the God-fearing Christian Byzantines (al-Rūm) were defeated by the fire-worshipping Sassanids, the pagan Arabs took this as a good omen, declaring that they, too, would prevail over the God-fearing Arabs of the peninsula. As regards this event, the Qur'an gives precise information:

*The Romans have been defeated in the nearer land, and they, after their defeat, will be victorious within ten years—God's command in the former case and in the latter—and on that day believers will rejoice.* (Sūra al-Rūm, XXX:2–4)

The events took place exactly as predicted, and both God-fearing groups, the Byzantine Christians and the Arabian Muslims, prevailed over their respective enemies (Iranian Sassanids and the pagans of Quraysh). Thus we find at the end of the verse a reference to the happiness of the believers, for these two victories were simultaneous.

The Qur'an has spoken of the lives of the Prophets and of past communities, in a number of Sūras and in various ways. It might be said that, being the final Revelation, the Qur'an clarifies much of the information found in previous Scriptures pertaining to the Prophets of the past, their missions, and their communities. In the Qur'anic accounts of the lives of the Prophets, there is not the slightest divergence either from the dictates of the intellect or of innate human nature, on the one hand, or from what the supreme status of the Prophets implies, on the other.

## Article 74

**Evidence and Testimony of the Prophethood of the Holy Prophet**

The assembling of evidence and testimonies, as stated earlier, is one means by which the veracity of the claim of the Prophet can be proven. Here we shall briefly allude to some of this evidence which shows clearly the authenticity of his claim.

1. The quality of the life of the Prophet prior to his receiving his mission. The Qurayshi tribesmen referred to the Prophet as al-Amīn, 'the Trustworthy', before he received his call, entrusting to his safe-keeping their most precious possessions. When they were re-building the Kaʿba, a dispute broke out between four tribes as to which would have the honour of fixing the Black Stone in its place. All agreed that this act be accomplished by the most honourable of the Quraysh, that is, the Holy Prophet, on account of his virtue and his purity of soul.[50]
2. The fact of being untainted by the impurities of his ambience. The Prophet of Islam was raised in an environment dominated by idolatry, gambling, the burying alive of female babies, the eating of carrion and various other forms of impropriety. Nonetheless, the Prophet was an exemplary figure, standing above his environment, remaining unsullied in any respect by the moral and spiritual corruption around him.
3. The content of his call. When we examine the content of the Prophet's call, it is striking that he was calling people to the very opposite of the norms prevailing in their society. They were idol-worshippers and he called them to *Tawḥīd*; they denied the afterlife, and he made belief therein one of the tenets of the faith; they buried alive their daughters and considered women to be of little importance, but he restored to women their intrinsic human dignity; they were greedy for riches and usury, and he prohibited usury; wine-drinking and gambling were rife, and he called these things the handiwork of the devil, and abstention from both were made obligatory.
4. The means by which the call was made. The ways and means by which the Prophet issued his call were essentially humane and moral. He never used inhumane methods in his conduct of warfare—such as blocking and polluting his enemies' water-supplies, cutting down trees or the like. Rather, he ordered that no women, children or old people were to be harmed, that no trees were to be cut, and that hostilities against the

enemy were not to commence until an ultimatum had been delivered. There was no trace of the Machiavellian maxim, 'the end justifies the means,' in his approach. For example, at the battle of Khaybar, he refused to take the advice of a Jew to poison the water-supplies of the enemy to force them to surrender. The history of his mission is, indeed, replete with noble acts towards his enemies.

5. The qualities of his followers. A careful consideration of the spirituality, the intellectuality and the morality of those who believed in the Prophet also confirms the veracity of his Message. It is clear that whenever a message has an effect on the most excellent members of a community, this is a sign of its veracity and authenticity; while, if the most worldly types are attracted by it, this is a sign of its deficiency. Amongst the true followers of the Prophet were such supreme figures as the Commander of the Faithful, ʿAlī b. Abī Ṭālib, Jaʿfar b. Abī Ṭālib, Salmān al-Fārisī, Abū Dharr al-Ghiffārī, Miqdād b. ʿAmr, ʿAmmār b. Yāsir, Bilāl b. Rabāḥ, Muṣʿab b. ʿUmayr, Ibn Masʿūd—in regard to all of whom history records eminent personal qualities: asceticism, piety, purity, righteousness, resolution, generosity.

6. The evident effect on the environment, the founding of a mighty and glorious civilization. Over a period of twenty-three years, the Prophet of Islam transformed the entire situation of the Arabian peninsula. He changed bandits into believers and raised up monotheists from pagan idolators; he trained them to such an extent that not only did they found a glorious civilization in their own homeland, but also spread the unrivalled majesty of Islamic culture to other parts of the world. Jaʿfar b. Abī Ṭālib, one of the Muslims of the Golden Age of Islam, stressed this very point in the answer he gave to the King of Ethiopia: 'O King, God has raised up amongst us a Prophet who led us from idolatry and gambling to prayer and charity, justice and piety, generosity to one's kin; and who prohibited all forms of corruption, lewdness and oppression.'[51]

This and other such evidence leads us to accept the veracity of his Message and the justice of his cause. It is certain that someone with such qualities as were possessed by him must be truthful in his claims to prophecy, and in his avowal of a connection with the unseen, just as the other evidence brought forward emphatically and with precision uphold these claims.

## Article 75

### Confirmation by the Previous Prophet

One of the ways by which the truth of a prophetic claim is affirmed is by confirmation given by the previous Prophet. For it is to be assumed that the prophethood of the previous Prophet was proven with conclusive evidence; so, naturally, his words can be the basis for evaluating the prophethood of the succeeding Prophet. Some verses of the Holy Qur'an indicate that the People of the Book recognized the Prophet of Islam just as clearly as they had recognized their own children; in other words, the distinguishing signs of his prophethood were clearly indicated in their revealed scriptures. The Prophet of Islam claimed to be the Prophet prophesied in their scripture and none denied the truth of his claim, as it is said in the Qur'an:

*Those unto whom We gave the Scripture recognize* [the Prophet] *as they recognize their sons. But lo! a party of them knowingly conceal the truth.* (Sūra al-Baqara, II:146)

The Prophet of Islam claimed that the Prophet Jesus gave good tidings regarding his own advent when he said:

*Lo! I am the Messenger of God unto you, confirming that which was* [revealed] *before me in the Torah, and bringing good news of a Messenger who cometh after me, whose name is Aḥmad.* (Sūra al-Ṣaff, LXI:6)

The People of the Book did not refute this claim, even though they refused to acknowledge its truth.

In passing, it is interesting to note that the Gospel, despite having been subjected to centuries of interpolations and alterations, still contains the prophecy of Jesus pertaining to a person named

Parakletos (meaning 'the Praised', thus 'Muḥammad') in the Gospel of St John, chapters 14–16, to which researchers can refer.[52]

### Article 76

As previously noted, the miracles of the Holy Prophet cannot be limited to the fact that the Qur'an was revealed through him; rather, in various circumstances, for the sake of convincing certain persons, he performed a number of miracles. Here, we must firmly establish in our minds, on the basis of the following simple inquiry, the fact that the Prophet did accomplish miracles other than that of the revelation of the Qur'an itself. The Qur'an speaks of nine miracles in connection with Moses,[53] five in connection with Jesus;[54] it is hardly conceivable, then, that the final Prophet, the seal (*khātam*) of all previous Prophets, should not perform miracles also, even if the pre-eminent miracle remains that of the revelation of the Holy Qur'an.

A number of miracles are, in fact, mentioned in the Qur'an:

1. The cleaving of the moon. When the idolators made their faith contingent upon the splitting of the moon in two by the Prophet, he, with the permission of God, did exactly that; as the Qur'an says:

   *The hour drew nigh and the moon was rent in twain. And if they behold a sign they turn away and say: prolonged illusion.* (Sūra al-Qamar, LIV:1–2)

   The last verse clearly shows that what is meant in the reference to the cleaving of the moon is not the cleaving that takes place at the Resurrection, but its being cleft in two at the time of the Prophet.
2. The *Miʿrāj* (ascent to Heaven). Another of the miracles of the Prophet is that he travelled from the Sacred Mosque in Mecca to the Mosque of al-Aqsa in Jerusalem, and from thence to the heavenly realms; this astonishing journey taking place one evening, in the course of a very short space of time. This is also related in the Qur'an. The power of God is such that no

existential factors could be a hindrance in the Prophet's ascent through the Heavens.[55]

3. The *Mubāhala* (trial by mutual imprecation). In order to prove his authenticity, the Prophet invited a group of Christians to perform the *Mubāhala*,[56] saying: 'Come, bring yourselves, your children and your women and invoke the curse of God on the liars amongst us.' It is obvious that such a mutual imprecation would end in the destruction of one of the two parties, but the Prophet declared his readiness to enter into such a contest. Eventually, the Christians withdrew, and accepted the Prophethood of the Prophet, after witnessing his resolution and his justice, and after seeing that he had brought his dearest folk with him to the appointed place.

## Article 77

**Distinctive Features of the Prophethood of the Prophet of Islam**

The prophetic mission of the Holy Prophet of Islam has certain distinctive features, of which four are the most important; these will be addressed in the following three articles.

The mission of the Prophet of Islam is universal, it is for all peoples, all places and all times, as the Qur'an says:

*And We have not sent thee save as a bringer of good tidings and a warner unto all mankind* ... (Sūra Saba', XXXIV:28)

And again:

*We sent thee not save as a mercy for the worlds.* (Sūra al-Anbiyā', XXII:107)

We see here that his mission and call is to all 'the people' (*al-nās*):[57]

*O people! The messenger hath come unto you with the truth from your Lord, so believe, it is better for you.* (Sūra al-Nisā', IV:170)

Of course, at the time when he began his mission, it was natural that he first make his admonitions to his own people before warning a people to whom no previous Prophet had been sent:

*... that thou mayst warn a folk to whom no warner came before ...* (Sūra al-Sajda, XXXII:3)

But this does not mean that he was sent only to a specific group. We occasionally see that the Qur'an, while clearly establishing a particular community as the recipient of the mission, immediately follows this with a statement indicating that all those who receive the message are invited to follow it:

*And this Qur'an hath been inspired in me, that I may warn therewith you and whomsoever it may reach.* (Sūra al-An'ām, VI:19)

It is clear that all the Prophets were charged to invite first of all their own people to follow the religion revealed to them, whether the scope of their mission was universal or delimited. In this regard, the Qur'an states:

*And We never sent a Messenger save with the language of his folk, that he might make* [the message] *clear for them.* (Sūra Ibrāhīm, XIV:4)

But, as we have said, the fact that the Prophet of Islam was sent with the language of his own people does not mean that his mission was limited to them alone.

### Article 78

The Prophethood of the Prophet of Islam was the Seal (*khātam*) of Prophethood, just as the divine law he brought placed the seal of finality upon all divine laws, and the Revelation that came through him was the seal of all previous revelations. In other words, after him no more Prophets will arise, and the law established by him will prevail until the Day of Resurrection. That is, there will be no further revealed laws; hence all claims to revealed status for any subsequent Law are null and void.

The question of finality has been clearly expounded in Qur'anic verses and hadiths, and cannot be refuted. We allude to some of these below.

*Muḥammad is not the father of any man among you, but he is the Messenger of God, and the Seal of the Prophets; and God is ever aware of all things.* (Sūra al-Aḥzāb, XXXIII:40)

Here, the word for 'seal', *khātam*, means literally a ring; for at the time of the Revelation, the stamp or sign of individuals was communicated by the carved stone in a ring. They would use these rings to seal their letters, indicating thereby that they had come to the end of the letter. Taking this into account, the import of the verse quoted above becomes clearer: with the advent of the Prophet of Islam, the 'scroll' of prophethood and prophecy has received its terminal seal, and the 'book' of prophetic revelation is brought to an end.

Insofar as the *risāla* (the divine message) means the disseminating and receiving of messages by means of revelation, it is clear that the end of prophethood also means, *ipso facto*, the end of the sending [by God] of divine messages.[58]

Amongst the various hadiths on this subject, it suffices to note the one referred to as Hadith *al-Manzila* ('the [Spiritual] Rank'). The Holy Prophet appointed ʿAlī as his representative in Medina before leaving for the battle of Tabuk; he said to him: 'Are you not happy that your station in regard to me is that of Aaron in regard to Moses, except that there is no Prophet after me?'[59]

Apart from this hadith—regarded as *mutawātir*[60]—many other equally strong hadiths have been recorded on the question of the finality of prophethood with the Prophet of Islam.

## Article 79

### The Islamic Shariʿa

The mystery of the perpetuity of the Islamic Shariʿa is hidden in two things: First, this Shariʿa is the most complete plan for securing the natural and spiritual needs of man according to divine guidance; nothing more complete than Islam can be conceived of. Second, in the realm of practical rulings, Islam offers a range of comprehensive principles and universal norms capable of responding to the most diverse needs of man. Clear testimony to this is found in the fact that the schools of *fiqh* (jurisprudence) have been able to respond creatively to the practical legal needs of different Muslim societies over the course of fourteen centuries; and, to this day, no matter has arisen that Islamic *fiqh* has been incapable of resolving. In this achievement, the following elements have been important and effective:

1. Intellectual self-evidence. In those legal areas where it has competence, intellectual reasoning forms one of the means by which the obligations of man can be deduced throughout his life.
2. Discerning between degrees of importance in cases of conflicting demands. We know that the legal rulings of Islam arise out of a series of existential properties inherent in the nature of things—properties that are either wholesome or corrupting, substantially or accidentally—some of which are grasped by the intellect, others being indicated by revealed law. In cases where conflicting interests arise, the *faqīh* (jurist) can, by means of exploring these essential properties, resolve the difficulty by giving priority to that which is most important.
3. Keeping open the 'door' of *ijtihād*.[61] To keep this 'door' of independent reasoning open for the Muslim *umma*—which is one of the distinguishing and honourable features of Shiʿism—is itself one of the factors which guarantee the finality of the religion of Islam, in that a vibrant and permanent *ijtihād* is capable of judging and resolving new problems and events, always in accordance with universal Islamic principles.
4. Secondary rulings. In Islamic Shariʿa, there are, in addition to its primary rulings, a series of secondary rulings capable of resolving many problems. For example, when the application of a given ruling becomes the source of hardship and injury for some, a principle such as the rule of prohibiting hardship or loss can assist the Shariʿa in breaking through apparent dead-ends (taking due account of the conditions laid down by *fiqh*). The Qur'an affirms:

> … *and He hath not laid upon you in religion any hardship.* (Sūra al-Ḥajj, XXII:78)

The Prophet also declared: '[There should be] no injury; and nobody should injure.' The school which upholds and applies these two principles and their like will never find itself confounded in a juristic dead-end.

**Article 80**

One of the special features of the Shariʿa is the simplicity and the balanced nature of its rulings, a feature which renders them easy to understand. It might be said that this feature is one of the most important factors in the penetration and spread of Islam among diverse peoples and nations of the world. As regards the worship of God, Islam offers a pure and clear concept of Divine Unity, far removed from all ambiguity or sophistry. The Sūra al-Tawḥīd (also called al-Ikhlāṣ), alone, bears witness to the truth of this assertion. Likewise this sacred Book places such emphasis on the principle of piety in its consideration of the spiritual rank and station of man, that it constitutes, in itself, a means of restoring to man all his most noble qualities: the nobility of man being brought to full fruition by his relationship with the divine. In the area of practical rulings, we see the way in which Islam prohibits all forms of hardship and injury; indeed, the Prophet makes himself known as one who brings an 'easy' law: 'I have come with a law that is easy (*sahla*) and tolerant (*samḥa*).'

Impartial and objective scholars—even amongst the non-Muslims—acknowledge that the most important factor in the rapid spread of Islam was the clarity and comprehensiveness of its guiding principles and its rulings. For example, the famous French scholar, Gustav LeBon writes: 'The secret of the advance of Islam resides in its extreme simplicity and ease. Islam is free of all those qualities which the healthy mind finds impossible to accept, and which other religions have in abundance. You could not conceive of a religion with simpler principles than those of Islam, which assert: God is One; all men are equal before God; by performing certain religious duties man attains felicity and Paradise, while violation of these duties leads to Hell. The clarity and ease of Islam and its rulings considerably facilitated its progress throughout the world. More important, though, was that strong faith that Islam casts into the hearts of its adherents, a faith to which no doubt can have access. Islam, just as it is the religion most disposed to scientific discovery, is also the greatest of all religions in respect of building upon the foundations of the past, and thereby fostering refinement of the soul and character of men.'[62]

## Article 81

The revealed scriptures brought by previous Prophets have, unfortunately, been gradually subjected to alteration and interpolation over the years. In addition to what is said in the Qur'an to this effect, there is historical evidence to corroborate this fact. In contrast, nothing has been added to or taken from the Holy Qur'an itself. The Holy Prophet of Islam received 114 chapters of the Qur'an, and this constitutes, among other things, an eternal memorial of himself, and he delivered them intact into this world. The scribes of the Revelation, especially Imam ʿAlī, who wrote down the revealed verses from the very beginning, have preserved it ever since from all interpolation. Despite the passage of fourteen centuries since its descent, not a single verse or chapter has been added to or taken away from the Holy Qur'an. We allude below to some of the reasons why the Qur'an has, of necessity, remained free of any alteration.

1. How could the Qur'an possibly be subject to alteration when God Himself has guaranteed its preservation and protection? It is said:

   *Truly, We, even We, reveal the Reminder* [that is, the Qur'an], *and verily We are its guardians.* (Sūra al-Ḥijr, XV:9)

2. God has prohibited the entry of any kind of falsehood into the Qur'an:

   *Falsehood cannot come at it from before it or from behind it. A revelation from the Wise, the Owner of praise.* (Sūra Fuṣṣilat, XLI:42)

   As God has denied all possibility of falsehood entering the Qur'an, this means that anything that might lead to the weakening of the Qur'an—such as adding words or verses, or taking them away—is likewise excluded; thus, one can say with absolute certainty that this Scripture has not been altered in any way.

3. History shows us that the Muslims were graced in a special way as regards learning and memorizing the Qur'an. At the time of the Revelation, the Arabs were famed for their excellent, powerful memories, so much so that after hearing a long sermon just once, they were able to repeat it by heart afterwards. In such a context, where there were so many people who knew the Qur'an by heart, how could anyone claim that it might have been altered?
4. There is no doubt that Imam ʿAlī had a difference of opinion, in certain matters, with the other three caliphs, and that he expressed these differences in a clear and logical manner, in for example, the sermon entitled *Shiqshiqiyya*, one of his most famous discourses.[63] But we observe that this great soul, to the end of his life, never said anything about even a single word of the Qur'an having been altered. If, God forbid, such an alteration had in fact taken place, a person such as he would never have remained silent. Rather, we see the contrary: that he continuously called upon people to meditate upon the Qur'an: 'O people, for whosoever follows the Qur'an, there is no poverty or indigence; and without following the Qur'an, there is no riches or freedom from want. So throughout your lives, sow the seed of the Qur'an [in your hearts] and follow it.'[64]

For these, and other reasons, the great scholars of the *ahl al-bayt*, from the beginning of Islam to the present day, have stressed the immunity of the Qur'an against any alteration (*taḥrīf*). It must be stressed that this has been the position of all Shiʿi authorities in all periods; and to this day, all the Shiʿi leaders without exception uphold this position.[65]

### Article 82

In some books of Hadith and Qur'anic exegesis, there are certain narrations which have given grounds for the idea that some alteration of the Qur'an has in fact taken place, but the following points should be borne in mind:

1. Most of these narrations are transmitted by persons and in books that are not trustworthy, such as the *Kitāb al-qirā'a* of Aḥmad b. Muḥammad Sayyārī (d. 286 AH). His narrations are classified as weak by those versed in knowledge of transmitters of hadith (*ʿilm al-rijāl*); and his legal school is classified as corrupt.[66] Another such book is that of ʿAlī b. Aḥmad al-Kūfī (d. 352 AH), about whom the same scholars said: 'At the end of his life, he took the path of fanaticism (*ghulūw*).'[67]
2. Those parts of these narrations that ostensibly relate to alteration are more akin to commentaries on verses. In other words, the content of a given verse is brought together with it's meaning in a single narration, and some have wrongly supposed that the commentary is part of the verse, having elided it therewith. For example, the '*straight path*' of the Sūra al-Fātiḥa is read in some narrations along with its commentary, 'the path of the Prophet and his family'. It is clear that such commentary is a way of affirming the sublimity of the Prophet.
3. Imam Khumaynī has divided those narrations on the basis of which alteration is deemed to have taken place, into three categories: (a) weak reports, in which nothing is proven; (b) forged reports, in which interpolations are clearly evident; and (c) strong reports, which, if their import be carefully considered, reveal that what appears to be an alteration of Qur'anic verses is in fact a comment upon the meanings of these verses, not a change in the literal wording of the Qur'an.[68]
4. Anyone wishing to attain a true understanding of the actual beliefs of a given school of thought must study the authoritative books on doctrine and belief as found in that school, rather than looking at some books of narrations compiled by those whose aim was but to gather up material, leaving to others the task of verification and evaluation. Similarly, referring to a few

unusual opinions held by some followers of the school is insufficient for arriving at a sound knowledge of the school, as is basing oneself on the words of one or two people who oppose the majority of the authoritative scholars in the school of thought.

To conclude this discussion on alteration, it is necessary to note the following points.

Any mutual recrimination by the adherents of different schools of law in Islam, especially in the current age, has as a result only the weakening of the unity of the *umma.*

If some Shiʿi scholars have written books in which the alteration of the Qur'an is mentioned, we observe that, after the publication of such books, Shiʿi scholars have written many refutations of the errors contained in them. In like manner, when an Egyptian scholar published the book *al-Furqān* in 1345/1926, in which he tried to prove that the Qur'an had been altered—basing himself upon certain narrations found in the books of the Sunnis, concerning the abrogation or writing of certain Qur'anic verses—the Shaykhs of al-Azhar repudiated the opinion and banned the book.

The revealed Book for all the Muslims of the world is the Glorious Qur'an, consisting of 114 Sūras, of which the first is the Sūra al-Fātiḥa, and the last is the Sūra al-Nās. In this book of divine speech, the name 'al-Qur'an' has been mentioned with certain qualifying adjectives, such as Glorious (*majīd*), Noble (*karīm*) and Wise (*ḥakīm*).[69] Muslims occasionally refer to it as the *muṣḥaf,* which in Arabic denotes any collection of written pages gathered up as in a scroll. It is related that after the passing away of the Prophet, when all the Sūras of the Qur'an had been collected in a single compilation, it was proposed by certain companions to keep it in this form.[70] Therefore, the *muṣḥaf* came to refer to the collected, written pages of a document, gathered in the form of a single book, whether it be the Qur'an or any other document. The Qur'an refers to the record of deeds as a *ṣuḥuf*:

*And when the pages (ṣuḥuf) are laid open.* (Sūra al-Takwīr, LXXXI:10)

It also refers to other scriptures as *ṣuḥuf:*

*The Books of Abraham and Moses.* (Sūra al-Aʿlā, LXXXVIII:19)

These verses show that the words *ṣuḥuf* or *muṣḥaf* had a broad meaning, and so came to be regarded as one of the names of the Qur'an after the passing away of the Prophet. It should come as no surprise that the writings from the hand of the Prophet's daughter are also referred to as *muṣḥaf.* The nature and content of this *muṣḥaf* is described by Imam Ṣādiq in the following narration: 'Fāṭima lived for seventy-five days after the death of the Prophet, in a state of great sorrow. Gabriel, by God's command, came to her and told her of the Prophet's rank in the divine proximity, thus consoling her. He also told her of events that would take place after her [death]. Imam 'Alī wrote, at Fāṭima's dictation, what Gabriel had said, and it is to this piece of writing that the *muṣḥaf* of Fāṭima refers.'[71]

Abū Jaʿfar relates from Imam Ṣādiq: 'The *muṣḥaf* of Fāṭima has nothing in it of the Qur'an; rather its contents were cast unto her [through inspiration] after the death of her father.'[72]

There are exalted individuals who, while not being Prophets or Messengers, nonetheless are spoken to by angels. These individuals are called *muḥaddath* [literally: 'spoken to'] and the blessed daughter of the Holy Prophet was a *muḥaddath.* We shall have occasion to return to this term below.

## IV. IMAMATE (IMĀMA)

After twenty-three years of struggle and effort in the cause of the faith of Islam, and in the endeavour to establish the Medinan community, the Holy Prophet passed away, at the beginning of the eleventh year after the Hijra. With the departure of this great soul, the Qur'anic revelation and the cycle of prophecy came to an end; no further Prophet would arise, nor would there be any subsequent religious dispensation. However, the responsibilities that had been incumbent on the Prophet (apart from those pertaining to the conveyance of the Revelation) naturally did not come to an end. It was thus essential, after his death, that enlightened and upright persons should, in each succeeding age, undertake these responsibilities, as successors and vicegerents, and as Imams and leaders of the Muslims. This much will be readily accepted by all Muslims; but there is a difference of perspective as between Shiʿas and the Sunnis as regards certain qualities that are deemed necessary in the successor to the Prophet, and also in the means of appointing him. Below, we shall address first of all the meaning of the term 'Shiʿa' and its background, and then we shall turn to discussion of the Imamate.

**Article 83**

The term 'Shiʿa' means 'follower', and now refers, conventionally, to the group of Muslims who, after the death of the Holy Prophet, believed that the function of leadership in the Islamic community was the prerogative of ʿAlī and his successors, regarded as *maʿṣūm*.[73] According to the historical record, the Prophet repeatedly spoke, throughout his life, and on different matters, about the virtues of ʿAlī, of his nobility, and also of his leadership qualities, second only to the Prophet's own. These sterling tributes and commendations of ʿAlī resulted, according to well-attested narrations, in the formation of a group around ʿAlī, in the very lifetime of the Prophet; a group that became known as *Shīʿat ʿAlī*, 'the followers of ʿAlī'. This group, after the death of the Prophet, remained true to their earlier conviction; they could not have favoured anyone above the person they believed to have been designated by the Prophet of God as his successor. Thus it was that in his lifetime and after his death a group became known as the Shiʿa. This fact has been amply recorded by writers of different perspectives.

One writer, Nawbakhtī (d.310 AH) writes as follows: 'The word "Shiʿa" is a term referring to those who, in the time of the Prophet of God and after him, regarded ʿAlī as the [rightful] Imam and caliph,[74] breaking away from others and attaching themselves to him.'[75]

Abū'l-Ḥasan al-Ashʿarī says: 'The reason why this group is called "Shiʿa" is because they were followers of ʿAlī, giving him precedence over the other companions.'[76]

Al-Shahrastānī writes: 'The word "Shiʿa" refers to those who followed ʿAlī in particular, believing that he had been designated as heir, Imam and caliph [by the Prophet].'[77]

Therefore, the history of this group is embedded in the history of Islam itself, its commencement not being separable from the origins of the religion itself; Islam and Shiʿism manifest themselves concurrently. In Article 86, we will show how the Prophet, from the first days of his open preaching, gathered together his clan, the Banū Hāshim, declaring to them that ʿAlī was his heir and successor; and afterwards, on various occasions, especially at the day of Ghadīr, formally proclaimed ʿAlī to be his successor.

Shiʿism, then, was neither the result of the conspiracy of the people of Saqīfa, nor did it come about through the events associated with the murder of ʿUthmān; it has nothing to do with such phenomena or any other such imaginary causes:[78] rather, it was the Prophet himself who, under divine guidance, and by means of repeated declarations, planted the seed of Shiʿism in the hearts of his companions, and gradually cultivated this seed, such that a group of eminent companions, such as Salmān al-Fārisī and Abū Dharr al-Ghiffārī, became the 'Shīʿat ʿAlī' or partisans of ʿAlī. Qurʾanic commentators relate from the Prophet that those signified by this verse are ʿAlī and his Shiʿa:[79]

*Verily, those who believe and do good works are the best of created beings.* (Sūra al-Bayyina, XCIX:7)

In historical accounts, mention is made of the names of the followers of ʿAlī, those among the companions who asserted their conviction that he was the true caliph after the death of the Prophet; we shall not recount all of their names in this short summary.

Throughout the history of Islam, the Shiʿa, side by side with the other Muslim *madhhabs*, performed their duty of spreading Islam, playing, indeed, a major part in its expansion. They have established different branches of learning, founded important states and dynasties, produced distinguished personalities in the domains of science, philosophy, literature and politics, thereby contributing greatly to Islamic culture and society. Today they are represented in most parts of the world.

### Article 84

As we shall see shortly, the question of the Imamate pertains to the divine domain. The appointment of a successor to the Prophet must be based on a divine revelation to the Prophet. But before entering into the traditional reports and formally religious aspects of this matter, let us suppose that we have no direct religious proof-texts to consult, and ask ourselves what verdict the human intellect would deliver on this question, taking due account of the conditions of those times. It seems clear that an intellectual evaluation would proceed along the following lines: If a great reformer struggled earnestly for many long years, and arrived at a plan that would benefit human society, it is natural that, in order that his plan continue to be implemented after his death, so as to bear fruit in the long-term, he would seek some effective way of perpetuating the system he had established. Or, to put it differently: it is not conceivable that a person should take great pains to construct some great building, and then leave it completely unprotected, appointing no watchmen or supervisors to maintain and preserve it.

The Holy Prophet is one of the greatest persons in human history who, by bringing forth a new religious dispensation, effected a profound transformation in the world, laying the foundations of an entirely new, global civilization. Evidently, this exalted individual, through whom an eternally valid religion was established, and who provided leadership to his own society, must have made it clear how this religion was to be preserved, how it was to be protected against the dangers and misfortunes that might confront it. He must also have said something about how the everlasting Muslim *umma* should be led and administered; and he must have indicated the qualities of leadership that should prevail after his passing away. In this light, it is inconceivable that he would first establish a religion that was to last till the end of time, and then fail to provide clear guidance as to how the leadership of that religion, after his death, was to be determined and organized.

Again, it is inconceivable that a Prophet who did not withhold his guidance as regards even the smallest question pertaining to human welfare should have neglected to provide guidance on so crucial a matter as the leadership of Islamic society, thus leaving the Muslims to their own devices, not knowing what their obligations were in regard to this fundamental issue. It is, therefore, impossible to accept the proposition that the Prophet departed from this world without having given any instructions regarding the leadership of his community after his death.

## Article 85

If we consider the history of this foundational epoch of Islam, and take into account the regional and global context at the death of the Prophet, the necessity of appointing someone to the position of Imam will be readily apparent. For, in the tumult following upon the Prophet's death, Islam faced a three-fold threat: on the one side, there was the Byzantine Roman Empire, on another was the Sassanid Persian Empire, and, from within, there was the danger posed by the group known as the 'Hypocrites'. As regards the first threat, suffice to note that the Prophet was concerned about it right up to his last days, mobilizing a large contingent of Muslims under the command of Usāma b. Zayd, to confront the Romans, despite the protests of those who were opposed to such a move. As for the second threat, the Sassanid emperor was clearly a malicious enemy who, having torn up the letter sent to him by the Prophet, himself wrote a letter to the governor of Yemen instructing him either to capture the Prophet or send to him his severed head. As for the third enemy, these persons had always been causing trouble for the Prophet, in Medina and elsewhere, their various plots being so many thorns in his side; their machinations and schemes are mentioned in various places in the Qur'an; indeed, an entire Sūra—one in which their evil thoughts and actions are commented upon—is named after them.

Now it might be asked: in the face of this triple danger, with enemies ready to ambush the Muslims from all sides, would the Holy Prophet have left the religion of Islam and the Muslim community without a leader, leaving the Muslims without any clear guidance?

This should also be considered: there is no doubt that the Prophet understood that the life of the Arabs was dominated by tribal loyalty, with members of a tribe seeing their own lives as bound up with that of their chief. Thus, leaving the task of appointing a leader to such tribesmen could only lead to factional disputes and inter-tribal rivalry, allowing the enemies of Islam to take advantage of the divisions opened up in the ranks of the Muslims. It is on this basis, precisely, that Ibn Sīnā writes: 'The appointment of a successor by means of explicit designation (*naṣṣ*) by the Prophet is closer to the truth [of the question of the caliphate], for by such designation, every kind of dispute and opposition is uprooted.'[80]

## Article 86

Now that it is clear that the wisdom of the Prophet must, of necessity, have led him to offer guidance on the principle of leadership of the Islamic *umma*, we should consider the solution proposed by him. Here, we shall critically address the two main perspectives on this question: [either] (a) the Holy Prophet, under divine command, chooses a great individual, one eminently qualified for the task of leadership of the *umma*, publicly appointing him as his successor; [or] (b) the Holy Prophet leaves to his people the responsibility for choosing a leader after his death.

It should be clear which of these two perspectives is corroborated by the Qur'an, the Sunna and the events in the life of the Prophet. A close examination of the life of the Prophet—from the day he was commanded to proclaim the new faith first to his near of kin, then to all mankind—reveals that he repeatedly made clear the distinctive qualities of his successor, thereby indicating that the means by which the leadership of the community was to be established was that of explicit designation (*tanṣīṣ*) and not election by the people. This point can be proven by the evidence we offer below:

1. Hadith: *Yawm al-Dār* ('The Day of the Home'). Three years after the beginning of the Prophet's mission, he was commanded by God to proclaim openly his call, with the revelation of this verse:

   *And warn thy tribe of near kindred.* (Sūra al-Shuʿarāʾ, XXVI:214)

   The Prophet invited the chiefs of the Banū Hāshim and said to them: 'I have brought for you the best of this world and the next. God has commanded me to invite you to this [religion of Islam]. Which of you will help me establish this religion, to be my brother and my successor?' He repeated this question three times, and each time it was ʿAlī, alone, who stepped forward, declaring his readiness to help the Prophet. Then the Prophet said: 'Truly, this is my brother, my heir and my successor among you.'[81]
2. Hadith: *al-Manzila* ('The [Spiritual] Rank'). The Prophet, on various occasions indicated that the station and rank of ʿAlī in relation to him was that of Aaron in relation to Moses, denying ʿAlī only one degree comprised in the station of Aaron, that of prophethood. The Prophet said in a hadith that is almost *mutawātir*. 'O ʿAlī, your rank [*manzila*] in relation to me is that of Aaron in relation to Moses.'[82] Now, according to the Qur'an, Aaron had the rank of a Prophet,[83] a caliph[84] and a minister (*wazīr*)[85] at the time of Moses, and this hadith proves that ʿAlī clearly had the rank of a caliph and a minister, like Aaron, but not that of a Prophet. Naturally, if the meaning were other than that of affirming, in regard to ʿAlī, all the ranks apart from prophethood, there would have been no need to make an exception of prophethood alone.
3. Hadith: *al-Safīna* ('The Ark'): The Prophet likened his *ahl al-bayt* to Noah's ark, saying: 'Is not the likeness of my *ahl al-bayt* among you like the ark of Noah among his folk? Whoever takes

refuge therein is saved and whoever opposes it is drowned.'[86] We know that Noah's ark was the sole place of refuge for people seeking to save themselves from the Deluge. Thus, according to this hadith, the *ahl al-bayt* of the Prophet is the sole refuge for those seeking protection against the tenebrous phenomena—sources of delusion and confusion—that confront humanity.

4. Hadith: *Amān al-umma* ('Security of the community'): The Prophet made it known that he saw his *ahl al-bayt* as a source of unity and a means of distancing his *umma* from divisiveness, saying: 'Just as the stars are a means of securing (*amān*) the people of the earth against drowning,[87] my *ahl al-bayt* is a means of securing (*amān*) my *umma* from division. If a tribe among the Arabs opposes them, they fall into dispute and become part of Satan's minions.'[88]
5. Hadith: *al-Thaqalayn* ('The Two Precious Things'): This hadith is one of those classified in Islam as *mutawātir*, and is found in many books written by scholars of both branches of Islam. In this hadith, the Prophet is preaching to the whole community: 'Verily, I am leaving with you two precious things, the Book of God and my progeny, my *ahl al-bayt*; for as long as you cling to these two, you will never go astray; and truly they will not be parted from each other until they join me at the *Ḥawḍ* [a pool of Paradise, identified with *al-Kawthar*].'[89]

This [last] hadith places side by side the authoritative knowledge of the *ahl al-bayt* and the Qur'an, thereby requiring Muslims to hold fast in matters of faith both to the Qur'an and the *ahl al-bayt.* But it is a great pity that some people knock on all doors except the door of the *ahl al-bayt*! The hadith *al-Thaqalayn*, upon whose authenticity both Shi'a and Sunni alike are in agreement, can help to bring about a truly unified *umma* among the world's Muslims; for if the two groups differed over the question of political leadership and authority after the Prophet's death, they are still able, despite this difference over historical interpretation, to be as one as regards the sacred significance of the *ahl al-bayt.* The Prophet provided no grounds for a schism to occur between the two groups; on the contrary, there ought to have been—according to this universally acknowledged narration—unison of will and singleness of purpose.

In general, during the period of the caliphate, the caliphs themselves referred to ʿAlī as their source of authoritative knowledge, and disputes over religious matters were resolved by recourse to him. In truth, from the time the *ahl al-bayt* of the Holy Prophet was set aside as a source of religious authority, a spirit of sectarianism set in, and groups with different names crystallized, one after the other.

## Article 87

In the hadiths quoted above, the Holy Prophet clearly indicated who was to be his successor, either in a general or a specific way, such that any one of them would suffice as proof for those who objectively seek after the truth. Nonetheless, in order that his message on this issue reach the ears of all the Muslims, far and wide, and in order to foreclose any possibility of doubt or hesitation on this score, the Prophet halted the great mass of pilgrims returning from the Hajj at a place called Ghadīr Khumm, telling his companions that he had received a command from God to deliver a message to them. This divine message pertained to the accomplishment of a momentous obligation, one so great that if he did not carry this out, the Prophet would not have performed his duty. As the Qur'an says:

*O Messenger, make known that which hath been revealed to thee from thy Lord, for if thou do it not, thou wilt not have conveyed His Message. God will protect thee from the people.* (Sūra al-Mā'ida, v:67)[90]

A pulpit was erected; he stood upon it and then proclaimed: 'Shortly, I shall be answering *labbayk* ['at Thy service'] to my Lord's call; what will you say of me?'

In reply, the people assembled said: 'We bear witness that you have conveyed unto us the religion of God; you wished only for our well-being, and you exerted yourself to the utmost. May God bestow the best of rewards upon you!'

Then he asked: 'Do you testify to the Oneness of God, to my message, and the reality of the Day of Resurrection?'

All those present so testified. Then he said: 'I shall enter the Pool (*al-Kawthar*) before you; take care how you treat two precious things that I am leaving behind.'

Someone asked what was meant by the 'two precious things'. The Prophet replied: 'The one is the Book of God, and the other is my progeny. And God, the Subtle, the Aware, has told me that these two will not be separated until the Day of Judgement, when they shall join me. Do not come too close to these two things, lest you perish; and do not stray too far from them, lest you perish.'

Then he clasped the hand of 'Alī, raising it aloft, so that all could see the two hands together, and spoke as follows: 'O people, who has a greater claim[91] over the believers than their own souls?' They replied: 'God and His Messenger know best.' [The Prophet said:] 'Truly God is my *Mawlā*[92] and I am the *mawlā* of the believers, and I have a greater claim over them than their own souls.' Then he said three times: 'For whoever has me as his *mawlā*, 'Alī is his *mawlā*.'

Then he said: 'My Lord, be the friend of whoever is 'Alī's friend, and the enemy of whoever is 'Alī's enemy; love whoever loves him and hate whoever hates him; help whoever helps him and abandon whoever abandons him, wherever he may be. Let those who are present convey this to those who are absent.'

## Article 88

The hadith of Ghadīr is accounted *mutawātir* (most authenticated) being related by companions, the followers of the companions, and countless narrators of Hadith down through the ages. A total of 110 companions, 89 of those in the succeeding generation, and 3500 scholars of Hadith have transmitted this hadith, so there can be no question of disputing its authenticity. Also, a group of scholars have written books on this hadith, amongst which the one which brings together most comprehensively all the chains of transmission for the hadith is *Sharīf al-Ghadīr*, by 'Allāma 'Abd al-Ḥusayn Amīnī (1320–1390/1902–1970).

At this point, we must address the question of what exactly is meant by the term *mawlā*, in respect both of the Prophet and of ʿAlī. There is considerable evidence to show that the meaning of this term is authority and leadership. We allude to some of this evidence below:

1. Upon the occasion of Ghadīr, the Prophet halted the caravan of pilgrims at a place that had neither water nor pasture, in the middle of an extremely hot day. The heat was so intense that those present wrapped one part of their cloak over their heads and the other part beneath them, to protect themselves against the heat. In such circumstances, the halt must have signified that the Prophet meant to speak about a matter of the utmost importance for the guidance of the *umma*; a key address that was to affect the destiny of the community—and indeed, what could be more crucial to the destiny of the *umma* than the issue of determining the successor to the Prophet, an issue which, properly resolved, would be a source of unity for the Muslims and of the safeguarding of the community?
2. Before expressing ʿAlī's status of *wilāya*, that is, his being made *mawlā*, the Prophet spoke of the three principles of *Tawḥīd*, Prophecy and the Afterlife, eliciting from the Muslims acknowledgement that he had indeed conveyed the divine message. By associating his message with the elicited confession by the Muslims of these three principles, he indicated the importance of the message he was about to deliver, the momentous nature of the issue he was to raise; it could not be about something so trivial as a recommendation to be the 'friend' of some person.
3. At the beginning of the discourse, the Prophet spoke of his impending death, thus indicating his concern over the state his *umma* would find itself in after his passing away. What could be more appropriate than providing for his followers a means of charting their course, according to his design, through the dangerous, stormy seas that lay before them?
4. Before conveying the divine message concerning ʿAlī, he spoke of his own quality of being a *mawlā*, his *mawlawiyya*, and his own precedence (*awlawiyya*), saying: 'God is my *Mawlā* and I

am the *mawlā* of the believers, and I am closer to them than they are to their own selves.' This shows that 'Alī's status as *mawlā* derives from the same root as the *mawlawiyya* and *awlawiyya* of the Prophet; it is by divine decree, then, that 'Alī's *awlawiyya* was confirmed.

5. After conveying the message, the Prophet instructed those present to report it to those who were absent.

**Article 89**

History tells us that the enemies of the Prophet tried in many ways to thwart his divine mission—from accusing him of being mad, to being possessed by a demon, to attempting to kill him in his bed. But God's protective grace ensured that these evil schemes of the idolators came to naught. The last hope for these enemies was that with the death of the Prophet, the religion he brought would come to an end also (as he had no male offspring to succeed him):

*Or say they: a poet, for whom we await the accident of time?* (Sūra al-Ṭūr, LII:30)

This was the thought that dominated many of the idolators and hypocrites. However, with the designation of such a worthy successor, who had proven throughout his life so pure in faith and constant in devotion to Islam, the hopes of the enemies were transformed into despair. By this act, the continuity of the religious community was secured, its foundations set firm, and the blessing of Islam, with the designation of such leadership, was brought to completion. It is for this reason that, after the appointment of 'Alī as successor to the Prophet, the verse relating to the 'perfecting of religion' was revealed on the day of Ghadīr:

*This day are those who disbelieve in despair of* [ever harming] *your religion; so fear them not, fear Me. This day have I perfected your religion for you and completed My favour unto you, and have chosen for you Islam as religion.*[93] (Sūra al-Mā'ida, V:3)[94]

Apart from the authentic hadiths cited—which go to prove that the issue of succession to the Prophet was a matter to be determined by God, rather than being left to the will of the community—various historical accounts also indicate that the Prophet, even when he was still in Mecca, not having yet established the Medinan state, regarded the issue of succession as one which pertained to God's decree. For instance, the chief of the tribe of Banū ʿĀmir came to the Prophet at the season of Hajj and asked him: 'If we pay allegiance to you, and you conquer your enemies, will we benefit from any share in the leadership [of your community]?' In reply, the Prophet said: 'That is for God to decide; He will entrust leadership to whomever He will.'[95]

It is evident that if the issue of leadership were to be determined by the choice of the people, the Prophet would have had to say: 'This question pertains to the *umma*,' or that 'It is up to the "folk who loose and bind"[96] to decide'; but the words of the Prophet in this connection are akin to those of God as regards the Message of Islam itself:

... *God knoweth best with whom to place His Message.* (Sūra al-Anʿām, VI: 124)

**Article 90**

The idea that the *umma* had no method for determining the successor to the Prophet was held by some of the companions. Instead of the designation of God and His Prophet, they followed the designation given by the previous caliph, each caliph receiving his appointment at the hands of his predecessor, except in the case of the first caliph. The idea that the designation by Abū Bakr of ʿUmar was not so much a definite order as a form of advice runs contrary to the historical evidence. For while the first caliph was still alive, the said designation was opposed by various companions, such as Zubayr; it is clear that if it were a question merely of advice, there would be no reason for the companions to oppose it at this stage. Turning from this appointment of ʿUmar by Abū Bakr to the third caliph, ʿUthmān, we see that he was appointed by a council of six persons who were all appointed in turn by the second caliph; this was also, therefore, a form of designation, as it involved restricting the ability to consult public opinion.

In principle, the idea of consulting public opinion or the notion of election of the caliph by the *umma*, was entirely absent from the minds of the companions; and whatever has been claimed to the contrary comes from later interpretations by others. For it is clear that the companions believed that the caliph was to be appointed by his predecessor. For instance, when the second caliph was injured, 'Ā'isha, a wife of the Prophet, sent him a message through his son, 'Abd Allāh b. 'Umar, saying: 'Give my greetings to your father and tell him not to leave the Prophet's *umma* without a shepherd.'[97]

Even though there was a crowd of people at his father's bed, Ibn 'Umar asked his father to appoint a successor, saying: 'People are talking about you, thinking that you are not going to appoint a successor. If a shepherd, entrusted with the responsibility of looking after your sheep and camels were to leave them alone in the desert, without assigning anyone the duty of taking care of them, would you not reproach him? Taking care of human beings is more important than taking care of sheep and camels.'[98]

## Article 91

At the beginning of our discussion of the Imamate, we pointed out that the Imam and caliph of the Prophet, from the point of view of the Muslims, is one who is charged with the responsibilities of the Prophet—save that of establishing the religion. We shall mention below the most important of these responsibilities in order to highlight the rank and significance of the Imamate.

1. Explaining the meanings of the Holy Qur'an and resolving its complexities was one of the responsibilities of the Prophet. As the Qur'an says:

   ... *And We have revealed unto thee the Remembrance that thou mayst explain to mankind that which hath been revealed for them.* (Sūra al-Naḥl, XVI:44)

2. Explaining the rulings of the Shariʿa was another of the Prophet's responsibilities, which he discharged partly through reference to Qurʾanic verses and partly by his own actions, the Sunna. Such explanation was given gradually, in harmony with the unfolding of daily events; the nature of this responsibility was such that it needed to be continued, for the number of hadiths of the Prophet regarding legal rulings does not exceed five hundred;[99] and this quantity of juristic traditions is insufficient for [a comprehensive system of] jurisprudence.
3. The avoidance of divisiveness. Since the Prophet was the pivot of God's truth, and he illuminated all matters, such that any kind of deviation in the beliefs of the *umma* was forestalled, no kind of sectarianism saw the light of day during his life-time.
4. Responding to all religious and theological questions was another of his responsibilities.
5. Training his followers by means of his speech and his actions.
6. Establishing justice, equity and security in the nascent Islamic society.
7. Protection of the frontiers and the lands of Islam against its enemies.

Now if the last two responsibilities can be carried out by a leader chosen by the people, it is obvious that the previous ones require a leader of exceptional knowledge and ability, one who, in his mode of awareness and of activity, follows in the footsteps of the Prophet, one who must be appointed by means of a special grace from God. He must bear within himself intimate knowledge of the prophetic message, and he must be free from all types of error and sin in order to discharge the aforementioned obligations and thereby fill the place vacated by the Prophet. But it must be stressed that such a person, despite possessing certain prophetic sciences, is not a Prophet, nor the founder of a divine law, the rank of Imam never being equated with that of a Prophet.

## Article 92

In the previous articles we have pointed out that an Imam is not an ordinary leader who simply has to rule a country and protect its borders; rather, in addition to this duty, he has other weighty responsibilities, alluded to above. The fulfilment of these tasks—such as commenting on the Qur'an, explaining religious rulings, replying to theological questions, and forestalling all forms of doctrinal deviation and legal confusion—all of this presupposes a comprehensive and inerrant knowledge; for an ordinary person trying to carry out such responsibilities would not be immune from sin and error.

Of course, *ʿiṣma* (inerrancy) is not to be identified exclusively with prophethood, for a person may be *maʿṣūm*, protected against sin and error, while not having the rank of a Prophet. A shining example of this is the Virgin Mary,[100] whom we mentioned earlier in the discussion of the *ʿiṣma* of the Prophets. In addition to the intellectual arguments already given for the necessity of the *ʿiṣma* of the Imam, there are other reasons, some of which we mention below.

1. The explicit and definite desire, on the part of God, to purify and cleanse the *ahl al-bayt* of all defilement, as the Qur'an says:

   *God's desire is but to remove impurity far from you, O people of the household* (ahl al-bayt), *and purify you with an utter purification.* (Sūra al-Aḥzāb, XXXIII:33)

   This verse indicates the *ʿiṣma* of the *ahl al-bayt* in that this special divine will to purify the *ahl al-bayt* of all impurity is tantamount to their being protected against the commission of all sin. The meaning of impurity (*rijs*) in this verse might be understood as pertaining to all forms of mental, moral and spiritual impurity, for sin flows forth as a result of these impurities. Also, since this divine will is specifically related to these people and not to all members of the *umma*, it follows that God's universal desire for all people to be pure must be distinguished from this particular mode of the expression of this will. The universal divine will for the purification of all Muslims is a religious (*tashrīʿī*) will[101] [that is, one that operates through the religion itself], and it is possible that through disobedience certain people will not accept this [divine will that they be purified]. On the other hand, the will to purify the *ahl al-bayt* is a creative or existentiating (*takwīnī*) will, and this kind of will or desire on the part of God is inseparable from the object desired—purity from all sin. It should be noted that this creative will to establish the *'iṣma* of the *ahl al-bayt* does not deprive them of their free will, any more than the *'iṣma* of the Prophets deprives them of theirs (as was discussed earlier).

2. According to the hadith *Thaqalayn*, which says 'I verily am leaving with you two precious things, the Book of God and my progeny,' the Imams of the *ahl al-bayt* are ranged alongside the Qur'an; this means that, just as the Qur'an is immune against all types of error, so are the Imams immune from all mental and volitional sin. This can be seen more clearly in the light of the rest of this hadith: (a) '... for as long as you cling to these two, you will never go astray'; (b) '... and truly they will not be parted from each other until they join me at the Pool.' It is perfectly clear then, that to which one must hold fast for guidance, dispelling all error, and which will not be separated from the Qur'an, must definitely be protected against all type of sin.
3. The Holy Prophet likened his *ahl al-bayt* to Noah's ark: 'Truly the People of my House (*ahl baytī*) in my community (*ummatī*) is like Noah's ark: whoever takes refuge therein is saved and whoever opposes it is drowned.'[102] Taking into account these reasons—which we have presented here in summarized form—the *'iṣma* of the *ahl al-bayt* is a clear and proven reality; needless to say, the traditional grounds for upholding this principle are by no means exhausted by what we have mentioned here.

## Article 93

### The Twelve Imams

Knowledge of the Imam can be attained in the following two ways: (a) the Prophet, under divine command, specifically refers to the Imamate of the designated individual; (b) the present Imam indicates the identity of the Imam to succeed him.

The Imamate of the twelve Imams of Shi'ism has been established by both of the above methods. According to certain hadiths, the Prophet referred to the Imamate of these twelve leaders; also, each Imam made known who was to be his successor.

For the sake of brevity, we shall restrict ourselves to citing just a single hadith in this regard.[103] The Prophet not only established the rank of ʿAlī, rather, he said that there would be twelve leaders through whom the dignity of the faith would be upheld. 'The religion (*dīn*) will always remain unassailable through [thanks to the presence of] twelve *khalīfas*.' In another recension we have: 'The religion (*dīn*) will always remain glorified through [thanks to the presence of] twelve *khalīfas*.'[104] It should be said that this hadith, indicating the existence of twelve caliphs, is found in some of the most authentic canonical collections of the Sunnis.[105] Evidently, these twelve caliphs, to whom the dignity of Islam is attached, are not other than the twelve Imams of Shiʿism. For neither the Umayyad nor the Abbasid caliphs were sources of dignity for the faith; and, additionally, their number does not correspond to that given in the hadith. The twelve Imams of Shiʿism are as follows:

1. Imam ʿAlī b. Abī Ṭālib, *Amīr al-Mu'minīn*, 'Commander of the Faithful' (born two years before the beginning of the Prophet's mission; died 40/660); buried in Najaf.
2. Imam Ḥasan b. ʿAlī, *al-Mujtabā*, 'The Chosen' (3–50/624–670); buried in Jannat al-Baqīʿ, Medina.
3. Imam Ḥusayn b. ʿAlī, *Sayyid al-Shuhadā'*, 'Lord of the Martyrs' (4–61/625–679); buried in Karbala.
4. Imam ʿAlī b. al-Ḥusayn, *Zayn al-ʿĀbidīn*, 'Prince of the Worshippers' (38–94/658–711); buried in Jannat al-Baqīʿ.
5. Imam Muḥammad b. ʿAlī, *Bāqir al-ʿIlm*, 'He who Splits Open Knowledge' (57–114/675–732); buried in Jannat al-Baqīʿ.
6. Imam Jaʿfar b. Muḥammad, *al-Ṣādiq*, 'The Sincere' (73–148/692–765); buried in Jannat al-Baqīʿ.
7. Imam Mūsā b. Jaʿfar, *al-Kāẓim*, 'The Self-controlled' (128–183/744–799); buried in Kazimayn, Baghdad.
8. Imam ʿAlī b. Mūsā, *al-Riḍā*, 'The Content' (148–203/765–817); buried in Mashhad.

9. Imam Muḥammad b. ʿAlī, *al-Jawād*, 'The Magnanimous' (195–220/809–835); buried in Kazimayn, Baghdad.
10. Imam ʿAlī b. Muḥammad, *al-Hādī*, 'The Guide' (212–254/827–868); buried in Samarra.
11. Imam Ḥasan b. ʿAlī, *al-ʿAskarī*, 'The Warrior' (232–260/845–872); buried in Samarra.
12. Imam Muḥammad b. Hasan, *al-Ḥujja / al-Mahdī*, 'The Proof/The Guided' (255/869). This is the twelfth Imam of the Shiʿa, who is deemed to be still living, but in a state of occultation (*ghayba*), until the time when God commands him to come forth and—according to clear promises given in the Qurʾan (in the following verses: Sūra al-Nūr, XXIV: 54; al-Tawba, IX: 33; al-Fatḥ, XLVII: 28; al-Ṣaff, LXI: 9) and the most authentic hadiths —he will establish the authority of Islam throughout the entire world.[106]

**Article 94**

Love of the Prophet's family is stressed both in the Qurʾan and the Sunna. The Qurʾan says:

*Say; I ask of you no reward for this, save love for the kinsfolk* (al-mawadda fīʾl-qurbā). (Sūra al-Shūrā, XLII:23)

The reference of the Arabic *qurbā* here is to those 'close' to the Prophet, as is evidenced by the fact that it is the Prophet himself who is making this request.

Loving his noble family, in addition to being a great honour, is a cause of remaining always in their proximity, emulating them in their exemplary virtues and their remoteness from any vice. In certain *mutawātir* hadiths, it is related that love of the Prophet's *ahl al-bayt* is a sign of faith, and enmity towards them a sign of faithlessness and hypocrisy. Whoso loves them, loves the Prophet and God, and whoso opposes them, opposes God and His Prophet.

In principle, loving the family of the Prophet is one of the obligations of the faith of Islam, about which there is no doubt or confusion; and all Muslims are at one as regards this principle, except for one group, known as the *Nawāṣib*,[107] who are, for this very reason, regarded as having left the faith of Islam.

## Article 95

### The Twelfth Imam: His Occultation and Manifestation

It is beyond the scope of this book to speak in detail of each of the twelve Imams. The only question we feel it is necessary to broach here is the belief in the existence of the Imam of the [present] age, his state of being hidden behind the veil of occultation, and belief in his re-appearance, at God's command, to establish justice throughout the world. We shall address this issue in the following eight articles.

The coming forth of a man from the family of the Prophet, one who is destined to establish the rule of universal justice in an age wherein injustice and oppression prevail, is an axiom of Islamic belief, and as such, agreed upon by the whole community of Muslims, the hadiths on this matter reaching the highest level of authenticity, that of *tawātur*. According to the estimates of the scholars, there are 657 hadiths on this subject, of which we shall cite just one, which has been transmitted in the *Musnad* of Ibn Ḥanbal. The Prophet said: 'If there were only one day left in the life of the world, God would prolong that day until a man come forth from my descendants, who will fill the world with justice and equity, just as it had been filled with injustice and oppression.'[108]

Therefore, there is complete agreement among all Muslims, Shiʿa and Sunni alike, upon the fact that a man from the Prophet's family will arise, in the manner indicated in the hadith, in the Last Days.

## Article 96

The distinctive features of this global reformer, as expressed by hadiths in both branches of Islam, are summarized below:

1. He will be of the Prophet's *ahl al-bayt* (389 hadiths).
2. He will be a descendant of Imam ʿAlī (214 hadiths).
3. He will be a descendant of Fāṭima al-Zahrā' (192 hadiths).
4. He will be from the ninth generation after Imam Ḥusayn (147 hadiths).
5. He will be a descendant of Imam Zayn al-ʿĀbidīn (185 hadiths).
6. He will be a descendant of Imam Ḥasan al-ʿAskarī (146 hadiths).
7. He will be the twelfth Imam of the Imams of the *ahl al-bayt* (136 hadiths).
8. Narrations giving reports about him (214 hadiths).
9. His life will be prolonged (318 hadiths).
10. His occultation will be prolonged (91 hadiths).
11. With his appearance Islam will rule the world (27 hadiths).
12. He will fill the earth with justice and righteousness (132 hadiths).

On the basis of these narrations, there is no dispute in Islam as to the fact that such a global reformer will arise; what is, however, subject to dispute is whether he was born in the distant past and is still alive today, or whether he will come to this world at some future time. The Shiʿa, along with a group of Sunni scholars, uphold the first position, believing that this personage was born in the year 255/868, and is still alive today; while a section amongst the scholars of the Sunnis believe that he will be born in the future.

As we, the Shiʿa, believe that he has been alive since the year 255 AH, we must mention, within the limits imposed by this book, certain principles pertaining to the occultation and longevity of this personage.

### Article 97

From the Qur'anic point of view, there are two types of saints of God: the outwardly manifest saint, who is known by the people; and the saint who is hidden from view, unknown by people, even though he lives among them and is aware of them. In the Sūra al-Kahf, both types of saint are mentioned in the same place: one was Moses b. ʿImrān, the other was his travelling companion, by land and at sea, known by the name of al-Khiḍr.[109] This saint of God was such that even Moses did not know his true identity, and it was only through God's guidance that he came to know who he really was, and come to benefit from his actions, as it is said:

*Then they found one of Our slaves, unto whom We had given mercy from Us, and had taught him knowledge from Our Presence. Moses said to him: May I follow thee, so that thou mayst teach me right conduct, of that which thou hast been taught?* (Sūra al-Kahf, XVIII:65–66)

The Qur'an then relates the useful and beneficial actions of this saint, making it absolutely clear that though the people did not know him, they nonetheless benefited from his influence and his holiness. The Imam of this age is akin to the companion of Moses, being unknown even while being a source of beneficence for the *umma*.[110] Thus, the occultation of the Imam does not imply any separation from the community; rather, he is described in a hadith related from the *ahl al-bayt*, as being '... like the sun hidden behind a cloud, unseen by the eyes, but nonetheless bestowing light and heat upon the earth.'[111]

In addition, throughout history, there have been many among the pious and the pure of heart—souls worthy of being honoured by him—who have been made aware of his presence, and have benefited—and continue to benefit—from it; and through them, others have also come to receive the blessings of this Imam.

**Article 98**

The customary means of governance in human collectivities involves a leader performing certain actions alone, and delegating other actions to his representatives. It is true that since the Imam's occultation, which was the result of various factors, people have been deprived of direct, physical contact with him; but it is still possible for the followers of the Imam to benefit from his presence and guidance in a variety of ways, spiritual, moral and legal—through those who represent him in these different spheres, as well as directly, as mentioned in the last article.

**Article 99**

The reason behind the occultation of the Imam of the Age is steeped in divine mystery; and it is possible that we will never be able to fathom it in all its profundity. The temporary occultation of a spiritual leader is not without precedent; examples of this phenomenon are to be encountered in previous religious communities. Moses was hidden from his people for forty days, which he spent in the place appointed for him by God (Sūra al-Aʿrāf, VII:142). Jesus concealed himself, by God's will, from his community; and his enemies, intent on killing him, could not find him (Sūra al-Nisāʾ, IV:157). The Prophet Jonah also was concealed from his people for a certain period (Sūra al-Ṣāffāt, XXXVII:140–142).

In general, even if one is unable fully to grasp the mystery of a particular phenomenon, whose authenticity is however fully confirmed by traditional sources, there should be no reason to doubt or deny the phenomenon; otherwise, a large part of the divine rulings, pertaining to essential axioms of the Islamic faith, would be subject to doubt also. The occultation of the Imam of the Age is no exception to this rule, and the absence of information on the mysterious reality of this phenomenon does not give one license to doubt or deny it. Nonetheless, it can be said that the mystery of occultation can be understood within the limits imposed by human thought; and we would present the case thus:

This Imam is the last of the divinely guided and protected personages; he is to bring about the final consummation of the great and ardent hopes of the Muslims—the inauguration of universal justice and the unfurling of the flag of *Tawḥīd* throughout the world. The fulfilment of this hope requires a certain passage of time, so that the requisite intellectual preparedness, and spiritual readiness on the part of humanity be attained; only then can the world properly receive the just Imam and his followers. Naturally, should the Imam appear before these preliminary conditions are in place, he might well meet with the same fate as that which befell the other Imams, namely, martyrdom; and thus, he would leave this world without having witnessed the realization of the great hopes vested in him. The wisdom inherent herein has been alluded to in certain hadiths. Imam Bāqir said: 'There is an occultation ordained for the *Qā'im* [lit. 'the one who rises up'] prior to his appearance.' The narrator of this hadith asked the reason for this. The Imam replied: 'To prevent his being killed.'[112]

In addition to this narration, there are hadiths mentioning [the need for the] trial and purification of humanity, which means that mankind, during the period of the occultation, will have to undergo trials imposed by God, in order to test the firmness of their faith and beliefs.[113]

**Article 100**

Theological arguments demonstrate that the existence of a *maʿṣūm* Imam in the midst of society is a great blessing from God, and a source of authentic guidance for people. It is clear that if people are receptive to this manifestation of divine grace, they would benefit from all the blessings inherent in his being; but, in the absence of this receptivity, they would be deprived of this blessing, the cause of this deprivation emanating from the people themselves, not from God or the Imam.[114]

**Article 101**

The Imam of the Age, having seen the light of day in the year 255 AH, is now over eleven centuries old. In the light of the vast power of God, accepting such a proposition is not difficult; for, in truth, those who find this idea hard to accept forget that the divine power is infinite:

*And they rate not God at His true worth.* (Sūra al-Anʿām, VI:91)

In addition, one should recall that in past communities there were many persons of exceeding old age, such as the Prophet Noah, whose prophetic mission lasted for some 950 years, according to the Qur'an (Sūra al-ʿAnkabūt, XXIX:14). Indeed, if God, who is omnipotent, can keep the Prophet Jonah alive in the belly of a whale until the Day of Resurrection (Sūra al-Ṣāffāt, XXXVII:143–144), can He not bestow a long life on the Imam who is His 'proof' on earth, sustaining him through His blessings and His grace? The answer is clearly in the affirmative. In the words of a poem:

Almighty God who does with ease
the whole wide world sustain,
Can with His Might, should He so please,
His proof on earth maintain.

### Article 102

Nobody knows the time when the Imam will appear; this, like the time appointed for the Day of Resurrection, is known only to God. Therefore, one cannot believe anyone who claims to have this knowledge, or who specifies a given period within which the Imam will appear. Leaving aside the question of the precise moment of his appearance, we should note that in certain hadiths, mention is made of general signs indicating his appearance; these are divided into two categories, those that are deemed 'definite' and those that are 'indefinite'. Detailed elaboration on these signs will be found in books of theology and Hadith.

## V. THE HEREAFTER (MAʿĀD)

### Article 103

**The Resurrection**

All divinely revealed religions are in unison over the principle of faith in the reality of the Hereafter. The Prophets all affirmed, alongside their invitation to accept *Tawḥīd,* the reality of life after death, and the return to God in the Hereafter, these principles being of capital importance in their mission. Indeed, belief in the Resurrection is one of the pillars of the faith of Islam. Though the principle of the 'eschatological return' (*al-maʿād*) has been expressed in previous religions, it is given more comprehensive treatment in the Qur'an than in any other revealed scripture, a considerable portion of the verses of the Holy Book being devoted to this question. This 'return' is referred to by different names in the Qur'an, such as: the Day of Resurrection (*yawm al-*

*qiyāma*), the Day of the Account (*yawm al-ḥisāb*), the Last Day (*yawm al-ākhir*), the Day of the Rising (*yawm al-baʿth*), amongst others. The reason for attributing such importance to this question is that faith and piety cannot be fully brought to fruition without belief in the Resurrection.

### Article 104

The sages and theologians of Islam have brought forth different ways of proving the necessity of the principle of Resurrection and life after death, their principal source of inspiration being the Holy Qur'an. It is thus appropriate here to allude first of all to the Qur'anic proofs of the Hereafter.

God is the absolute Truth, thus His acts are all true, they are devoid of any kind of falsehood or vanity. Creating man without also bestowing upon him an immortal and meaningful life would be a vain and futile act, as the Qur'an says:

*Deemed ye then that We had created you for naught, and that ye would not be returned unto Us?* (Sūra al-Mu'minūn, XXIII:115)

The justice of God demands that the pious and the impious do not receive the same recompense in the Hereafter. However, we observe that the life of this world is such that perfect justice as regards the dispensing of reward and punishment is unrealizable, since the destinies of the two groups of souls are so intertwined that they cannot be completely disentangled from each other. From another angle, there are certain acts—good and bad—whose very intensity calls for a recompense that goes beyond the scope of this lower world: one only has to reflect on, for example, a person who is martyred after spending his entire life exerting himself to the utmost for the cause of the Truth, and another who kills innumerable pious souls.

It is clear then, that a world hereafter is necessary for the realization of the perfect justice of God; for this absolute justice requires a realm of infinite possibility; as the Holy Qur'an says:

*Shall We treat those who believe and do good works as those who spread corruption in the earth; or shall We treat the pious as the wicked?* (Sūra Ṣād, XXXVIII, 28)

It also says:

*Unto Him is the return of all of you; it is a promise of God in truth. Verily, He produceth creation, then reproduceth it, that He may reward those who believe and do good works with equity; while, as for those who disbelieve, theirs will be a boiling drink because they disbelieved.* (Sūra Yūnus, X:4)

Man is created in this world from a minute particle, growing by degrees into a fully-formed body. Then a point is reached when the Spirit is breathed into that frame, and the Qur'an, having in view the perfection of this most excellent creation, refers to the Creator as '*the best of Creators*'. Then man, at death, is transported from this to another world, which is the ultimate completion of his previous resting place. The Qur'an puts it thus:

... *then We produced it as another production; so blessed be God, the best of Creators. Then, verily, after that ye surely die. Then, verily, on the Day of Resurrection ye are raised up.* (Sūra al-Mu'minūn, XXIII:14–16)

This verse indicates that the renewal of life is a necessary corollary of the creation of life from an infinitesimal particle.

## Article 105

During the period when the Qur'an was revealed, the disbelievers expressed their doubts about the Resurrection; the Qur'an responds, and in the course of doing so, elucidates the evidence for the reality of the Resurrection. Below, we cite some of the relevant verses:

In one place, the Qur'an stresses the absolute power of God:

*Unto God is your return, and He is able to do all things.* (Sūra Hūd, XI:4)

Elsewhere, it is recalled that the One who is capable of creating man in the first place is not incapable of re-creating him anew. It is related that those who disbelieved in the Resurrection ask who would cause them to be re-born; the answer comes:

*Say: He who created you at the first.* (Sūra Banī Isrā'īl, XVII:51)

In other places, the bestowing of life upon man is likened to the revival of the earth in the season of spring after the sleep of winter:

*And thou seest the earth barren, but when We send down water thereon, it doth thrill and swell and put forth every lovely kind* [of growth]...

After the allusion to this recurrent feature of the natural world, the reality of the Resurrection is expressed:

... *and He giveth life to the dead.* (Sūra al-Ḥajj, XXII:5–6)

The doubters ask: When man dies and his body has rotted away, with his bodily parts scattered in the earth, how shall those parts be re-assembled, so that a body like the first one be reconstituted? The Qur'an replies by stressing the infinite knowledge of God, saying:

*Yea, He is the All-knowing Creator.* (Sūra Yā Sīn, XXXVI:81).

In another verse, this infinite knowledge is put thus:

*We verily know that which the earth taketh of them, and with Us is a recording Book.* (Sūra Qāf, L:4)

It has been thought that man is nothing more than the sum of his material, bodily parts, and that after death this body decomposes and becomes dust. According to this view, the question is asked how it can be that the individual who is brought to life at the Resurrection is the same as the one who had previously died. In other words: how is the unity of the two bodies preserved? The Qur'an relates the words of the disbelievers thus:

*When we are lost in the earth, are we really then to be created anew?*

The Qur'an answers:

*Say: The angel of death who hath charge over you, will gather you* (yatawaffākum), *and afterward unto your Lord ye will be returned.* (Sūra al-Sajda, XXXII:10, 11)

The word *yatawaffā* in this verse means the taking or gathering up of the soul at death. Understood thus, there is, at the moment of death, in addition to the material substance that remains on earth and becomes dust, something else that exists, something that the angel of death takes, and that is the spirit of man. In this light, the purport of the answer given by the Qur'an is that the preserver of the unity and the identity of the two bodies is that very spirit which the angel of death takes; so that 'the one who is made to return' (*al-muʿād*) is identical to 'the one who was first originated' (*al-mubtadā*). From this and similar verses it is clear that the person raised up at the Resurrection is the same person who was previously alive on earth, and will thus receive the appropriate reward or punishment. Another verse refers to this oneness of personality:

*Say: He will revive them Who produced them at the first, for He is the knower of every creation.* (Sūra Yā Sīn, XXXVI:79)

### Article 106

Both the Qur'an and the Hadith show that the Resurrection is both of the body and the soul. The purpose of bodily resurrection is that the body be raised up in another domain and, once more, be connected to a soul, in order that it might experience the delights or torments—as reward or punishment—that are of a perceptible, sensible nature, and which cannot be experienced in the absence of a body and its sense-faculties. The purpose of spiritual resurrection is that, in addition to the tangible rewards and punishments that are of a bodily nature, there is a whole series of rewards and punishments that are of a spiritual order, beyond the senses, that are in store for the righteous and the wicked, respectively, for the perception and assimilation of which the spirit has no need of a body or its faculties of sense-perception. The perception of the divine beatitude (*riḍwān*) is one example; the Qur'an relates, after mentioning certain tangible paradisal rewards, that:

... *the beatitude of God is greater. That is the supreme triumph.* (Sūra al-Tawba, IX:72)

Likewise, there are modes of grief and sorrow that bring anguish to the soul, as the Qur'an says:

*And warn them of the day of anguish when the case hath been decided. Now they are in a state of heedlessness and they believe not.* (Sūra Maryam, XIX:40)

## Article 107

Death is not the termination of life, but a transferral from one domain to another, a domain which is permanent and everlasting, one in which the Resurrection takes place. Between this world and the Resurrection there is an intermediary world, the Barzakh [literally, 'barrier'], in which man resides for a certain period after death. The real nature of life in the Barzakh is unclear to us, and the only data we have regarding this is that which is given us by the Qur'an and Hadith. Below, we bring attention to bear upon the indications given by the Qur'an:

1. When death comes to an idolator, he says:

   *My Lord! Send me back, that I may do right in that which I have left behind!*

   The answer is given:

   *But nay! It is but a word that he speaketh; and behind them is a Barrier* (Barzakh) *until the Day when they are raised.* (Sūra al-Mu'minūn, XXIII, 99–100)

   These verses indicate that souls have a real existence after death, but are unable to return to this world.
2. Regarding the martyrs it is said:

   *And call not those who are slain in the way of God 'dead'. Nay, they are living, only ye perceive not.* (Sūra al-Baqara, II:154)

   In another verse, the life of these martyrs in the way of God is described:

*Joyous* [are the martyrs] *because of that which God hath bestowed upon them of His bounty, rejoicing for the sake of those who have not joined them but are left behind: that no fear shall come upon them neither shall they grieve.* (Sūra Āl ʿImrān, III:170)

3. Regarding the sinners, especially the people of Pharaoh, we are told that before the Day of Resurrection, they are exposed each morning and evening to fire; and that at the Resurrection, they will be subjected to the most intense form of suffering:

*The Fire—they are exposed to it morning and evening; and on the Day when the Hour upriseth* [it is said]: *Cause Pharaoh's folk to enter the most awful doom.* (Sūra al-Mu'min, XL:46)

## Article 108

The first stage of the soul's life in the Barzakh begins with the withdrawal of the spirit from the body. At the time that man is buried, according to many hadiths, the angels question him on *Tawḥīd*, Prophecy, and a series of other principles pertaining to belief and religion. Obviously, the answers given by a believer will differ from those given by a disbeliever, and in consequence, the grave and the Barzakh will be places wherein divine mercy manifests for the believer, and divine wrath, for the disbeliever. The questioning by the angels and the dispensing of mercy and wrath, respectively, to the believers and disbelievers in the grave, pertain to basic beliefs of our religion; the grave constitutes the commencement of 'Barzakhī' life, which will persist until the Day of Resurrection.

Imami scholars have expounded these questions in books of theology. Shaykh Ṣadūq, in his book *Tajrīd al-iʿtiqādāt*, says: 'Our belief as regards the questions in the grave is this: it is true, and whoever gives the correct answers to these questions will be granted divine mercy, and whoever gives the wrong answers will be subjected to divine punishment.'[115]

Shaykh Mufīd, in his book *Taṣḥīḥ al-iʿtiqād*, writes: 'Strong hadiths of the Holy Prophet tell us that the people of the graves will be questioned regarding their religion; and some hadiths indicate that two angels are charged with this task of interrogation, and they are called Nākir and Nakīr.' He says further: 'The interrogation in the grave shows that those in the graves are alive, remaining thus until the Day of Resurrection.'[116]

Naṣīr al-Dīn Ṭūsī writes: 'The punishment of the grave is real, it is an intelligible possibility, and there are the most authentic hadiths confirming its reality.'[117]

Reference to theological works of the other schools of Islam will reveal that there is unanimity on this issue, the only person of note denying its reality being Darār b. 'Amrū.[118]

## Article 109

From the observations above, it will have been made clear that the reality of the Resurrection consists in this: the spirit, after having been separated from the body—by the will of God—is once again returned to that body in which it had lived previously; this, in order to experience, in another realm of existence, the reward or punishment elicited by his actions on earth.

Certain groups within different religions, and others outside the pale of all religion, deny the notion of Resurrection such as it is found in heavenly-inspired religions, but have accepted the principle of reward and punishment of actions, doing so in connection with the idea of reincarnation (*tanāsukh*). They claim that the spirit attaches itself to a foetus, through the unfolding of whose life the spirit returns to this earth, going through the stages of childhood, maturity and old age; but, for one who had been virtuous in his previous life, a sweet life results, while for those who were wicked in their previous lives, a wretched life lies in store.

It must be understood that if all human souls traverse the path of reincarnation for ever, there can be no place for the principle of Resurrection; while by both intellectual and traditionally transmitted evidence, belief in the Resurrection is an obligation. Indeed, it must be said that those who believe in reincarnation do so because they are incapable of conceiving of the Resurrection in a proper manner, and so have replaced it with the idea of reincarnation. There are extensive discussions regarding the falsity of this belief, and its incompatibility with Islam; we summarize some of these arguments below.

The soul of man attains at death a certain degree of completion. Thus, to be attached once more to a foetus requires, according to the principle of necessary harmony between the soul and the body, a descent of the soul from a degree of completeness to a degree of deficiency, and a return from a state of actuality to one of potentiality—something which contradicts the normal principle of the order of the created universe, an order based upon the movement of things towards their perfection, from potentiality to actuality.[119]

If we accept the fact that a soul, after being separated from a body, finds itself joined to a different, living body, this would imply a plurality of souls within a single body, and a twofold personality; whereas such a phenomenon is clearly at odds with the perception that each person's conscience yields, that of possessing a single personality.[120]

A belief in reincarnation, in addition to being contrary to the principles of order in the universe, can also be used by oppressors and opportunists as a means of legitimizing themselves, by claiming that their power and privilege are the consequences of their previous lives of virtue and rectitude; and that the misfortunes of the oppressed are, likewise, the consequences of their previous lives of wickedness. By such means they attempt to justify their evil actions and the inhuman injustices of the society over which they rule.

## Article 110

To conclude this discussion on reincarnation, it is necessary to answer two questions. The first is this: According to a clear Qur'anic description, past communities were subject to transformation (*maskh*)—some persons became pigs, others monkeys:

*God hath turned some of them to apes and swine* ... (Sūra al-Mā'ida, v:60)[121]

If reincarnation is false, how could such transformations occur?

The answer is as follows: Transformation differs fundamentally from reincarnation as commonly understood. For, according to reincarnation, the spirit is joined, after separation from one body, with another body, or to a foetus; whilst in transformation, the spirit does not become separate from its body—rather, it is simply that the appearance and form of the body is transformed, so that the person is able to see his sins in the form of monkeys and pigs, and suffer thereby. In other words, the soul of a person who was a sinner does not descend from the state of humanity to that of animality. For, were such the case, the persons so transformed would not be able to grasp their suffering and punishment as such, whereas the whole point of this kind of transformation, as the Qur'an says, is that it be an exemplary punishment for sinners.[122]

In this regard, Taftāzānī says: 'The true import of reincarnation is that souls of human beings become attached, after their separation from their respective bodies, to other bodies for the sake of governing over and possessing them, in this very world; it does not mean that the appearance of the body changes, as is the case in transformation.'[123]

ʿAllāma Ṭabāṭabāʾī also says: 'People who have been transformed are those who, while retaining their human spirit, are transformed as regards their form; transformation does not mean that the human soul is transformed also, becoming the soul of [for example] a monkey.'[124]

The second question: Some writers have presumed that the idea of the 'return' (*rajʿa*) has been derived from that of reincarnation.[125] Does belief in the 'return' require belief in reincarnation? As we shall be seeing below, the doctrine of the 'return', according to most of the Shiʿi scholars, consists in this: A number of believers and disbelievers will return to this world in the Last Days; and their manner of 'returning' is akin to the way in which the dead were brought to life by Jesus;[126] or like the reviving of Uzayr after 100 years.[127] Thus, belief in the 'return' has nothing to do with reincarnation. In our discussion below, further clarification of the meaning of the 'return' will be given.

### Article 111

In the discourse of the scholars, based on the Qurʾan, there is an issue known as 'portents of the Hour' (*ashrāṭ al-sāʿa*) which refers to the signs preceding the Resurrection. These signs are divided into two types: (a) Events which occur before the Resurrection and the collapse of the created order; these events take place when people are still living on earth. The phrase 'portents of the Hour' refers, in the main, to this type of phenomenon. (b) Events which are the cause of the collapse of the created order, most of which are mentioned in the following Sūras: al-Takwīr (LXXXI), al-Infiṭār (LXXXII), al-Inshiqāq (XXXIV) and al-Zilzāl (XCIX).

The signs of the first type can be summarized as follows:

1. The raising up of the last Prophet (Sūra Muḥammad, XLVII:18).
2. The breaking up of the barriers, [hitherto restraining] Gog and Magog (Sūra al-Kahf, XVII: 97–99).
3. The covering over of the sky by thick smoke (Sūra al-Dukhān, XLIV: 10–16).
4. The descent of the Messiah (Sūra al-Zukhruf, XLIII:57–61).
5. The emergence of a beast from the belly of the earth (Sūra al-Naml, XXVII:82).

Explanation of these signs can be found in books of exegesis and Hadith.

As regards the signs of the second type, the Qurʾan speaks in detail of the transformation of the existential conditions of the universe: the collapse of the sun, the moon, the oceans, the mountains, the earth and the sky; in sum, the existing order will be rolled up as a scroll, and a new order will arise, thus manifesting God's all-encompassing power, as it is said:

*On the day when the earth will be changed to other than the earth, and the Heavens* [also will be changed], *and they will come forth unto God, the One, the Irresistible.* (Sūra Ibrāhīm, XV:48)

### Article 112

The Holy Qurʾan describes an event named 'the blowing of the trumpet', which will occur twice: (a) the first blast of the trumpet causes the death of all living creatures in the heavens and the earth (except those for whom God wills otherwise); (b) the second blast will revive the dead and bring them all before God,[128] as it is said:

*And the trumpet is blown, and all who are in the heavens and all who are in the earth swoon away, save him who God willeth. Then it is blown a second time, and behold them, standing, waiting.* (Sūra al-Zumar, XXXIX: 68)

The Qur'an specifically says in regard to the gathering and the resurrecting of mankind on the Day of Judgement:

... *they come forth from the graves as though they were scattered locusts.* (Sūra al-Qamar, LIV: 7)

**Article 113**

After the revival of the dead and their entrance into the domain of the Resurrection—but before they proceed to Heaven or Hell—various events come to pass, events which the Qur'an and Hadith describe:

1. Each person's reckoning will be conveyed in a particular way, one of these is the presentation to each of the record of his deeds (Banī Isrā'īl, XVII:13–14).
2. Apart from the recording of all deeds, small or great, being registered in the account of each person, there will also be, on the Day of Resurrection, witnesses from within and without man, that will testify to his actions on earth. The external witnesses consist of God (Āl 'Imrān, III:98); the Prophet of each religious community (al-Naḥl, XVI:89); the Prophet of Islam (al-Nisā', IV:41); the foremost among the Islamic community (al-Baqara, II:143); God's angels (Qāf, L:18); and the earth (al-Zilzāl, XCIX:4–5). The internal witnesses consist of the members and limbs of man (al-Nūr, XXIV:24); and the embodied forms of his own acts (al-Tawba, IX:34–5).
3. In order to take account of the actions of human beings, in

addition to what has been mentioned, there will be scales of justice set up, and each person will receive his exact due:

*And We set up a just Balance on the Day of Resurrection so that no soul is wronged in anything. Though it be of the weight of a mustard seed, We bring it. And We suffice as reckoners.* (Sūra al-Anbiyāʾ, XXI:47)

4. It is narrated in certain hadiths that there is a path that all must traverse on the Day of Resurrection. In these hadiths, this path is called *al-Ṣirāṭ*; exegetes have identified it with what is referred to [implicitly] in Sūra Maryam, verses 71–72.[129]
5. Between those in Heaven and Hell there is a barrier which the Qurʾan calls a *ḥijāb.* On the Day of Resurrection, eminent individuals will be raised up to a high place from which they will see the inhabitants of Heaven and Hell by their respective marks, as it is said:

   *Between them is a veil, and on the heights are men who know them all by their marks.* (Sūra al-Aʿrāf, VII:46)

   These eminent souls, according to hadiths, are the Prophets and their noble successors.
6. When the rendering of account has been completed and the fate of souls is known, God hands to the Prophet a flag called *Lawāʾ al-ḥamd* (Banner of Praise), and he then leads to Heaven those destined for it.
7. In numerous hadiths, mention is made of the pool of al-Kawthar, present in the domain where the Resurrection takes place; the Prophet comes before all others to this pool, and then those in the community who are saved drink at the pool, through the mediation of the Prophet and his *ahl al-bayt.*

## Article 114

**Intercession**

Belief in the intercession of intercessors on the Day of Resurrection, with God's permission, is axiomatic in Islam. Intercession pertains to those individuals whose connection with God and religion has not been totally ruptured, and who are capable, despite being defiled by certain sins, of being embraced by the Mercy of God through the blessed prayers of intercessors. Belief in intercession derives from the Qur'an and the Sunna, as we indicate below.

There are verses in the Qur'an which indicate the reality of the principle of intercession on the Day of Resurrection; and this noble Scripture elucidates both this principle and its dependence on the permission and good pleasure of God:

... *and they cannot intercede except for him whom He accepteth.* (Sūra al-Anbiyā', XXI:28)

In another verse it is said:

*There is no intercessor save by His permission.* (Sūra Yūnus, X:3)

It is clear that the principle of intercession is, from the Qur'anic perspective, both real and definitive. But now we must ask: who are the intercessors? From certain verses we learn that the angels are among those with the power to intercede:

*How many angels are in the heavens whose intercession is of no avail except after God giveth leave to whom He chooseth and accepteth!* (Sūra al-Najm, LIII: 26)

Exegetes have commented that the meaning of the '*praised station*' [in the following verse] is the station of intercession proper to the Prophet of Islam:[130]

... *it may be that thy Lord will raise thee to a praised station* (Sūra Banī Isrā'īl, XVII:79)

The principle of intercession is mentioned also in many of the Prophet's sayings, some of which we mention below.

The Prophet said: 'My intercession is especially for the perpetrators of major sins in my community.'[131] It would seem that the reason why this should be the case is that God has explicitly promised that if people avoid major sins, they will be forgiven (Sūra al-Nisā', IV:31), hence there would be no need for intercession or the like. He [the Prophet] has also said: 'I have received five gifts from God, [one of which] is that of intercession, which I have in store for my community. My intercession is for those who have not associated any partner with God.'[132]

Those wishing to investigate further the identity of the intercessors on the Day of Resurrection, apart from the Prophet (such as the *maʿṣūm* Imams, sages and martyrs) and also those who are subject to their intercession, should refer to the books on theology and Hadith. For now, it must be noted that belief in intercession, like belief in the acceptance by God of repentance, must not become a means of emboldening people to commit sins; rather, it should be seen as a ray of hope, in whose light forgiveness can be sought, so that one who has committed certain sins might be led back to the Straight Path, and not be reduced to despair, like those who feel that the divine mercy has passed them by and that they can never revert to the path of rectitude.

Given what has been said above, it will be clear that the effect of intercession is not confined to the elevation of the rank of those granted intercession, as certain groups in Islam (such as the Muʿtazilites) have claimed.[133]

## Article 115

As has been stated, then, belief in the principle of intercession in the Hereafter, within the framework of divine authorization, is an axiom of the Islamic faith, and nobody has the right to cast doubt upon it. Now, it must be asked: can one also seek, even in this world, the intercession of intercessors such as the Prophet? In other words: is it correct for a person to say: 'O Prophet of God, intercede for me with God!'

The answer to this is as follows: The legitimacy of such a practice was acknowledged unanimously, by all Muslims, until the 8th/14th century, after which a number of persons opposed the practice, regarding it as impermissible; this, despite the fact that Qur'anic verses, prophetic sayings, and the established conventional practices of the Muslims all attested to its permissibility. For the intercession of the intercessors is, in essence, a prayer on behalf of others, and there is no doubt that asking for the prayers of the pious—and especially the Prophet—is both permissible and laudable.

A hadith of the Prophet, related by Ibn ʿAbbās, makes it clear that the intercession of a believer consists in the making of a petition on behalf of others: 'If a Muslim dies, and forty believers in the unity of God pray for him, God accepts their intercession on his behalf.'[134] It is thus clear that the intercession of forty believers in the funeral prayer of a dead person is nothing other than a prayer for him to be forgiven by God.

A glance at the pages of history reveals that the companions of the Prophet asked him in their own lifetimes for his intercession. Tirmidhī relates from Anas b. Mālik: 'I asked the Prophet to intercede for me on the Day of Judgement. He said: "I shall do so." I asked him, "Where will I find you?" He replied: "By the side of the *Ṣirāṭ*."'[135]

The reality of seeking intercession, then, is nothing other than the request for prayers from the intercessor. Examples of this practice can be found in the period of the Prophets, as related in the Qur'an:

1. The sons of Jacob, after the disclosure of their wicked acts, asked their father to implore God's forgiveness of them. Jacob accepted their petition and promised to do so at the appointed time.[136]
2. The Qur'an says:

   *And if, when they had wronged themselves, they had but come unto thee and asked forgiveness of God, and the Messenger had sought forgiveness for them, they would have found God Forgiving, Merciful.* (Sūra al-Nisā', IV: 64)

3. Likewise it says, regarding the hypocrites:

   *And when it is said unto them: Come! The Messenger of God will ask forgiveness for you, they avert their faces, and thou seest them turning away, disdainful.* (Sūra al-Munāfiqūn, LXIII:5)

It is evident that being averse to asking the Prophet to seek forgiveness for one—that is, asking for his intercession—is a sign of hypocrisy and pride; conversely, making this request is a mark of faith and humility before God.

Our aim in this discussion has been to affirm the validity and legitimacy of seeking intercession. Now, the fact that the intercessor, in the verses quoted, is no longer alive does not detract from the argument propounded. Even if it be supposed that these verses pertain to the living and not the dead, this still does not diminish the validity of the principle. For, if seeking intercession from the living is not *shirk* (polytheism) then, naturally, seeking intercession from the dead will not be so either; the question of whether the intercessor is alive or dead is immaterial as regards the distinction between *Tawḥīd* and *shirk*. The only question is whether, when these blessed souls receive requests for intercession, they can hear them; this is a question that relates to the reality and the benefit of the connection between the two groups, the petitioners and those petitioned, and it will be addressed below, in the debate on *tawassul*.

Here it should be noted that seeking the intercession of the Prophets and the saints by true, monotheistic believers differs fundamentally from the requests by the polytheistic idolators for the intercession of their idols. For the monotheists make their request for intercession from the saints while acknowledging two principles:

1. The station of intercession is the preserve of God, and is determined according to His disposition, as it is said:

   *Say: Unto God belongeth all intercession.* (Sūra al-Zumar, XXXIX:44); *Who is it that can intercede with Him save by His leave?* (Sūra al-Baqara, II:255).

2. The intercessors to whom the monotheist believer extends his hands, seeking their prayers, are purified slaves of God, blessed by their proximity to Him, and thus those whose prayers are accepted.

Taking due note of these two principles, the difference between the monotheists seeking intercession and the polytheistic idolators alive at the time of the Prophet becomes readily apparent. Firstly, the polytheists believed in setting no kind of limits or conditionality on the making of their requests for intercession. The monotheists, on the other hand, following the guidance of the Holy Qur'an, know that the station of intercession is the exclusive preserve of God, and the success of the intercession of other intercessors is totally contingent upon His permission and good pleasure.

Secondly, the polytheists alive at the time of the Prophet believed that their idols, though fashioned by their own hands, were gods and lords, imagining in their deluded folly that these lifeless objects had been endowed with a share in divinity and lordship. The monotheists, on the contrary, consider the Prophets and the Imams as slaves of God, and continuously chant phrases such as 'His slave and His Prophet' and 'The righteous slaves of God'. The vast distance that separates these two divergent attitudes towards intercession could hardly be clearer.

Therefore, the attempt to prove the illegitimacy of the principle of intercession in Islam by reference to verses that invalidate the seeking of intercession by the idolators from their idols, is nothing but an utterly misplaced analogy, a piece of baseless sophistry.

## Article 116

### Repentance

One of the teachings of Islam—and indeed of all religions of heavenly origin—is that sinners always have the possibility of repentance before them. When a man is genuinely remorseful in regard to his sins, and his spirit turns him towards God in humility, and with a pure heart he resolves never to repeat his sins, then God, who is infinitely kind, accepts his repentance. The Qur'an says:

*And turn all together in repentance unto God, O believers, that ye may succeed.* (Sūra al-Nūr, XXIV:31)

Those who are unaware of the reforming influence of repentance and the belief in intercession imagine that opening up these two doors for sinners is a kind of invitation to them to commit sin! Those who think thus seem to be oblivious to the fact that many people are, in different ways, besmirched with some sin; rarely can one find a person who, throughout his life, has never sinned. Who, indeed, has never sinned in this world? Therefore, if the door of repentance (and of intercession) were not open, those souls who might be ready to renounce a life of sin—and to resolve, henceforth, to lead lives of purity and goodness—such people would say to themselves: 'We shall have to endure the punishment of Hell because of the sins we have committed; so why not spend the rest of our lives gratifying our souls' desires and losing ourselves more completely in the bosom of illicit pleasure?' In this way, the closing of the door of repentance opens wide the entrance of the pit of despair as regards the mercy of God; behaviour will then follow the downward path of concupiscent desire, rather than the upward path of fervent hope.

The positive effects of the principle of repentance become clearer when we understand that the acceptance of repentance in Islam requires the fulfilment of certain conditions, as the sages and the scholars of our religion have explained. The most important such condition is that one no longer performs the sins of which one repents. The Qur'an says clearly and explicitly, as regards the door of repentance:

*... Thy Lord hath prescribed for Himself mercy, that whoso of you doeth evil through ignorance and repenteth afterward thereof, and doeth right, truly, He is Forgiving, Merciful.* (Sūra al-Anʿām, VI:54)

## Article 117

### Reward and Punishment

Both intellectual evidence and traditional authority alike attest to the fact that on the Day of Resurrection, each person will behold the reward for his good actions. The Qur'an says:

*And whoso doeth good an atom's weight, will see it then.* (Sūra al-Zilzāl, XCIX:7)

And also:

*... and that his effort will be seen. And afterward he will be repaid for it with fullest payment.* (Sūra al-Najm, LIII:40–41)

From these verses it is clear that the wicked deeds of man do not obliterate his good deeds. Nevertheless, it must be understood that those who indulge in certain sins (such as disbelief or polytheism), or become apostates, will experience the 'nullification of action', and consequently will find their good deeds wiped out; they are then subject to perpetual punishment:

*And whoso among you becometh an apostate and dieth in his disbelief, such are they whose works are nullified both in the world and the Hereafter. Such are the rightful owners of the Fire, abiding therein.* (Sūra al-Baqara, II:217)

Taking all of the above into consideration, it is clear that each person of faith will behold the consequences of his good and bad acts in the next world, unless those bad acts take the form of apostasy and the like, in which case, according to the Qur'an and Hadith, all good deeds are negated and lost.

In conclusion, it is necessary to insist on the following point: Although God has 'promised' to reward the good deeds of the believers and, conversely, has 'threatened' to punish bad acts, there is a significant difference between the two principles—promise and threat (*waʿd* and *waʿīd*). For the necessity of keeping a promise is a self-evident intellectual principle, and the breaking of a promise is also, self-evidently, a sin. But as regards a 'threat', the meting out of the punishment threatened is a right possessed by the punisher, but he can also refrain from exercising this right. Thus, there is nothing preventing certain good actions from, as it were, covering over the ugliness and consequences of bad deeds, this being called *takfīr*.[137] In the Qur'an, certain good acts are deemed means whereby this 'covering-over'[138] by God of bad action is effected, one of these means being the avoidance of major sins:

*If ye avoid the major sins which ye are forbidden, We will remit from you your evil deeds, and make you enter at a noble gate.* (Sūra al-Nisā', IV:31)

Certain acts such as making repentance, giving charity in secret, speaking truthfully, and the like, also have this effect; that is, they too attract God's 'covering over' of man's sins.

**Article 118**

Abiding in the punishment of Hell is the fate apportioned to the disbelievers, while for believers who have sinned—even though being alive to the truth of *Tawḥīd*—the path of forgiveness and removal from the Fire is never barred:

*Verily, God forgiveth not that a partner should be ascribed unto Him. He forgiveth* [all] *except that to whom He will. Whoso ascribeth partners to God, he hath indeed forged a tremendous sin.* (Sūra al-Nisāʾ, IV:48)

This verse, explicitly presenting the possibility of forgiveness for all sins—except that of polytheism—undoubtedly envisages the bad acts of persons who die unrepentant. For, in repentance, all sins—even polytheism—are forgiven; and, taking due note of the fact that this verse distinguishes between the polytheists and others, we have to conclude that it indicates the forgiving of those who depart from this world without having repented. It is clear that were such a person a polytheist, he would not be forgiven; but if he is not a polytheist, then there is hope that he may be forgiven, but not in an unconditional way; rather, it would be according to the proviso '*to whom He will*'. In other words, only he is forgiven whom God wills to be forgiven. This proviso in the above verse (which expresses the vastness of God's mercy) maintains sinners in a state between fear and hope, heightening their resolve and desire to avert the danger inherent in sin, and to repent before they die. Thus, the promise expressed above, by keeping man away from the two precipices of despair and audacity, guides him back to the Straight Path.

The seventh Imam Mūsā al-Kāẓim said: 'God does not place in perpetual Hell anyone other than the disbelievers, the deniers, and the misguided polytheists.'[139] Ultimately, then, all people other than those mentioned will benefit from the reward of their good acts:

*And whoso doeth good an atom's weight, will see it then.* (Sūra al-Zilzāl, XCIX:7)

### Article 119

We believe that, even now, Heaven and Hell are existent realities. Shaykh Mufīd says: 'Heaven and Hell are even now real; hadiths bear testimony to their current actuality, and religious scholars are unanimous on this issue.'[140] The Qur'an also attests to the actuality of Heaven and Hell:

*And verily he saw him yet another time, by the Lote-tree of the utmost boundary, nigh unto which is the Garden of the Abode.* (Sūra al-Najm, LIII:13–15)

Elsewhere, in regard to the glad tidings and warnings given respectively to the believers and disbelievers, it declares that Heaven is already prepared for the former and Hell for the latter. Heaven has been '*made ready for the pious*' (Āl 'Imrān, III:133); as for Hell, we find the following admonition:

*And guard yourself against the Fire made ready for the disbelievers.* (Sūra Āl 'Imrān, III:131)

Nevertheless, the location of Heaven and Hell are not known to us, and it is only by means of certain verses that we are able to assume that Heaven is located in a supremely exalted dimension of reality; we are told, for example:

*And in the Heaven is your sustenance, and that which ye are promised.* (Sūra al-Dhārīyāt, LI:22)

THREE

# Faith, Disbelief and Other Issues

### I. FAITH AND DISBELIEF (ĪMĀN WA KUFR)

#### Article 120

Correctly situating the boundary that separates faith from disbelief is one of the most important of all theological issues. Faith (*īmān*) signifies 'confirmation' (*taṣdīq*), while disbelief (*kufr*) literally signifies 'covering over'; hence, one also calls a farmer a *kāfir*, that is, one who 'covers over' the seed of wheat by the earth. But in theological parlance, faith signifies belief in the Oneness of God, in the Day of Judgement, in the message of the last Prophet; and, of course, belief in the message of the Prophet of Islam implies acknowledgement of the prophecies brought by all previous Prophets and revealed books, while following all the doctrines and rulings brought by the Prophet of Islam.

The true locus of faith is the heart of man, as the Qur'an says:

... *they are those upon whose hearts He hath written faith.* (Sūra al-Mujādila, LIX: 22).

Also, in relation to the bedouin of the desert who submitted to the power of Islam, but whose hearts were devoid of the light of true faith, the Qur'an says:

... *for the faith hath not yet entered into your hearts.* (Sūra al-Ḥujurāt, XLIX:14)

But of course, one can only form some kind of judgement about the faith of a person if the person in question positively expresses his faith, or the lack of it, either by way of speech or other means. The Qur'an says in regard to those who disavow their faith:

*And they denied them* [Our signs], *though their souls acknowledged them* ... (Sūra al-Naml, XXVII:14)

Whenever a person denies the Oneness of God, or the Day of Judgement, or the Message of the Prophet, evidently, such a one will be judged an unbeliever, since denial of one of the axioms of the religion, implying therewith denial of the integrity of the Message, is tantamount to disbelief.

## Article 121

### Degrees of Faith

Although the reality of faith pertains essentially to heartfelt belief, it must not be supposed that this measure of faith suffices in itself for salvation; rather, the individual is obliged to act in consequence of his faith, accomplishing the obligations that flow from faith. For in many Qur'anic verses and hadiths, the person of true faith is defined as one who is bound by the concomitants of faith and fulfils the religious duties incumbent upon him. Thus, we find in the Sūra al-'Aṣr, that all men are accounted as being in a '*state of loss*', excepting only:

*those who believe and do good works, and exhort one another to truth and exhort one another to patience.* (Sūra al-'Aṣr, CIII:2–3)

Imam Bāqir relates that a man asked Imam 'Alī: 'Is it the case that anyone who testifies to the Oneness of God and to the message of Muḥammad is a believer?' The Imam replied: 'Where, then, are the obligatory duties one owes to God?' The Imam also said: 'If faith were but a matter of [uttering the double testimony, consisting of] words, then fasting, prayer, and [the distinction between] the permissible and the prohibited, would not have been revealed [as part of the religion].'[1]

From the above we can conclude that there are various degrees of faith and each degree has a particular sign. Belief in one's heart, conjoined with some outward manifestation—or at least, in the absence of any denial thereof—is the lowest degree of faith, from which a series of religious and temporal duties proceed. The other degree of faith, which is the source of man's salvation both in this world and the next, is dependent upon the fulfilment of the necessary active corollaries of faith.

It would be appropriate here to make the following point: Certain hadiths posit the accomplishment of religious obligations as part of the pillars of faith. The eighth Imam, 'Alī b. Mūsā al-Riḍā, relates from his father, and through his forefathers, from the Prophet himself, the following saying: 'Faith is knowledge of the heart, confirmation by the tongue and action by one's limbs.'[2]

In some hadiths, such actions as performing the daily *ṣalāt* prayers, paying *zakāt*, keeping the fast of Ramadan and performing the Hajj, are specified, alongside the double testimony of faith.[3] This type of hadith either has in view the means whereby Muslims can be distinguished from non-Muslims, or else affirms that the salvific value of the double testimony of faith is dependent upon the accomplishment of religious duties flowing from faith, among which the aforesaid duties are the most important.

Taking into account these two principles of inner faith and consequent outward expression, no Muslim school should accuse another of being *kāfir* solely on account of differences as regards certain secondary religious duties. For the only basis upon which one can legitimately accuse someone of being a *kāfir* is if he deny one of the three fundamental principles of Islam: (a) attestation of the Oneness of God, (b) belief in the message of the final Prophet, and (c) belief in the Resurrection in the Hereafter. Believing in these principles implies faith and denial of them implies disbelief. Also, true faith is undermined if one denies something which strictly entails a denial of one of these three principles—this is the case only if such a denial be clearly and irrefutably incompatible with a confession of belief in the principles of Islam.

From this point of view, it is fitting that Muslims in all parts of the world take care to preserve the brotherhood of Islam, and ensure that differences of opinion—ones that do not pertain to essential principles—are not used as sources of dispute, mutual recrimination or ostracism; even in cases of intellectual or theological differences, Muslims should resort to reasoned debate, based on scholarly research, and guard against senseless outbursts of bigotry, fanaticism and the hurling of false accusations which only leads to mutual anathematization.

**Article 122**

Insofar as the Muslims of the world are unanimous as regards the three fundamental principles of Islam, there are no grounds for one group of Muslims anathematizing another group simply because of differences in respect of certain secondary applications or details. For many of the principles over which there are differences of opinion pertain to theological questions that were expounded some considerable time after the period of the Revelation, each group having for its own position certain arguments and supporting evidence. Therefore, there should be no reason whatsoever for these questions becoming the cause of mutual anathematization or recrimination, which rupture the unity of Islam. The best way of resolving differences, as stated above, is rational debate and discourse, eschewing the illogicality of intolerance and fanaticism. The Qur'an says:

*O ye who believe, when ye go forth in the way of God, be careful to discriminate, and say not unto one who offereth you* [the greeting of] *peace: Thou art not a believer* ... (Sūra al-Nisā', IV: 94)

The Holy Prophet, in the course of explaining the foundations of Islam, said that no Muslim has the right to declare another Muslim a *kāfir* or a *mushrik* only on account of the commission of sin by the latter.[4]

## II. INNOVATION (BIDʿA)

**Article 123**

The Arabic word *bidʿa* signifies etymologically a new or original action that has no precedent, one by which a degree of excellence or perfection in the performer of the action is demonstrated;

thus, one of the Names of God is *al-Badīʿ*, 'The Marvellously Original':

*The Originator of the heavens and the earth.* (Sūra al-Baqara, II:117)

But the conventional meaning of the term refers to any action which is deemed to fall outside the boundaries of the Shariʿa; the most concise definition would be as follows: establishing a practice as part of the religion when it is not so.

Committing *bidʿa* is a major sin; there is not the slightest doubt about its being prohibited. The Holy Prophet said: 'Every newly originated thing is a *bidʿa,* and every *bidʿa* is a going astray, and every going astray ends up in the Fire.'[5] But the important point as regards the issue of *bidʿa* is to define and describe it in a way that makes clear what it includes and what it excludes, so that it can be distinguished clearly from what it is not. To grasp aright the true nature of *bidʿa,* the following two points should be borne in mind:

Firstly, *bidʿa* is a type of wilful interference with religion, effected by means of adding something to the Shariʿa or removing something from it. Therefore, if a given innovation has nothing to do with religion, but is rather derived from traditional custom or convention, it will not necessarily be a *bidʿa*—its legality will depend upon whether the innovation in question is permitted or prohibited by the Shariʿa. For example, in respect of housing, clothing and such matters, people are constantly resorting to innovations—especially in our times, witness the radical transformations in the ways of living, or the new forms of recreation and leisure activities. It is clear that all of this constitutes *bidʿa* in the literal sense of 'innovation', but has no necessary relation with *bidʿa* in the Shariʿite sense. As we have said above, the permissibility of such innovations depends upon whether or not they violate the rulings and principles of the Shariʿa. For example, the intermingling of improperly dressed men and women at gatherings in public places is illicit (*ḥarām*), but it is not a *bidʿa,* for those participating in such gatherings do not maintain that what they are doing is religiously permitted, something for which Islam gives its support; indeed, it is often quite the opposite. But it can happen that such persons become conscious of what they are doing, that is, breaking a religious rule, and resolve not to attend such gatherings again.

To explain this further, if a nation decides that a specified day be a holiday, but does not claim that this action is a religious obligation, then, again, this action is not a *bidʿa*; its permissibility must be determined from another point of view, according to religious principles and rulings. In the light of these considerations, it should be clear that many innovations of mankind in such fields as art, sport and manufacturing, do not pertain in fact to the issue of *bidʿa,* but are rather to be considered from a different angle altogether: that is, whether they are permissible or prohibited, this evaluation being based on a set of clear criteria and principles.

Secondly, *bidʿa* in religious terms basically entails the presentation of a particular action as a religious obligation, whilst in fact there is no basis for it in the principles or rules of religion. But an action performed as a religious act and for which there are clear supports in terms of religious law—whether in the form of specific rules or universal principles—cannot be considered as *bidʿa.* In this regard, ʿAllāma Majlisī, a great Shiʿi scholar writes: '*Bidʿa* in religion pertains to an affair that is originated after the Holy Prophet, one for the permissibility of which there is no supportive ground either in specific or general terms.'[6]

Ibn Ḥajar al-ʿAsqalānī, a renowned scholar of the Sunnis also says: '*Bidʿa* is an affair which arises (after the Prophet) and for which there is no principial support in terms of the Shariʿa; but an action which is upheld by a religious principle is not *bidʿa.*'[7]

Indeed, whenever we can establish a relationship between a given action and religion, on the basis of a particular indication or a universal rule, then it is obvious that such an action cannot be regarded as *bidʿa.* In respect of a particular religious ruling (legitimizing the action), no further comment is needed. What does stand in need of explanation, however, is the second case, that of legitimacy acquired through universal religious rules, for it is possible that many an action that appears outwardly as newly originated and lacking any precedent in Islamic history, can nonetheless be perfectly acceptable if its essential nature is subsumed by a universal rule or principle of the Shariʿa. For example, universal conscription is a practice that has become current in many countries. The policy of calling upon the youth to serve in the army beneath the banner of their country as part of their religious duty, despite being a recently originated practice, cannot be regarded as *bidʿa*, as it is buttressed by a religious principle and foundation; for, as the Qur'an says:

*Make ready for them all thou canst of* [armed] *force* ... (Sūra al-Anfāl, VIII: 60)

From the above explanation, many of the unfounded doubts which have entangled a large number of people can be resolved. For example, multitudes of Muslims throughout the world celebrate the birthday of the Holy Prophet, while certain groups brand such celebrations as *bidʿa*; but, according to the principles we have given above, there are no grounds for regarding these actions as *bidʿa*. Even if we were to suppose that this type of veneration of the Prophet and this way of expressing love for him, is not strictly speaking a part of religious law, nonetheless the expression of love for the Prophet of Islam and his family is a self-evident principle of Islam, a universal principle of which these kinds of celebrations and religious gatherings are specific manifestations. The Holy Prophet said: 'None of you is a believer until I am more beloved unto him than his wealth, his family and all of mankind.'[8]

It is clear that those who participate in the commemoration of the birthday of the Prophet and his family, expressing thereby their happiness on such occasions, do not at all maintain that the particular way in which they organize these celebrations today is enjoined as such by religious law; on the contrary, such people believe simply that the outward manifestation of love for the Prophet and his family is a universal principle, one which is stressed in Scripture and tradition, and which possesses a range of possible expressions and accentuations. The Holy Qur'an states:

*Say: I ask of you no reward for this, except loving-kindness among kinsfolk.* (Sūra al-Shūrā, XLII:23)

This principle can be expressed in various ways, in both the individual and collective life of the Muslims. The holding of celebrations on the occasion of the birthday of the Prophet and members of his family is but a means of recalling the divine descent of mercy and blessings upon these days; it is also a means of expressing gratitude to God. Such celebrations are, moreover, to be found in previous religions. According to the Qur'an, Jesus requested of God that He cause to descend a heavenly table of food (a *mā'ida*) for him and his companions, so that the day of this descent might be for him and his followers—among future generations—a commemorative feast:

*Jesus, son of Mary, said: O God, our Lord, send down for us a table spread with food from heaven, that it may be a feast for us, for the first of us and the last of us, and a sign from Thee ...* (Sūra al-Mā'ida, v:114)

As we have said above, *bid'a* consists of a type of tampering with religion, one for which no sound warrant from any authoritative religious sources is forthcoming, either in universal or specific terms; and it must be recalled here that the sayings attributed to the Imams of the *ahl al-bayt* are, according to the authority of the *mutawātir* saying of the Prophet, referred to above as *al-Thaqalayn,* to be counted as sources of Shari'ite authority and grounds for religious rulings. Whenever these noble and impeccable personages explicitly permit or prohibit something, those who follow their guidance are doing nothing other than following the guidance of religion; thus there can be no question of appending the title of *bid'a* in such contexts.

To conclude: *bid'a* in the sense of an unwarranted interference with religion is always an ugly and forbidden act, referred to in the Qur'an as follows:

*... Hath God permitted you, or do you invent a lie concerning God?* (Sūra Yūnus, v:59)

When *bid'a* is understood in this sense, its subdivision into categories such as 'bad' and 'good', 'forbidden' and 'permitted', has no real meaning. But in the strictly etymological sense, *bid'a,* understood simply as a newly originated act or practice in human affairs, without any immediate connection with religious law, is susceptible of differentiated evaluation according to the five categories of Islamic law: obligatory (*wājib*), forbidden (*ḥarām*), discouraged (*makrūh*), recommended (*mustaḥabb*), and indifferent (*mubāḥ*).

## III. DISSIMULATION (TAQIYYA)

### Article 124

One of the teachings of the Qur'an is that a Muslim is permitted to conceal his belief in situations wherein, as a result of expressing it, his life, honour or property would be endangered. In religious terminology, such an act is referred to as *taqiyya* ('dissimulation'). It is not only on religious grounds that dissimulation is justified, but intelligence and human wisdom likewise reveal the necessity and propriety of the practice in certain sensitive situations. On the one hand, the preservation of life, property and honour are necessary, and on the other, acting according to one's beliefs is a part of one's religious duty. But in those cases where the outward expression of one's belief might endanger one's life, property or honour, and the two duties thereby clash, human intelligence naturally will give precedence to the most important of the two duties. In truth, dissimulation is a weapon in the hands of the weak in the face of merciless tyrants. It is obvious that in the absence of any danger a person will not need to hide his beliefs, nor act in opposition to his beliefs.

The Qur'an refers implicitly to ʿAmmār b. Yāsir (and all those who, whilst at war with the disbelievers, and despite the strength of their heartfelt faith, formally utter words of disbelief in order to save themselves) in the following verse:

*Whoso disbelieveth in God after his belief—except him who is forced to* [pretend to disbelieve] *and whose heart is secure in faith* ... (Sūra al-Naḥl, XVI:106)

In another verse it is said:

*Let not the believers take unbelievers for their friends in preference to believers. Whoso doth that hath no connection with God unless* [it be] *that ye are but guarding yourselves against them, taking security. God biddeth you beware of Himself. Unto God is the journeying.*(Sūra Āl 'Imrān, III:28)

In the light of these two verses, the Muslim commentators unanimously attest to the religious sanction given to dissimulation.[9] Indeed, anyone who has conducted a modicum of research into Qur'anic commentary and Islamic jurisprudence will know that the principle of dissimulation is justified within Islam. The verses above, and the actions of, for example, the believing folk of Pharaoh, who hid their faith, while outwardly denying it (see Sūra Ghāfir, XL: 28), cannot be overlooked. But dissimulation has, for the most part, been opposed. However, it must be said that despite the fact that the verses regarding dissimulation were revealed in respect of the possibility of dissimulating in the face of disbelievers, the principle established is not restricted in its applicability to those circumstances wherein the life, property and honour of Muslims are threatened only by disbelievers; for if the expression of one's beliefs, or action according to one's beliefs, gives rise to fear for one's life, property and honour, which are being threatened by a Muslim, then dissimulation in such a situation will be upheld by the same principle that allows for dissimulation before disbelievers.

This point has also been made by others. For example, Rāzī says: 'The Shafi'ite *madhhab* establishes that whenever the Muslims find themselves in a situation vis-à-vis each other similar to that pertaining between Muslims and disbelievers (in war), then dissimulation for the sake of the preservation of life is permitted. Dissimulation is not confined to circumstances in which loss of life [is feared]; it is also permitted in the face of the possibility of loss of property. For the sacredness of property is akin to the sacredness of the blood of the Muslims, and if one is killed in this path [that is, the path of protecting the lives or the property of Muslims] he is accounted a martyr.'[10]

Abū Hurayra said: 'I have received from the Prophet two types of knowledge and instruction: one of them I have transmitted to people, but the other I have kept to myself, for had I conveyed it to you, I would have been killed.'[11]

The historical record of the Umayyad and Abbasid caliphs is full of injustice and oppression. In those days, it was not only the Shiʿa who, as a result of manifesting their beliefs, were rejected and banished [and were thus forced to resort to dissimulation], Sunni scholars of hadith were also compelled, during the rule of Ma'mūn, to take the path of dissimulation over the question of the 'createdness of the Qur'an'; all of them, except one (Aḥmad b. Ḥanbal), outwardly accepted the edict of Ma'mūn on this question, even while being inwardly opposed to it, the story of which can be read in history books.[12]

## Article 125

From the point of view of Shiʿism, dissimulation is necessary in certain conditions but forbidden in others; in the latter case, one cannot resort to dissimulation on the pretext that one's life or property might be endangered. Certain groups believe that the Shiʿa uphold the necessity of dissimulation in an unconditional manner: such a belief is completely erroneous, and the leading authorities of Shiʿism have never entertained it. Such leaders have always taken note of the conditions of their time, paying careful attention both to the requirements of the general welfare of the Muslims and to the avoidance of whatever is to the detriment thereof, and have thus chosen an appropriate path. Therefore, we see that in fact there have been times when the Shiʿa have not taken up the path of dissimulation, but have on the contrary sacrificed their lives and their property in the cause of bearing witness to their beliefs.

In fact, the *maʿṣūm* Imams of Shiʿism have for the most part been martyred, having met their death either through the sword or the poison of their enemies. Without doubt, if they had presented a smiling face and offered up sweet words to the rulers of their times, they would have been regaled with the highest positions of power and privilege; but these Imams knew all too well that dissimulation (for example, in the face of a Yazīd [the caliph held responsible for the killing of the grandson of the Prophet, Ḥusayn, at Karbala]) would have given rise to the disappearance of true religion and the effacement of the correct application of the faith.

In contemporary conditions also, there are two types of religious obligation incumbent upon the religious leaders of the Muslims: in certain circumstances to resort to dissimulation, and in others—wherein the fundamentals of the faith are endangered—to be prepared to give up one's life and face death.

In conclusion, let us recall that dissimulation is a personal affair, and that it pertains to individuals placed in a position of weakness in the face of powerful enemies; they dissimulate insofar as they consider that if dissimulation is not made, not only do they lose their lives, but also no positive advantage is derived from their being killed. But there is no place for dissimulation in regard to the teaching and clarification of the doctrines and rulings of religion—for example, no scholar can write a book, on the basis of dissimulation, in which deviant doctrines are presented in the guise of Shiʿi belief, and disseminated as such to the public. Therefore, no book has been written in the field of beliefs and rulings on the basis of dissimulation throughout the course of the history of Shiʿism; on the contrary, even in the most difficult times, Shiʿi scholars have always made manifest the true beliefs of this perspective. Of course, there are differences of opinion as regards certain principles and issues, but never has there been any Shiʿi scholar who has written a book or treatise contradicting—under the pretext of dissimulation—any clear and important aspect of Shiʿi belief; nor have any such scholars expressed one thing in public and something contrary in secret: anyone who employs such methods of discourse puts himself outside the pale of Imami Shiʿism.

For those who find it difficult to understand or digest the idea of dissimulation, or who have been subject to the propaganda of the enemies of Shiʿism, we would strongly recommend that they study the historical experience of the Shiʿa during the reign of the Umayyads, the Abbasids, and even during that of the Ottomans in Turkey and Syria, and discover what a high price they paid for upholding and following the beliefs of the *ahl al-bayt*, what sacrifices they made and what bitter tribulations they endured. The Shiʿa underwent such a fate, despite having recourse to dissimulation; what, one wonders, would have been their lot if they did not have recourse to this principle? One might well also ask: in such a case, that is, without the practice of dissimulation, would there be anything left of Shiʿism today?

In principle, if there is cause for any blame to be attached to dissimulation it is solely on account of those who compel its practice; that is those persons deserve to be blamed who, instead of conducting themselves according to the Islamic principles of justice and kindness, waged the most severe and murderous policy of suppression, both political and religious, against the followers of the family of the Prophet. It is such people who are culpable, not those who out of sheer necessity took refuge in dissimulation, in order to preserve their lives, their property and their beliefs. What is astonishing is that some people, rather than blaming those who compel recourse to dissimulation—namely, the oppressors—blame instead those who resort to it—namely, the oppressed, accusing them moreover of hypocrisy. In truth, the difference between dissimulation and hypocrisy is as great as that between Heaven and earth. The hypocrite is one who is inwardly in a state of faithlessness while outwardly professing faith; whereas Muslims who resort to dissimulation have hearts overflowing with faith, while outwardly expressing the contrary, only out of fear for the harm that the oppressor may bring upon them.

## IV. RESORTING TO INTERMEDIARIES (TAWASSUL)

### Article 126

**Intermediary Causes**

The life of man is constructed on the basis of making use of various intermediary means (*wasāʾil*, sing. *wasīla*) and causes of nature, each of which has its own special features. When we are thirsty we drink water, when hungry we eat food. Fulfilling our needs by recourse to natural means—on condition that such means are not regarded as independent causes in their own right—is inherent in *Tawḥīd.*

There are some who hold that *shirk* means 'connecting oneself with, and resorting to, what is other than God'. Now this is true only on condition that such intermediary causes and means be given the status of independent and autonomous agency; if on the other hand, we take these factors as means with which—by the will and authority of God—we can attain certain ends, then the principle of *Tawḥīd* is not violated. In general, the life of man, from the day of his birth onwards, is founded on just such a basis; that is, he takes advantage of the extant ways and means at his disposal. Indeed, the progress of science and industry proceeds on this very principle.

The legitimacy of making *tawassul* [i.e., resorting to intermediary causes and means] in respect of the means offered by nature is clearly indisputable; the question here pertains to causes that are beyond nature, causes which man can only come to know about through divine revelation. Every time something is introduced in the Qur'an or Hadith literature as a 'means' (*wasīla*), making use of that thing derives from the same authority that is the basis for *tawassul* in respect of natural causes. Therefore, there are times when we are allowed, given a proper religious motivation, to seek to take advantage of factors beyond the natural realm, while bearing in mind the following two points:

1. The factors in question must be clearly established, either in the Qur'an or the Hadith literature, as means that can lead to the attainment of goals in this life or the Hereafter.
2. The means and causes are not regarded in any fashion as having principial autonomy or independent status; rather, we must understand that their capacity to yield results is utterly contingent upon the authority and will of God.

The noble Qur'an invites us to benefit from various spiritual means:

*O ye who believe, be mindful of your duty to God, and seek the means* (al-wasīla) *of approaching Him, and strive in His way in order that ye may succeed.* (Sūra al-Māʾida, v:35)

It should be noted that 'means' (*wasīla*) does not mean the same thing as 'drawing near' (*taqarrub*); rather, it refers to anything that is a source of drawing near to God; struggling in the cause of God, as mentioned in the verse quoted above, is one among many such means of drawing close to the divine.[13]

**Article 127**

In the previous article we maintained that *tawassul,* in respect of causes of natural and supernatural provenance, pertains to true *Tawḥīd* (on condition that these causes are not given even a hint of independent authority). There is no doubt that carrying out the obligatory duties and recommended practices of religion—such as prayer, fasting, almsgiving, Jihād, and so on—are all so many means by which man can approach his goal, which is none other than attaining proximity to God. In the light of these practices, man grasps the reality of his slavehood, and in consequence, comes closer to God. But it must be noted that the means of supernatural provenance are not confined to the performance of acts of worship; for a whole series of means are made known in the Qur'an and Hadith literature, resort to which gives rise to the answering of one's prayers. Below, we mention some of these:

1. Resorting to the 'Most Beautiful Names and Qualities of God', as is said in the Qur'an:

   *Unto God belong the Most Beautiful Names, so supplicate Him by means of them.* (Sūra al-Aʿrāf, VII:180)

   Resorting to the Divine Names and Qualities is frequently encountered in the collections of Islamic personal supplications (*duʿāʾ*).
2. Resorting to the *duʿāʾ* of righteous souls, the most lofty kind of such *tawassul* being in respect of the Prophets and saints: one asks them to pray for one in the divine presence.

[Regarding the second point], the Qur'an instructs those who have wronged their own souls (the sinners) to go to the Prophet and then ask for pardon from God themselves, and ask the Prophet also to seek forgiveness for them:

*If only they had come to you* [O Prophet] *after they had wronged their souls, and then had sought forgiveness from God, and the Prophet had sought forgiveness for them, they would verily have found God relenting, merciful.* (Sūra al-Nisā', IV: 64)

In another verse, a complaint is made of the hypocrites who are called to come to the Prophet and seek his prayers:

*And when it is said unto them: come, the Messenger of God will seek forgiveness for you, they avert their faces and thou seest them turning away, disdainful.* (Sūra al-Munāfiqūn, LXIII:5)

Other verses show that such a perspective prevailed in previous religious communities also. For example, the sons of Jacob asked their father to plead for forgiveness from God for their sins; and Jacob complied with their request:

*They said: O our father, ask forgiveness of our sins for us, for truly we were sinful. He said: I shall ask forgiveness for you of my Lord. Truly, He is the Forgiving, the Merciful.* (Sūra Yūsuf, XII:97–98)

It might be asked: *Tawassul*, in the sense of seeking the prayers of the righteous, can be regarded as consistent with *Tawḥīd* (or at least, efficacious) as long as the person whom we ask to pray for us be alive; but how can such requests be regarded as useful and consistent with *Tawḥīd* if those from whom one seeks assistance are dead? To answer this question, or this objection, we must bring the following two points to bear on the discussion:

1. Even if we suppose that the necessary condition for *tawassul* in respect of a Prophet or saint be that the person in question be alive, requesting prayers from them after their death will then only be an inoperative or ineffectual act, not a source of *shirk*; this point is for the most part forgotten in such discussions, and the question of whether a person be alive or dead comes

to be regarded as a boundary separating *Tawḥīd* from *shirk*. If we were to accept the condition that the personage resorted to by others for prayers be alive, the question of whether the personage be alive or not becomes the criterion only of the efficacy of *tawassul*, not a means of determining whether the act expresses *Tawḥīd* or *shirk*.

2. As regards the efficacy of *tawassul*, this depends only upon two conditions: (a) the personage from whom prayers are sought must possess knowledge, wisdom and power; and (b) there must be an established relationship between those making the request for prayer and those to whom the request is made.

In regard to making such requests from Prophets and saints who have passed away, both of these conditions are fulfilled, as can be clearly seen in the light of both intellectual (*ʿaqlī*) and traditional (*naqlī*) evidence.

The reality of life in the realm of the Barzakh is well attested both in the Qur'an and the Hadith literature, as we saw in Articles 105 and 106 above. Since, according to clear Qur'anic evidence, those martyred in the path of God are alive, it is obvious that the Prophets and the saints—many of whom were also martyrs—partake of an even greater degree of life.

As regards the relationship between us and the saints, there are many factors from which its reality can be adduced, amongst which we shall mention below the following:

1. All Muslims address the Prophet of Islam at the end of their *ṣalāt* prayers, by saying: 'May peace be with you, and the mercy of God and His blessings, O Prophet' (*al-Salāmu ʿalaykum ayyuhā'l-nabīyyu wa raḥmatu'llāhi wa barakātuhu*). Are they all merely paying lip-service by so doing; does the Prophet not hear or reply to all these greetings?
2. The Prophet gave instructions at the Battle of Badr that all the bodies of the polytheists be cast into a well. Then he spoke to all of them. One of his companions asked him: 'Are you talking to the dead?' The Prophet replied: 'You are not better able to hear than they.'[14]
3. The Prophet frequently visited the Baqīʿ graveyard and

addressed the souls of those buried there, saying: 'Peace be with the people of the homes of the believing men and the believing women.' In another narration he is reported to have said: 'Peace be with you, abode of believing folk.'[15]

4. It is narrated in Bukhārī's *Ṣaḥīḥ* that on the day that the Prophet died, Abū Bakr went to the house of 'Ā'isha. Then he went to the Prophet's body, took the cloth from his face, kissed him, cried, and then said: 'My father be your ransom, O Prophet of God, God has not decreed two deaths for you; the one that was decreed for you has come to pass.'[16] If the Prophet were not alive in the Barzakh, and there were consequently no possible relationship between us and him, how could Abū Bakr have addressed him thus?
5. When Imam 'Alī was washing the body of the Prophet, he said to him: 'My father and mother be your ransom, O Messenger of God! With your death something is brought to an end which is not brought to an end with the death of anyone else: the stream of prophecy, the revelation of heavenly knowledge and tidings ... remember us with your Lord and keep us close to your heart.'[17]

Finally, let us note that *tawassul* in respect of the Prophets and saints takes various forms, on which detailed commentaries can be found in theological treatises.

## V. CHANGE OF DESTINY (BADĀ')

### Article 128

The divine decree as regards human destiny is of two types: (a) a definitive and unconditional destiny, which is not susceptible of any kind of alteration; and (b) an open-ended and conditional destiny, which, in the absence of certain conditions, can be altered, such that another destiny will replace it.

Taking this into account, let us note that all groups in Islam regard *badā'* as a tenet of the faith, even if not all actually use the term. But this quibbling over terms does not detract from the proposition itself, for what matters is the meaning of the essential content [of the term] and not its name.

The reality of *badāʾ* is founded upon two principles. The first is that God has absolute power and authority over the whole of existence, and whenever He wills, He can replace a given destiny with another one; both types of destiny mentioned above are contained within His foreknowledge, and there can be no kind of alteration in respect of His knowledge. Therefore, the first type of destiny does not in any way imply a limitation of God's power, such as would strip Him of the ability to change this destiny. God, in contrast to the belief of the Jews that '*the hand of God is tied*', has infinite power; in the expression used by the Qur'an:

*Nay, His hands are spread out wide ...* (Sūra al-Māʾida, v: 64).

In other words, God's creativity and the actions deriving from His power are continuous; and by the authority of the words: '*Every day He is acting upon an affair*' (Sūra al-Raḥmān, LV:29) God has not disengaged Himself from the work of creation, rather, the process of creation is a continuous one.

Imam Ṣādiq comments as follows upon the above quoted verse wherein the Jews claim that '*the hand of God is tied*': 'The Jews say that God has disengaged Himself from the work of creation; He has nothing to do with such matters as increasing or diminishing daily sustenance, the length of life, and so on. Denying this, God has said: "*Their hands are tied, and they are accursed for saying so. Nay, His hands are spread out wide. He bestoweth as He will*".' (Sūra al-Māʾida, v:64) Then he adds: 'Do they not hear the words of God: "*God effaceth what He will and establisheth* [what He will], *and with Him is the Mother of the Book*".' (Sūra al-Raʿd, XIII:39)

The conclusion from the above points is as follows: Islamic belief is based on God's infinite power, absolute authority and perpetual creativity; God is capable, at any time He so wishes, of bringing about a transformation in the things destined for man, such as his life-span or his daily bread, causing one destined thing to replace another thing previously destined, both things destined having been previously inscribed in the *Umm al-kitāb* ('Mother of the Book').

The second principle regarding *badāʾ* is that acts of supreme power and authority issue from God; and when He brings about the replacement of one destiny for another, it is not without wisdom and rectitude. Some of these changes of destiny are brought about by man himself, who can— through his free will, his decisions and his way of life—lay the groundwork for a change in his destiny.

Let us suppose, for example, that a man does not accomplish his duties towards his parents. Naturally, this shortcoming is improper and will have a detrimental impact upon his destiny. Now if he should repent of his actions, and thereafter diligently perform all of his responsibilities, he lays the foundations for a change in his destiny, opening himself to the grace expressed in the verse:

*God effaceth what He will and establisheth what He will.* (Sura al-Raʿd, XIII:39)

The inverse case can also be envisaged according to this principle. We shall now mention some of the many verses and sayings on this issue:

1. *Truly, God changeth not the condition of a people until they change that which is in their hearts.* (Sūra al-Raʿd, XIII:11)
2. *And if the people of the townships had believed and kept from evil, surely We should have opened for them blessings from the sky and from the earth. But they denied, and so We seized them on account of what they used to earn.* (Sūra al-Aʿrāf, VII:96)
3. Suyūṭī writes in his Qurʾanic commentary that Imam ʿAlī asked the Prophet to explain the verse '*God effaceth what He will*'. The Prophet responded: 'I shall enlighten your vision and that of my *umma* with the explanation of this verse. Giving alms in the path of God, being virtuous towards one's father and mother, performing pious acts—[such deeds] transform misfortune into good fortune, prolong one's life and prevent a bad death.'[18]
4. Imam Bāqir said: 'Respecting the ties of kinship purifies one's acts and bestows blessings upon one's wealth; it also protects one against adversity, renders one's [final] reckoning easy, and pushes further away one's death.'[19]

Taking these two principles into account, it is clear that the concept of *badāʾ* pertains to an evident aspect of Islamic belief. Leaving aside the question of the expression or the term itself, all the schools of Islam are at one in accepting that meaning to which the term refers.

Finally, in order to clarify why this Islamic belief is expressed by the term '*badāʾ Allāh*' we offer the following two points for consideration. Those who employ this term follow the Prophet's usage of it. Bukhārī relates in his *Ṣaḥīḥ* that the Prophet said, in regard to three persons suffering from the diseases of septacaemia, alopecia and blindness: 'God—Exalted and Glorified be He—has brought about [these diseases] in order to try them [thereby].' Then he related in detail the story of their lives, and showed how it was that God, on account of their denial of His blessings removed from two of these persons their previous good health and inflicted upon them diseases of their forefathers.[20]

This kind of usage [also] derives from the [linguistic] principle of resemblance and from conventional modes of speech in the language of the Arabs. It is customary for a person to say in Arabic, when he changes his mind about something, '*badā-lī*', that is, 'It has changed for me'. Religious leaders, wishing to speak the kind of language that will be understood by those to whom their speech is addressed, have used this expression in connection with God. It is worth mentioning in this regard that the Qur'an repeatedly refers to such attributes as plotting, scheming, deceiving and forgetting, in connection with God. But it is obvious that God's majesty infinitely transcends the possibility of perpetrating such actions—such as they are conventionally understood by man, and in the forms that they take amongst human beings. The attributes mentioned above are given in connection with God as follows:

*Lo, they plot a plot, and I plot a plot.* (Sūra al-Ṭāriq, LXXXVI:15–16)

*So they plotted a plot; and We plotted a plot.* (Sūra al-Naml, XXVII:50)

*Lo, the hypocrites seek to deceive God, but it is He Who deceiveth them.* (Sūra al-Nisāʾ, IV:142)

*They forgot God, so He hath forgotten them.* (Sūra al-Tawba, IX:67)

In any case, the scholars of Shiʿism, taking note of the impossibility of alteration in the knowledge of God, have carried out extensive research into the use of the term *badāʾ*, which we cannot summarize here; students wishing to investigate the matter in detail should refer to the books noted below.[21]

## Article 129

**The Return (*Rajʿa*)**

In the Arabic language, *rajʿa* means 'return'; in Shiʿi terminology it denotes the return of a group of Muslims to this world after the appearance of the Mahdi and before the Resurrection. Evidence for the possibility of such an occurence is forthcoming first and foremost from the Qur'an, which tells us, in the Sūra al-Naml (xxvii: 83, 87):

*And the Day when We shall gather out of every nation a host of those who denied Our Revelations, and they will be set in array...*

*And the Day when the trumpet will be blown, and all who are in the heavens and the earth will start in fear, except him whom God willeth. And all come unto Him humbled.*

As can be seen, the verses above speak of two days, the first of which turns one's attention to the second. As regards the first day, there is mention made of the revival only of a particular group, whilst as regards the second day, the death of the whole of mankind is mentioned; we observe, then, that the first day is other than the Day of Resurrection.

A comparison between these two verses in the Sūra al-Naml reveals that the world is awaiting two days, on one of which some, and on the other of which all, souls will be revived. Sayings transmitted in the Shiʿi tradition maintain that the first day pertains to the period after the appearance of the Mahdi and before the Day of Resurrection.

The return to life in this world of a group of righteous or wicked souls before the Resurrection should not, then, give rise to astonishment, for in previous communities also there were groups who, after their death, returned again to life, and after a time passed away for a second time.[22]

The return of persons to life in this world does not conflict with reason, nor with sources transmitted by tradition, for as we have seen, the Qur'an explicitly refers to this return in respect of past communities, and there can be no better evidence than this for upholding the possibility of this phenomenon. There are some who regard the 'return' to mean the same thing as 'transmigration' (*tanāsukh*); such an idea is utterly baseless, for transmigration holds that a soul, after dying, regains its life anew, either starting out from the embryonic state, or else by entering another body. The Return, on the other hand, has nothing to do with either of these false ideas. The principal authority for upholding the validity of the doctrine of the Return is derived from the revival of the dead in past communities, and the bodily Resurrection on the Day of Judgement; indeed, one might regard the Return as a minor foreshadowing of that ultimate Resurrection at which all without exception will be brought back to life.

There is an extensive debate regarding *rajʿa*, and detailed explanations of its different aspects, in the Shiʿi books of Qur'anic commentary, Hadith, and theology. In Shiʿi sources there are also transmitted sayings regarding this question that have the highest degree of confirmation (*tawātur*); more than thirty Hadith scholars in over fifty books have transmitted such sayings.[23]

## Article 130

### Respect for the Companions

The companions and friends of the Prophet who believed in him and who derived wisdom from his presence, receive from us, the Shiʿa, an especial reverence, whether they be amongst those martyred at the Battles of Badr, Uḥud, Aḥzāb and Ḥunayn, or of those who remained alive after the passing away of the Prophet. All of them, insofar as they were the companions of the Prophet and believed in him, deserve our respect, and there is no true Muslim in the world that would speak badly of the companions, or express unkind opinions about them; and should anyone claim that a group of 'Muslims' do in fact indulge in such criticisms, such claims would be baseless.

But alongside this issue there is another question which should be addressed without prejudice, sentimentalism or bitterness: were all the companions equally just, pious and devoid of sin? It is clear that seeing the Prophet and keeping his company, despite being a great honour, cannot be seen as rendering a person immune from sin; we cannot therefore regard all of the companions in exactly the same light, as being all equally just, pious and shorn of all sinfulness. For, according to the testimony of the Qur'an, in spite of their having the honour of being companions, they are divided into different categories as regards faith and hypocrisy, and in respect of obedience and disobedience to God and His Prophet. Taking due account of this differentiation, it cannot be said that they are all as one, each one of them being as just and as pious as the next.

There is no doubt that the Qur'an has praised the companions on several occasions.[24] For example, as regards those who made the oath of allegiance to the Prophet at the time of the negotiations leading to the Treaty of Ḥudaybiyya, the Qur'an expresses the satisfaction [of God]:

*God was well pleased with the believers when they swore allegiance to thee beneath the tree ...* (Sūra al-Fatḥ, XLVIII:18)

But this praise, their eliciting the good pleasure (*riḍwān*) of God, relates to them '*when they swore allegiance to thee*', and cannot thus be regarded as evidence of a guarantee of rectitude and deliverance from faults for all of them for the rest of their lives. For if one or more of them afterwards takes a wrong path, evidently, the previous pleasure of God cannot be pointed to as evidence of their continuing piety or of their being permanently devoid of faults: the rank and station of these companions who elicited the pleasure of God is not higher than that of the Prophet about whom the Qur'an says:

*If thou ascribe a partner to God thy work will fail and thou wilt indeed be among the losers.* (Sūra al-Zumar, XXXIX: 45)

This kind of verse expresses the virtue manifested by these persons in that particular state, and of course, should they maintain such virtue until the end of their lives, they would attain salvation.

On the basis of what has been said, whenever we have definitive evidence from the Qurʾan, the Hadith or from history, of the deviation of a person or persons, one cannot refute this evidence by reference to such instances of the kind of praise quoted above.

By way of example, the Qurʾan refers to some of the companions by the term *fāsiq*, that is, a miscreant:

*If a miscreant brings you tidings, verify it* ... (Sūra al-Ḥujurāt, XLIX:6)

In another verse, referring to one companion, we have:

*Is he who is a believer like him who is a miscreant? They are not alike.* (Sūra al-Sajda, XXXII:18)

This individual, according to definite historical evidence, was Walīd b. ʿUqba, one of the companions of the Prophet, who despite having the double merit of being a companion and of having made the Hijra with the earliest Muslims, was unable to preserve his good name, and through having lied about the tribe of Banū Mustaliq, earned from God the title of *fāsiq*.

Taking due note of this verse and other similar ones,[25] and with regard also to those hadiths in which certain companions are severely criticized,[26] and, likewise, taking into account the historical evidence pertaining to certain companions,[27] one cannot definitively regard all of the Prophet's companions—whose number exceeds one hundred thousand—as being equally just and pious.

What is at issue here is whether we can justifiably regard all of the companions as equally just; it is not a question of insulting them. Unfortunately, some people do not distinguish between the two issues, and accuse those who oppose the notion of equal justice in all the companions of falling into the error of insulting and criticizing the companions.

To conclude this discussion, we should like to stress that the Shiʿa of the Imami school do not believe that the respect we have for those who have had the privilege of companionship with the

Prophet should prevent us from objectively evaluating their actions. We hold that association with the Prophet cannot on its own give rise to immunity from sin for the rest of one's life. The basis for this evaluation by the Shi'a is derived from Qur'anic verses, sound hadiths, corroborated historical sources and from basic common sense.

## Article 131

### Love for the Prophet and his Family

The cultivation of love and affection for the Prophet and his family is one of the principles of Islam, stressed by both the Qur'an and the Sunna. The Qur'an says in this connection:

*Say: If your fathers, and your sons, and your brethren, and your wives, and your tribe, and the wealth ye have acquired, and your merchandise for which ye fear there will be no sale, and dwellings ye desire, are dearer to you than God and His Messenger and striving in His way: then wait till God bringeth His command to pass. God guideth not wrong-doing folk.* (Sūra al-Tawba, IX:24)

In another verse, it says:

... *those who believe in him* [the Prophet], *and honour him, and help him, and follow the light which is sent down with him: they are the successful.* (Sūra al-A'rāf, VII:157)

In this verse God refers to the successful as having four special features: (a) believing in the Prophet; (b) honouring and revering him; (c) helping him; and (d) following the light (that is, the Qur'an) that was revealed with him.

Taking note of the fact that helping the Prophet comes third in this list, it is altogether clear that honouring him, which is the same as venerating him, cannot be restricted in time to the period of his life, just as believing in him, also mentioned in this verse, cannot have any such restriction.

As regards loving his family, it suffices to note that the Qur'an establishes this as a 'reward' that believers owe him for the fact of having received from him the prophetic message (of course, it is given in the *form* of a reward and is not a reward in the strict sense), saying:

*Say: I ask of you no reward for this, save loving kindness to kinsfolk.* (Sūra al-Shūrā, XLII:23)

The principle of loving and honouring the Prophet is not only found in the Qur'an, it is also stressed in the hadiths, two of which we mention below:

1. The Prophet said: 'Not one of you is a believer until I am more beloved unto him than his own children and all of mankind together.'[28]
2. Another hadith says: 'There are three things which show that one has truly tasted the food of faith: that there is nothing more beloved to one than God and His Prophet; that being burned in the Fire is deemed preferable to forsaking his religion; that one loves and hates [only] for [the sake of] God.'[29]

Loving the family of the Prophet has been stressed also in hadiths, some of which we mention below:

1. The Prophet said: 'A slave [of God] is not a believer unless I am more beloved to him than his own soul; and my descendants are more beloved to him than his own descendants; and my family is more beloved to him than his own family.'[30]
2. In another hadith, he says this as regards loving his descendants: 'Whoever loves them, loves God, and whoever hates them, hates God.'[31]

Up to now, we have been considering the reasons for the principle of loving the Prophet and his descendants; now the following questions may be posed: (a) What benefit is derived for the *umma* from loving the Prophet and his descendants? (b) In what manner should the Prophet and his family be revered and loved?

As regards the first question, let us recall that love for a person of perfect virtue is itself a ladder leading one up to perfection; whenever someone loves a person with all his heart, he makes an effort to emulate him, to do whatever would bring happiness to that person, and to renounce whatever would grieve him.

It goes without saying that such a predisposition is a source of transformation, keeping one continuously upon the path of obedience, and ever vigilant against sin. One who verbally expresses love for a person, but whose actions oppose the beloved, is devoid of true love. The following lines of poetry attributed to Imam Ṣādiq allude to this point:

> You disobey God while claiming to love Him;
> I swear by my soul, this is indeed bizarre.
> If the lover is truthful, he obeys the Beloved
> And from His path would never stray far.[32]

Having brought to light some of the fruits of loving the Prophet and his family, we must now address the question of the manner in which this love should be manifested. Evidently, the substance of inward love cannot be completely deprived of some outward radiance of that love in action; rather, one of the aims of affection is that in one's speech and action there be a harmonious echo of that affection.

There can be no doubt that one of the ways in which love of the Prophet and his family radiates is through emulating them in action, as has been mentioned; but as for the other modes of radiance of this state, they can be summed up as follows: Those who express any speech or action that is universally understood as being a sign of such love and is an honourable means of manifesting it, will be regarded as acting in conformity with the principle of love of the Prophet, on condition that the means by which the Prophet is revered be in accordance with the law and not in violation of it.

Therefore, the honouring of the Prophet and his family, especially on such occasions as their birthdays and the days commemorating their death, is one of the means by which the love and esteem we have for their spiritual rank and station can be given expression. Decorating the streets on the occasion of the birthday of the Prophet, the lighting of candles, the flying of flags, the holding of religious gatherings for the sake of recalling the virtues and excellences of the Holy Prophet or of his family—all these are to be counted as signs of love for these personages, and channels through which this love flows. This affectionate means of glorifying the Prophet on the occasion of his birthday is now a strongly established tradition among most, if not all Muslims.

Diyār Bakrī writes as follows: 'The Muslims always celebrate the month in which the Holy Prophet was born, honouring his birthday by holding celebrations, feeding and giving alms to the poor, expressing great joy, telling the story of his birth: how many wonders are brought for them at this time!'[33] An identical description is given by another scholar, by the name of Aḥmad b. Muḥammad Qastallānī in his book.[34]

## Article 132

### Mourning of Religious Leaders

From what has been said, the philosophy behind mourning the death of religious leaders will be clear; for any kind of gathering held to commemorate the afflictions and tribulations of these personages is an expression of love and affection for them. If Jacob mourned for long years at the loss of his beloved Joseph,[35] weeping profusely, the root of this emotion was the depth of the love he had for his son. In this light one can more readily understand why those who bear love for the family of the Prophet should weep and shed tears on the days commemorating their death. They are but following the example of the Prophet Jacob.

In principle, the establishment of gatherings for bereavement of dear ones goes back to an action performed by the Prophet himself. When he noticed, after the Battle of Uḥud, that women were mourning the loss of their martyrs among the Anṣār [the Medinan 'Helpers' of the Prophet], he fell to thinking of the loss of his magnanimous uncle, and said: 'But nobody is crying for Ḥamza.'[36] When the companions of the Prophet sensed that the Prophet's wish was for his uncle to be mourned, they instructed their wives to organize a session of mourning for him. The session took place, and the Prophet, out of appreciation for this expression of compassion from the mourners, made a prayer on their behalf: 'May God have mercy on the Anṣār'. Then he asked the leaders of the Anṣār to tell their womenfolk to return to their homes.[37]

In addition, mourning for those martyred in the path of God has a 'philosophical' underpinning: maintaining the grandeur of such persons is a means of preserving their school of thought, thereby upholding the perspective which is founded upon sacrifice for the sake of religion, and upon the ideal of refusing to submit to humiliation and disgrace. The logic of this perspective is summed up thus: 'A red death is better than a humiliating life.' In every gathering of 'Āshūrā', the tenth day of the month of Muḥarram, commemorating the martyrdom of Imam Ḥusayn, this logic is revived, and entire nations have learnt and continue to learn a great lesson from his supreme act of self-sacrifice.

## Article 133

**Preserving Sacred Monuments**

Wise people all over the world make an effort to preserve the works of their ancestors, protecting such monuments against decay, doing so in the name of their 'cultural heritage'. They guard such works by spending large sums of money on what they now call 'national' monuments, for such monuments act as a link connecting the past to the present, giving an impetus to nations in their effort to trace out more clearly the path towards advancement and progress. When such ancient monuments pertain to the Prophets and saints, they have an influence over and above that of simply reminding people of their past: they also enhance faith and orientation towards these great individuals. Were such monuments not to exist, the spirit of doubt and scepticism would, after some time, afflict the followers of the personages associated with the monuments, causing them possibly to begin to question even the principles of the faith. This might be said to be a contributory factor to the decline of religious orientation in the West; today the very historical existence of Jesus is even being disputed by some sceptics.

The Muslims, on the other hand, have been able to proceed with dignity and honour in this regard, having successfully preserved the sacred places connected with the Prophet and his descendants from decay. They can claim that a holy personage was indeed selected to be a Prophet over fourteen centuries ago; that he launched an extremely advanced programme of social betterment; and brought about a profound spiritual and moral transformation, from the effects of which people all over the world still benefit to this day. And there can be no doubt whatsoever as regards the existence of this righteous individual and the veritable transformation he initiated. For his birthplace, the places where he prayed and worshipped, the very spot where he received his prophetic mission, the places where he preached, the areas where he defended honourable people, and the very material on which he wrote letters to the world leaders of his age, along with hundreds of other relics and traces of his life—all have been kept intact with special care as tangible, concrete signs of his presence. Taking note of the importance of this principle, Muslims throughout the world have a duty to take all possible measures to preserve these traces of his life.

The points raised above can help to clarify the importance of preserving sacred monuments from the point of view of social philosophy also. The Qur'an, incidentally, along with other clear textual evidence from the Prophet's life, confirms this principle. In certain verses, the Qur'an refers to 'houses elevated by God', as in the following:

*In houses which God hath allowed to be exalted, and in which His Name shall be remembered, therein do offer praise to Him at morn and evening men whom neither merchandise nor sale diverteth from remembrance of God and constancy in prayer, and paying the poor due; who fear a day when hearts and eyes will be overturned ...* (Sūra al-Nūr, XXIV:36–37)

It is clear that 'houses' in this verse does not mean 'mosques', for the two words are clearly distinguished in the Qur'an, the 'Sacred Mosque' (*al-Masjid al-Ḥarām*) being other than the 'Sacred House of God' (*Bayt Allāh al-Ḥarām*). According to hadiths, the meaning of houses here is 'houses of the Prophets', especially those of the Prophet of Islam and his pure progeny. Suyūṭī transmits a saying of Abū Bakr: 'When this verse was revealed to the

Prophet, we were all in the mosque. A man rose and asked the Prophet: "Whose houses are these?" The Prophet replied: "They are the houses of the Prophets." Then I rose and said: "Is the house of ʿAlī and [Fāṭima] Zahrā' also amongst these houses?" He said in reply: "Yes, it is amongst the best of them".'[38]

Now that the meaning of 'houses' has been clarified, we shall address what is meant by their being 'elevated' (*tarfīʿ*). There are two possible meanings to consider. The first is elevation in the sense of constructing and setting up; the Qur'an uses the word *rafʿ* in this sense, as in the following verse:

*And when Abraham and Ishmael were raising* (yarfaʿu) *the foundations of the House...*(Sūra al-Baqara, II:127)

Since the houses of the Prophets were already built, bringing such houses into being cannot be intended here; instead, it can only mean the safeguarding of such houses against ruin and desolation.

The second meaning of elevation is in the sense of being sanctified and protected. One understands that, in addition to preserving the houses against destruction, they are protected against any kind of impurity that would be incompatible with their sanctity.

Therefore, it is incumbent upon Muslims to honour and preserve houses connected with the Prophet, embracing this duty as a means of gaining proximity to him.

In this regard, it would be of benefit to consider the verse concerning the 'Companions of the Cave' (*aṣḥāb al-kahf*), when their concealed spot was discovered.[39] There were two groups who differed over the manner in which the spot was to be honoured. One group said that a memorial to them should be built over their graves, and the other group said that a mosque should be built over their graves. The Qur'an refers to both of these proposals with approval. If these two opinions were contrary to the principles of Islam they would have been related in the Qur'an in quite a different tone, or they would have been criticized outright. The verse is as follows:

*When* [the people of the city] *disputed their case among themselves, they said: Build over them a building; their Lord knoweth best concerning them. Those who won their point said: Verily we shall build a place of worship over them.* (Sūra al-Kahf, XVIII:21)

These two verses—along with the deeply rooted history, starting from the time of the Prophet and continuing to this day, of Muslims making every effort to preserve all traces of the Prophet and to safeguard and honour houses connected with him and his progeny—are clear testimony in themselves to the Islamic authenticity of the principle in question. Therefore, the construction of graves for the Prophets, of edifices connected with the Holy Prophet and his pure progeny, and the building of mosques over or alongside their graves—all of these actions proceed from this Islamic principle.

## Article 134

### Visiting Graves

Visiting the graves of Muslims, in particular, those of relatives and friends, is an established practice in Islam, one which brings about definite positive effects. For instance, the very witnessing of the stillness of the graveyard, coming to the place where the light of life of human beings has been extinguished, is a moving experience and contains a lesson for those willing to learn. Such persons may say to themselves: This transient life, whose end is to lie hidden beneath shovels of earth, is not worth wasting through unjust acts. They then might take a fresh look at their own lives and reform their spiritual and mental attitudes. The Holy Prophet said: 'Visit the graves, for truly this will remind you of the Hereafter.'[40]

In addition, the visiting of the graves of the great personages in our religion is a kind of propagation both of the faith and of the holy sites. The attention paid by people to the graves of these great souls strengthens the idea that it is the spirituality of these great ones that gives rise to this desire, on the part of others, to visit their graves; whilst those who possessed great power and wealth, but were devoid of spirituality, are simply buried in the earth and nobody pays them any attention.

During the last days of his life, the Prophet went to the graveyard of Baqīʿ [in Medina], and prayed for the forgiveness of those in the graves, and then said: 'My Lord has ordered me to come to the graveyard of Baqīʿ and to pray for forgiveness on behalf of those buried there.' Then he said, 'When you visit them, say: [Greetings of] Peace to those residing in this graveyard, from the Muslims and the believers; may the mercy of God be granted to those of us who have passed away and those who remain behind; and we shall, if God wills, be joining you.'[41]

In books of Hadith, visiting the graves of the saints and religious authorities is given as a strongly recommended practice (*mustaḥabb mu'akkad*); and the Imams of the *ahl al-bayt* always visited the grave of the Prophet and the graves of the Imams preceding them, inviting their followers to do likewise.

## Article 135

**Exaggeration (*Ghulūw*)**

The word *ghulūw* in the Arabic language means going beyond the limit. The Qur'an addresses the People of the Book thus:

*O People of the Book, do not exaggerate in your religion, nor utter anything concerning God save the truth.* (Sūra al-Nisā', IV:171)

They are criticised for *ghulūw* because they had made the rights of Jesus to exceed the bounds of truth, by referring to him as God or as the son of God.

After the death of the Prophet, certain groups likewise went beyond the bounds of truth in respect of the Prophet and some of the members of the *ahl al-bayt*, ascribing to them degrees of eminence that are the preserve of God alone. Thus, they were given the name of *ghālī* or *ghāliyān* [in Persian], as they had exceeded the bounds of the truth.

Shaykh Mufīd says: 'The *ghāliyān* are those who pretend to profess Islam, but who regard Imam 'Alī and his children as having the properties of divinity and prophecy, and presenting them as having qualities which go beyond the bounds of the truth.'[42]

ʿAllāma Majlisī says: '*Ghulūw* in regard to the Prophet and the [religious] leaders applies if we name them God, or that in our prayers and our worship we see them as partners with God, or that we see creation or our daily sustenance as being from them, or that we believe that God has incarnated Himself (*ḥulūl*) in them, or that we say that they know the secrets of the unseen without [needing] inspiration from God, or that we think of the Imams as [having the same rank as the] Prophet, or that we presume that knowledge and recognition of the Imams renders us beyond the need for any kind of worship and absolves us of all religious responsibilities.'[43]

Imam ʿAlī and his pure progeny always sought to distance themselves from the exaggerators, and even cursed them. Here we shall relate one sound hadith in which Imam Ṣādiq gives his followers the instruction: 'Warn your youth about the exaggerators, lest they ruin their religious beliefs, for truly the exaggerators are the worst of God's creatures; they try and belittle the majesty of God while claiming lordship for the slaves of God.'[44]

Their outward profession of Islam is thus valueless, and the religious authorities regard them as disbelievers. Let us note that, despite the fact that we must guard against the dangers of *ghulūw*, it must not be thought that all types of reverential belief regarding the Prophet and the saints pertain to this aberration; we must, as always, maintain circumspection and caution, and with the appropriate criteria, arrive at a proper evaluation of the beliefs in question.

## VI. TRADITIONS (HADITH)

### Article 136

In regard to their religious beliefs and legal rulings, the Imami Shiʿi school makes use of those hadiths of the Prophet that have been related by trustworthy and reliable sources, whether these sources be in the books of the Shiʿa or in those of the Sunnis. Thus, one will find references in Shiʿi books of jurisprudence to certain hadiths transmitted by Sunni sources. (In the fourfold division of hadiths in the Shiʿi jurisprudential system, this type of hadith is referred to as *muwaththaq*, 'reliable'). This shows the baseless nature of what certain hostile persons claim in regard to the Shi'a.

The foundations of Shi'i jurisprudence are the Scripture, the Sunna, the intellect and consensus (*ijmā'*). The Sunna refers to the speech and actions of the *ma'ṣūmīn*, at the head of whom stands the Prophet of Islam. Therefore, whenever a hadith is related by a trustworthy person and it consists in a report of an action or saying of the Prophet, it is considered as possessing credibility. The contents of the Shi'i books on jurisprudence bear sufficient witness to this assertion, and it must be said that in this respect there is no difference between the hadith books of the Shi'a and the Sunnis; if there is any discussion here it is over the means and criteria by which the reliability and credibility of the transmitters are established.

## Article 137

Those hadiths and narrations of the inerrant Imams of the religion that have a sound chain of transmission are considered by the Shi'a as religious proof-texts, on the basis of which one must act, and in conformity with which one must make one's *fatwā* ('religious decision'). The Imams of the *ahl al-bayt* were not *mujtahids* or *muftīs* in the current and conventional sense of these terms; for what they conveyed were so many truths [on the basis of which the *mujtahids* and the *muftīs* of later generations arrive at their jurisprudential decisions]. These narrations have come down to us by different paths, as described below:

### Transmission from the Prophet of God

The impeccable Imams (either directly or else through their great forefathers) received and transmitted to others sayings of the Holy Prophet. This type of narration, involving a given Imam, and going back from predecessor to predecessor to the Prophet himself, is often to be encountered in Shi'i books. If all of these hadiths of the *ahl al-bayt* reaching back to the Prophet were to be gathered together in one work, this would result in a major reference book, a veritable treasure for scholars of hadith and jurisprudence in Islam. For these narrations, deriving from such well established sources, would be unparalleled in the field of hadith studies. We shall allude to one instance of this kind of hadith, which might stand forth as altogether exemplary, and which goes by the name of *silsila al-dhahab* ('chain of gold')—and which is regarded, in terms of its blessings, as a veritable jewel in the treasury of those lovers of literature and promoters of culture in the Samanian dynasty [and elsewhere].

The venerable Shaykh Ṣadūq, in his *Kitāb al-tawḥīd*, relates the following narration by Abū Ṣalt al-Harawī. 'I was travelling through Nīshābūr with Imam ʿAlī b. Mūsā al-Riḍā when a group of hadith scholars from that city, including Muḥammad b. Rāfiʿ, Aḥmad b. Ḥarb, Yaḥyā b. Yaḥyā, Isḥāq b. Rāhawiyya and other seekers after knowledge, took the mount of the Imam and exclaimed: "We implore thee, by the rights of your pure forefathers, to relate to us some saying that you have heard from your father." The Imam put forth his head from his carriage and said: "My father, *al-ʿAbd al-Ṣāliḥ* Mūsā b. Jaʿfar told me: My father, *al-Ṣādiq* Jaʿfar b. Muḥammad told me: My father, Abū Jaʿfar Muḥammad b. ʿAlī *Bāqir ʿilm al-anbiyāʾ* [the full title of Imam Bāqir, lit. 'He who splits open the knowledge brought by the Prophets'] told me: My father, ʿAlī b. al-Ḥusayn *Sayyid al-ʿĀbidīn* told me: My father, *Sayyid Shabāb Ahl al-Janna* [lit. 'Lord of the youths of Paradise'] al-Ḥusayn told me: My father, ʿAlī b. Abī Ṭālib, said: I heard the Prophet say: I heard Gabriel say: I heard God—Glorified be His Majesty!—say: *Lā ilāha illāʾLāh* ('There is no god except God') is My fortress; so whoever enters My fortress will be safe from My wrath".'[45]

## Transmission from the Book of ʿAlī

Imam ʿAlī was a companion of the Holy Prophet throughout his Prophetic mission, thus benefiting from the grace of being able to record many sayings of the Prophet in a book (in fact, the Prophet dictated certain things to ʿAlī). The special features of this book, which remained with his family, after his martyrdom, have been described by the Imams of the *ahl al-bayt.* Imam Ṣādiq said: 'The length of this book is seventy cubits, and it was written by the hand of ʿAlī b. Abī Ṭālib at the dictation of the Prophet of God; and everything which the people need is described therein.'[46]

It should be said that this book was handed down from generation to generation in the family of Imam ʿAlī, and there are frequent references to it in the sayings of Imam Bāqir and Imam Ṣādiq, and the book itself was shown to certain of their companions. Even today, some of the hadiths contained in this book are to be found in the Shiʿi collections of hadith, especially the book *Wasāʾil al-Shīʿa* [by Muḥammad Ḥasan Ḥurr al-ʿĀmilī].

**Divine Inspiration**

The sciences of the Imams of the *ahl al-bayt* have yet another source, which is given the name 'inspiration' (*ilhām*). Inspiration is not the exclusive preserve of the Prophets; rather, history shows that certain eminent and saintly personages have also been graced with this gift. Despite not being Prophets, these individuals were inspired with knowledge of certain secrets of the hidden world. The Qurʾan bears witness to some of these individuals; for example, we have the companion of Moses (al-Khiḍr) by whom he was taught various sciences, as is said:

> ... *unto whom* [al-Khiḍr] *We had given mercy from us, and had taught him knowledge from our presence.* (Sūra al-Kahf, XVIII: 66)

We also have the following, in respect of one of the helpers of Solomon (Āṣif b. Barkhiyā):

> *One with whom was knowledge of the Book said* ... (Sūra al-Naml, XXVII: 40)

Such persons did not obtain their knowledge in the ordinary way; rather, in the expression used by the Qurʾan, they have what is called *ʿilm ladunī* ('knowledge through [divine] presence'), as in the verse cited above, '*We had taught him a knowledge from our presence* (*ʿallamnāhu min ladunnā ʿilman*).'

Therefore, the fact of not being a Prophet does not prevent certain exalted individuals from having the possibility of receiving inspiration from God. In hadiths related by both branches of Islam, this type of person is referred to as *muḥaddath* [lit. 'one who is spoken to'], that is, one who, despite not being a Prophet, is addressed by the angels.

Bukhārī relates in his *Ṣaḥīḥ* the following hadith from the Prophet: 'Verily there were before you, from amongst the People of Israel, persons to whom (the angels) spoke, without their being Prophets.'[47]

Thus, it can be understood how the Imams of the *ahl al-bayt*, in addition to being the source of authority for the *umma* in regard to the exposition of spiritual sciences and religious rulings, also received inspiration from God, answering thereby certain questions that could not be answered by reference to the hadiths of the Prophet or the book of Imam 'Alī.[48]

### Article 138

The hadiths of the Prophet, and his Sunna generally, are considered, together with the Qur'an, as primary sources of the system of Muslim belief and jurisprudence. After the passing away of the Prophet, a group of Muslims, under the pressure of the powers of the government of the time, neglected to write down the prophetic hadiths; but fortunately, the followers of the Imams of the *ahl al-bayt* vigilantly took up the task of recording these hadiths. In previous articles we have already mentioned the fact that a section of the hadiths of the Imams of the *ahl al-bayt* go back in fact to the Prophet himself.

Throughout history, those trained in the school of thought of the *ahl al-bayt* have compiled voluminous collections of hadith, which are mentioned in the category of works known as *kutub rijāl* [lit. 'books of the men' i.e. those who transmitted hadiths]. Large collections of hadith were compiled, especially in the 4th/10th and 5th/11th centuries, on the basis of books written in the time of the Imams, by their students; to this day, these collections remain pivotal as regards the religious beliefs and rulings of the

Shiʿa. Below we mention some of the titles and authors of these books:

1. *al-Uṣūl min al-kāfī* (8 volumes), by Muḥammad b. Yaʿqūb al-Kulaynī (d. 329/940).
2. *Man la yaḥḍuruhu'l-faqīh* (2 volumes), by Muḥammad b. ʿAlī b. Babawayh, known as Shaykh Ṣadūq (d. 371/981).
3. *Tahdhīb al-uṣūl* (2 volumes), by Muḥammad b. Ḥasan al-Ṭūsī, known as Shaykh Ṭūsī (d.385/995).
4. *al-Istibṣār* (4 volumes), by Shaykh Ṭūsī also.

These works constituted the second series of hadith collections brought together by the Shiʿa up to the 4th/10th and 5th/11th centuries. As already mentioned, in the very time of the Imams, that is, the 2nd/8th and 3rd/9th centuries, there were collections, known as the primary collections, which contained '*The Four Hundred Articles*' (*al-uṣūl al-arbaʿumiʾa*)[49] the contents of which were to be transferred into the second series of collections.

Since the science of Hadith literature has always been given serious attention by the Shiʿa, there also appeared in the 11th/17th and 12th/18th centuries a further set of collections, of which *Biḥār al-anwār* (by Muḥammad Bāqir al-Majlisī), *Wasāʾil al-Shīʿa* (by Muḥammad Ḥasan Ḥurr al-ʿĀmilī) and *al-Wāfī* (Muḥammad Muḥsin Fayḍ al-Kāshānī) are deservedly the most famous.

It is clear that the Shiʿa do not act according to just any hadith. In the field of belief, the narrations of ordinary individuals, or those that are contrary to the Qurʾan or the Sunna, will definitely not be accepted as proof-texts. Likewise, the existence of narrations in the hadith books is not necessarily a reason for trusting the author of those books; rather, the hadiths recounted in such books are divided by the scholars of Shiʿism cited above into four categories: *ṣaḥīḥ* ('sound'), *ḥasan* ('good'), *muwaththaq* ('reliable'), and *ḍaʿīf* ('weak'), each category having its own particular rules and criteria, the detailed explanation of which can be found in the science of Hadith studies.

## VII. JURISPRUDENTIAL REASONING (IJTIHĀD)

### Article 139

In the previous sections we alluded to the fourfold bases of Shiʿi jurisprudence, that is, the Qur'an, the Sunna, intellect and consensus. The act of deducing specific religious rulings from these principles, in accordance with particular conditions clarified in the science of jurisprudence, is called *ijtihād* ('applied reasoning').

Insofar as the Shariʿa of Islam is the last religious law to be revealed—with no further such dispensations coming after its promulgation—it must of necessity respond to all of the needs of mankind, in both the individual and collective domain. The Muslims of the Prophet's epoch, taking due note of the perfection and comprehensiveness of Islam, considered the Prophet's life as a model to be followed as scrupulously as possible in their own lives, such that in all the affairs of their lives they fixed their gaze upon the commands and prohibitions ordained by God and His Prophet.

From another point of view, it cannot be denied that since not all phenomena and events can have been encountered in this early epoch, and since continuous transformations in lifestyles have brought about phenomena that were altogether new, there has been a constant need for appropriate religious rulings to deal with the new situations. Taking this into account, it will be seen that keeping open the door of *ijtihād* for the jurisprudents throughout the course of Islamic history was a real necessity. Could it be conceived that Islam, this perfect and comprehensive religion, should remain silent in the face of new conditions, and leave mankind bewildered and rudderless in the turbulent sea-changes of history?

We know that the scholars of jurisprudence divide *ijtihād* into two categories: unrestricted *ijtihād*, on the one hand, and *ijtihād* within a specific *madhhab*, on the other. For example, when one applies *ijtihād* within the framework of the Ḥanafī *madhhab*, one will attempt to address the question in hand according to the perspective of Abū Ḥanīfa, and this will be termed *ijtihād* within a *madhhab*. But when a *mujtahid*, one who exercises *ijtihād*, does not confine himself to the method of a given individual or within the framework of a specific system of *fiqh*, applying himself instead to the principial sources of jurisprudence—whether the outcome is in accord with a given system or not—this is referred to as unrestricted *ijtihād*.

Unfortunately, from the year 665/1226, the door of unrestricted *ijtihād* has been closed to the scholars of the Sunnis;[50] so *ijtihād* has been confined within the delimited jurisprudential systems, this naturally resulting in a restriction of the scope of truth-seeking and open-minded inference from the divine sources of jurisprudence.

The jurisprudents of Shiʿism, basing themselves on the Qurʾan, the Sunna, consensus and intellect, have always conducted *ijtihād*, and their efforts to arrive at religious truths and sciences have not been restricted by anything other than these religious sources. Thus, the scholars of this *madhhab*, by virtue of this living and deeply rooted tradition of *ijtihād*, have developed a comprehensive system of *fiqh*, one which can adapt to the different and changing needs of human society; and they have assembled a veritable treasury of scholarly knowledge. A major factor making for this living and self-regenerative system of Shiʿi jurisprudence is the prohibition of following (*taqlīd*) a dead *mujtahid*: one can only follow a living *mujtahid* who has his finger on the pulse of the social conditions of his time.

Shiʿi *fiqh* is in accord with the other schools of law on a great number of issues; the book of Shaykh Ṭūsī, *al-Khilāf*, bears witness to this fact. It is only in minor *furūʿ*[51] that one finds a difference of opinion with one or other of the four schools, or with the jurists of the epoch preceding these four schools. It is in respect of a series of such *furūʿ* that the Shiʿi *fiqh* has a distinctive approach; we shall allude to some of these in the following Articles. For it is sometimes imagined that these special *furūʿ* have no religious grounds, or that they are opposed to the Qurʾan or the Sunna, whereas the very opposite is in fact the case.

### Article 140

The Sunna of the Holy Prophet has been recorded and transmitted by a group of his companions for future generations; his speech, his declarations and his actions are all so many divine evidences and are to be followed. Therefore, if a companion should relate a saying of the Prophet, and the requisite conditions of verification are fulfilled, it is to be accepted and acted upon accordingly.

Likewise, should a companion shed light on the meaning of some word in the Qur'an, or relate some event relevant to the age in which the prophetic mission was being accomplished, or some other matter, his narration is to be accepted, once the requisite conditions of verification are fulfilled.

But if a companion mentions some opinion or inference of his own in respect either of a Qur'anic verse or a hadith, or if some saying of his is transmitted and it is not clear whether this is a saying of the Prophet or his own opinion, then this will not be regarded as an evidence, since the opinion of one *mujtahid* does not carry any evidential weight for other *mujtahids*. Thus, when it comes to acting on the basis of these sayings, one must distinguish carefully between those statements of a companion pertaining to his own *ijtihād* and opinion, on the one hand, and those statements which relate the sayings of the Prophet, on the other. The Imami Shiʿa act on those statements of the companions which relate some aspect of the Sunna of the Prophet.

### Article 141

It is incumbent upon each Muslim to attain certainty in respect of those principles in which he has faith. It is not permitted to follow others without being certain of these principles oneself. Insofar as these principles of faith are few in number, and the intellect has access to clear evidence regarding each of them, the attainment of certainty in respect of these essential theological principles will be straightforward for most persons. But the applications of these principles, along with the different juristic rulings, are of a more voluminous nature, knowledge of which presupposes extensive preliminary study, such as is beyond the scope of most people. Thus, the majority of people, according to the dictates of human nature and the opinion of the wise alike, must refer to the *mujtahids* and scholars for guidance as regards the rulings of the Shariʿa, and thereby accomplish correctly their religious obligations.

In principle, man is a knowing agent, that is, his actions are based on a foundation of knowledge; should he gain knowledge himself, so much the better, but failing this, he receives help from the knowledge of others. Here we must note carefully that following a fully qualified *mujtahid* is an expression of the principle of referring to a specialist, and as such, has nothing to do with the fanatical and unthinking 'following' of the kind that flows from nationalism, racism or other forms of extremism.

## VII. SOME CONTESTED LEGAL RULINGS

The religion of Islam is composed of belief ('knowledge of reality'), and law ('commands and prohibitions'); these two elements are also expressed as *uṣūl al-dīn* ('principles of religion') and *furūʿ al-dīn* ('details of religion'). In the discussions above, we have tried to show the rational basis of some of the fundamental Shiʿi beliefs, and we have explained the Shiʿi perspective on the means of establishing the credibility of the hadiths of the Prophet and the *ahl al-bayt*. Now it is necessary to allude briefly to the juristic method of the Shiʿa, and to call attention to some of the issues in their jurisprudence which evince a distinctively Shiʿi perspective.

### Article 142

**Ablution (*Wuḍūʾ*)**

We are all aware that the ablution (*wuḍūʾ*) is one of the pre-requisites of performing the *ṣalāt* prayer. We read in the Sūra al-Māʾida (v:7):

*O ye who believe, when ye rise up for prayer, wash your faces, and your hands up to the elbows, and wipe your heads and your feet up to the ankles.*

In the first sentence, '*wash your faces, and your hands up to the elbows,*' the word *aydīy* used here is the plural of *yad*, meaning 'hand'. Now, in the first place, this word in the Arabic language is used in different ways: sometimes it refers only to the fingers of the hand, sometimes it means the fingers up to the wrists, sometimes it means the fingers up to the elbow, and finally, sometimes it means the whole arm, from the fingertips right up to the shoulder. Secondly, the part of the hands that must be washed for the ablution extends from the fingers to the elbow, as the Qurʾan says, clarifying the precise region to be washed, up to the elbows. Thus, the word *ilā*, in the phrase *'ilāʾl-marāfiq'* ('up to the elbows'), clarifies the part of the arms to be washed, not how the arms are to be washed (for example, from the elbow downwards or from the hand downwards). Rather, the manner of washing is to be connected with the customs and traditions of the people; now, the most common way of cleaning something is to do so from the top downwards. For instance, if a doctor were to order that the leg of a sick person be washed from the knee, it would be washed from the knee downwards, not inversely, from the foot to the knee. Thus, the Imami Shiʿa believe that in the ablution, the face and the arms should be washed from up down, and not the other way around.

Another contested issue is that of wetting the feet in the ablution. According to Shiʿi *fiqh*, the feet are to be wiped with water and not washed; the reason for this, in brief, is that the verse quoted indicates that the one wishing to pray has to perform two duties in respect of the ablution: the first is to wash (*ghusl*) the face and the arms; and the second is to wipe (*masḥ*) the head and the feet. This becomes clear upon comparing the two sentences of the verse: *'Wash your faces, and your hands up to the elbows'* and *'wipe your heads, and your feet up to the ankles... .'* Were we to present these two sentences to an Arabic-speaker, who was not aware of any particular juristic opinions on the matter, he would say without hesitation that, according to this verse, our duty is to *wash* our face and arms, and to *wipe* our heads and our feet.

As regards grammatical principles, the word *arjulakum* ('your feet') must follow the word *ruʾūsikum* both of which are to be wiped;

one cannot refer the word *arjulakum* back to the act of washing by making it follow the word *aydīyakum* ('your hands'). Thus, it is necessary to conclude that as between the word *arjulakum* and *aydīyakum* there is the obstructing sentence, '*so wipe your heads*', so there can be no conjunction between the two in terms of the principles of Arabic language; any attempt to make such a conjunction will lead to an erroneous meaning being attached to the verse.

It might also be noted in passing that whether we adopt one or the other of the two possible readings of the verse, the reading of *jarr* or that of *nasb*, the meaning remains the same, the word *arjulakum* still being ruled over by the property pertaining to *ru'ūsikum*.[52]

Verified narrations from the Imams of the *ahl al-bayt* indicate that the ablution is made up of two parts: two 'washings' and two 'wipings'. Imam Bāqir, in the course of describing the ablution performed by the Prophet relates that he wiped his feet.

It is worth noting that it is not just the Imams of the *ahl al-bayt* who performed this act of wiping of the feet; a group of companions and Muslims of the second generation also did the same. But for various reasons that are detailed and commented upon in books of *fiqh*, a number of Muslims among the Sunnis replaced the act of wiping with that of washing the feet.

## Article 143

### Prostration in Prayer

The Shiʿa are of the belief that, in the *ṣalāt* prayer, one must make the prostration on the earth, or on whatever may be on it, so long as the material on the ground not be made out of a substance that can be worn or eaten; prostration on anything else, when one has the choice, is not considered correct. This matter has been made clear in a hadith that the Sunnis also record in their books: 'The earth (*al-arḍ*) has been made for me a place of prostration (*masjid*)[53] and a means of purification (*ṭahūr*).'[54] The word *ṭahūr*, which envisages the *tayammum*,[55] shows that what is meant by *al-arḍ* in the saying is the natural substance of the earth, stone and the like.

Imam Ṣādiq said: 'The prostration is allowed only on the earth, or on what grows from the earth, except that which can be eaten or worn.'[56]

It was the general practice of the Muslims at the time of the Prophet to make their prostration on the ground of the mosque, which was covered by gravel and sand. During hot weather, when making the prostration on hot stones was difficult, they used to take up some gravel in their hands, hold it until it cooled, and then, when the time for prayer came, they would place that handful of gravel before them and make the prostration on it. The companion, Jābir b. 'Abd Allāh al-Anṣārī said: 'I was praying the noon prayer with the Prophet; I had a handful of gravel that I was moving from one hand to the other until it cooled, and made the prostration on it when the time for prayer came.'[57]

One of the Prophet's companions was avoiding getting his forehead rubbed into the earth; the Prophet said to him: 'Make your forehead dusty with earth!'[58] Likewise, if someone were by chance to prostrate upon a part of the cloth of his turban, the Prophet would take the material away from underneath the forehead.[59]

These hadiths all bear witness to the fact that at the time of the Prophet it was incumbent on the Muslims to make prostration upon the earth or stone, and they did not prostrate on carpets, cloth or even the material of their turbans. But it was later revealed to the Prophet that prostration could also be made on mats of straw and reed, and many narrations indicate that the Prophet did prostrate on such materials.[60]

Of course, in times of necessity, some companions used to prostrate on part of their clothes, as Anas b. Mālik says: 'We used to pray with the Prophet. Whenever one of us was prevented from prostrating on the earth, he would prostrate upon part of his turban or on a part of his clothes.'[61]

Therefore, the Shi'a have always felt themselves bound to maintain the principle of prostrating only upon the earth and what grows naturally from it, that is, reed, straw and the like, while avoiding any substances that are either worn or eaten. If they insist upon prostrating only upon such surfaces, it is for these reasons. It would indeed be advantageous for all mosques in the world where Muslims pray to be built in such a manner that enables the followers of all the *madhhabs* of Islam to accomplish their respective duties in an appropriate and dignified manner.

In conclusion, we should not omit to mention the following point: stones and earth are 'prostrated upon' (*masjūdun alayhi*) and not 'prostrated to' (*masjūdun lahu*); for it is sometimes wrongly supposed that the Shi'a actually prostrate *to* their stones! In truth, like all Muslims, prostration is solely to God. Our humility and effacement before the divine presence is given outward expression by this act of placing the forehead on the earth, while in the heart one says: 'Where is this dust, and where is the Lord of the Worlds!'

## Article 144

**Times of Prayer**

It is incumbent upon every Muslim to pray five times a day, at times prescribed by the Qur'an and the Sunna: from noon to sunset is the period for the *ẓuhr* and *'aṣr* prayers; from sunset to the late night is the period for the *maghrib* and *'ishā'* prayers; and from first light to sunrise is the time for the *fajr* prayer.

The Shi'a believe that in the period between noon and sunset, both the *ẓuhr* and the *'aṣr* prayers can be prayed together, the first four units of prayer pertaining to *ẓuhr* and the second set of four to *'aṣr*. Therefore, one is allowed to pray these two sets of prayers any time within the prescribed period, without necessarily having to pray each separately, at the preferred time; however, it is better to separate the two and pray each at the preferred time, as we shall explain below.[62]

Imam Bāqir said: 'When the sun begins to decline, the time for the *ẓuhr* and the *'aṣr* begins; and when the sun sets, the time for the *maghrib* and the *'ishā'* begins.'[63]

Imam Ṣādiq said: 'When the sun reaches its height, the time for both the *ẓuhr* and the *'aṣr* prayers begins, except that the *ẓuhr* prayer must be said before the *'aṣr*. You are able to perform the prayers any time before the sun sets.'[64]

Imam Bāqir relates that the Prophet used to pray the *ẓuhr* and the *ʿaṣr* prayers together, without there being any reason or special circumstances for doing so.[65]

In principle, the permissibility of joining the two prayers together is agreed upon, in certain circumstances, by all schools of *fiqh*. On the days of Arafat and Muzdalifa [during the Hajj], all are agreed that the two prayers of *ẓuhr* and *ʿaṣr*, as well as *maghrib* and *ʿishāʾ*, can be joined together; likewise, a majority of the Sunnis accept the joining of the prayers when travelling. What distinguishes the Shiʿa from the other schools is that they go one step further. Based on the reasons given above—and despite upholding the principle that it is preferable to pray the prayers separately and at their respective, specific times—they accept the permissibility of joining the prayers together in an unconditional manner. The wisdom of this position, as is evident in the hadiths brought forth in this regard, derives from the principle of making the religion of Islam easy to practise for the Muslims. For the Prophet himself, on numerous occasions, in the absence of any reason (such as travelling or sickness, and so on), prayed the two prayers together in order to make the burden of the religion light for his community, allowing him who so wishes to pray the prayers together, and him who so wishes to pray them separately.

In his *Ṣaḥīḥ*, Muslim relates: 'The Messenger of God prayed the *ẓuhr* and the *ʿaṣr* together, and the *maghrib* and the *ʿishāʾ* together, without his being a traveller or in fear [of being attacked by the enemy in war-time].'[66]

The wisdom of this position is revealed in certain narrations; in one such we read: 'The Prophet joined together the *ẓuhr* and the *ʿaṣr*, and the *maghrib* and the *ʿishāʾ*. When asked about this, he said: I did this lest my community find hardship [in the performance of the obligatory duties of Islam].'[67]

There are more than twenty-one narrations in the collections of sound hadiths that pertain to the Prophet's joining together of the two sets of prayers, some of them relate to times of travel, others to times of sickness, stormy weather and times when one is not travelling. The wisdom behind this practice, as seen above, derives from the principle of avoiding hardship and making the duties of religion easy to accomplish. It is on this principle that the Shiʿi school have made it permissible to join the two sets of prayer together in an unconditional manner. The way the two prayers are joined is just the same as the way in which they are joined, for all Muslims, when travelling and at the occasions of Arafat and Muzdalifa [during the Hajj].

It is sometimes thought that the reason for joining the two prayers together is that the *ẓuhr* prayer be prayed at the last possible time (within the preferred period, that is, when the shadow of the sun-dial's pointer is the same length as itself), and that the *ʿaṣr* be then prayed at the very beginning of its preferred time. In such a way, the one praying will be able to pray each prayer within the preferred time, the one at the end of its period and the other at the beginning of its period. But such an idea contradicts the meaning of the narrations. For, as has been said, the way in which the prayers are to be joined is the way they are joined by all Muslims at Arafat and Muzdalifa. In other words, at Arafat, both the *ẓuhr* and the *ʿaṣr* are prayed together at the time of *ẓuhr*, and at Muzdalifa, both the *maghrib* and the *ʿishāʾ* are prayed together at the time of *ʿishāʾ*.[68] Thus, for one who would join the two sets of prayers, it is this mode of joining the prayers performed by the Prophet that must be carried out; one cannot pray one prayer at the end of its preferred period and then the other at the beginning of its preferred period.

In some of the narrations, the wisdom of joining the prayers is presented in terms of the ease and comfort of the community, in others in terms of relief of difficulty; the principal point is that the one who prays should be allowed to decide for himself whether to join the two sets of prayers together, for the sake of relieving him of any difficulty. Also, one should note, on the basis of this explanation of the joining together of prayers, that the Prophet did not bring something new, insofar as a mode of joining the prayers was already permitted, even prior to his own action of joining the prayers: every Muslim could pray the *ẓuhr* at the end of its period and the *ʿaṣr* at the beginning of its period.

The *fuqahāʾ* [jurists] of Shiʿism have written extensively on this matter, and those interested can consult their treatises of *fiqh*.

## Article 145

**Temporary Marriage (*Mutʿa*)**

Shiʿi *fiqh*, on the foundations of the guidance provided by the Qur'an and Sunna, considers two types of marriage as being valid: 'permanent marriage' which needs no comment, and 'temporary marriage' or *mutʿa*, which can be commented on as follows.

A man and a woman who are not prevented by religious reasons (such as being related by blood or in terms of a common foster-mother) from marrying one another can, after agreeing upon a dowry and for a specified period of time, enter into wedlock; and after the elapse of the specified time, they separate from one another, without there being any need for the formalities of divorce. If in the meantime they have any offspring, these children are licit and are entitled to receive inheritance from both parents. After the specified period of time has elapsed, the woman must observe the period of *ʿidda* (seclusion) as prescribed in the Shariʿa; and if pregnant, she must wait until after the birth of the baby, and then she has the right to marry another man.

Temporary marriage is, in essence, at one with permanent marriage, and all the rules pertaining to the latter apply to the former. However, there are certain important differences between the two, and these can be summarized as follows: (a) the specification of a period of time in the case of temporary marriage, and (b) the absence of any need to pay alimony at the end of the specified period of a temporary marriage.

Since Islam is the final and most comprehensive religion, it must provide a solution for crises relating to sexuality. Let us take, for example, the case of a young man living away from his own country, either studying or else trying to find work, and he does not have the means to enter into a permanent marriage. What should he do? He has to choose one of the following three options: either exert self-control and deprive himself of sexual pleasure; or enter into illicit affairs with immoral women; or make use of the possibility of temporary marriage, according to strict conditions, with a virtuous lady.

It is clear that there is no fourth option for such a person.

Needless to say, we do not mean to imply that temporary marriage only applies in such circumstances; only that this kind of situation indicates well the religious wisdom behind the rule.[69]

It should be noted also that in the systems of *fiqh* of other schools of Islam a type of permanent marriage is allowed which, in reality, is but a form of temporary marriage: this is a marriage in which a man and woman marry, but either one or both of them know that after a certain time they must be divorced and separate from each other. The permissibility of such a marriage is equivalent to the permissibility of temporary marriage; only the names differ.

The Qur'an and Sunna alike indicate the religious validity of temporary marriage. The Qur'an says:

*And those* [women] *from whom ye seek satisfaction* [by marrying them], *give unto them their portions as a duty* ... (Sūra al-Nisā', IV:24)

Nearly all commentators of the Qur'an are in agreement that this verse relates to temporary marriage. In principle, there is no doubt that such marriage was permitted in [early] Islam; if there is any disagreement, it is over the question of whether the ruling that allowed temporary marriage had been abrogated or not. Narrations from both Shi'i and Sunni sources show that this ruling had not been abrogated by the Qur'an or by the Prophet, but that it was prohibited for certain reasons in the time of the second caliph ['Umar]. From the very words of the caliph in which he makes his judgement on the matter, it is clear that the practice was both permitted and current in the time of the Prophet, and indicates that his prohibition of it is based only on his own opinion. His words were as follows: 'O people, three things were current in the time of the Prophet which I now forbid and prohibit, and I punish [whosoever practises them]: temporary marriage, marriage during Hajj, and the exhortation *ḥayya 'alā khayri'l-'amal* ["hasten unto the best act," said as part of the call to prayer].'[70]

It is strange that to this day the caliph's prohibition as regards the first and last issues has remained in place, but marriage during Hajj—contrary to the caliph's wish—is being practised by all Muslims. The meaning of marriage during Hajj is that a pilgrim to the Ka'ba, during the period between his performance of 'Umra and the rites of the Hajj, leaves the state of *iḥrām* [the 'pilgrim-state'], thus rendering permissible those things that are prohibited in the state of *iḥrām.*

Clear evidence of the fact that the Prophet had never banned temporary marriage is also provided by the following narration. Bukhārī relates that ʿImrān b. Ḥasīn said: 'The verse relating to temporary marriage was revealed; at the time of the Prophet we used to practise it. No verse banning it was ever revealed, nor did the Prophet ever prohibit it in his lifetime. Then, a man said what he wanted in regard to it from his own opinion.'[71] The reference here is to the prohibition promulgated by the second caliph.

## Article 146

### Folding Hands in Prayer

The folding of hands in front by one who is praying is considered an innovation (*bidʿa*) and is forbidden in Imami *fiqh.* Imam ʿAlī said: 'The Muslim should not fold his hands in front of him while praying, standing before God; [for, should he do so] he would be like the disbelieving fire-worshippers.'[72]

Abū Ḥāmid al-Sāʿadī, a great companion, reported in front of a group of other companions—including such figures as Abū Hurayra, Sahl Sāʿadī, Abū Usayd Sāʿadī, Abū Qutāda, Ḥārith b. Rubʿī and Muḥammad b. Muslima—the precise manner in which the Prophet prayed, naming all the most subtle as well as the most basic recommended practices; but he said nothing about such a practice as the folding of one's hands in front of one.[73]

It is clear, then, that if the Prophet had prayed in such a manner, even occasionally, he [Abū Ḥāmid al-Sāʿadī] would have mentioned it, or at least, those present would have done so. Similar hadiths to this one have been transmitted to us from Imam Ṣādiq, through Ḥammād b. ʿĪsā, and are recorded in our books of Hadith.[74]

We can also usefully take note of the hadith of Sahl b. Saʿd which tells us, implicitly, that the folding of the hands in the prayer came about after the Prophet's death. He said: 'The people were ordered to do so'[75]—if this action were ordered by the Prophet, the order would have been explicitly connected to him.

## Article 147

### Optional Congregational Prayer during Ramadan (*Tarāwīḥ*)

The *tarāwīḥ* prayer is considered by some followers of the Prophet to be a recommended practice. In Shiʿi *fiqh*, it is recommended that one perform one thousand units of prayer during the nights of the month of Ramadan. But performing these prayers in congregation is considered to be an innovation, for these prayers should be said individually in the mosque, or better still, at home. Zayd b. Thābit relates that praying at one's home is better than praying at the mosque, except for the obligatory prayers, the performance of which in congregation, at the mosque, is deemed *mustaḥabb* ('recommended').[76]

Imam Bāqir said: 'Those prayers which are *mustaḥabb* [as opposed to those which are *wājib*, 'obligatory', namely, the five daily prayers] cannot be performed in congregation; every kind of innovation is a source of straying, and leads to the Fire.'[77] Imam Riḍā also mentions in his treatise, which is concerned with doctrines and practices, that *mustaḥabb* prayers cannot be performed in congregation, and if they are, it is a *bidʿa*.[78]

As is clear from the unfolding of the history of the congregational *tarāwīḥ* prayer, which is current today among the Sunnis, it has been given religious status by *ijtihād* operating on the basis of personal opinion; so it is given by the Sunnis the label *bidʿa ḥasana* ('a good innovation'). Those wishing to research this point further can consult the books mentioned in the note below.[79]

## Article 148

### The Tax of One-Fifth (*Khums*)

All the *fuqahāʾ* of Islam are of the belief that spoils obtained in war should be divided amongst the warriors, but a fifth of all spoils is to be given for certain other purposes, as the following verse states:

*And know that whatever ye take as spoils of war, then verily, a fifth thereof is for God, and for the Messenger, and for the kinsmen, and orphans, and for the needy and the wayfarer ...* (Sūra al-Anfāl, VIII: 41)

The *fuqahā'* of Shiʿism differ from those of other schools in that the latter regard this 'fifth' (*khums*) as being confined to spoils of war, and do not believe in giving over this share in any other circumstances, arguing that this verse relates only to spoils of war. But this position is incorrect, from two points of view.

Firstly, in the Arabic language, anything that one obtains without having worked for it, is referred to as *ghanīma*, and the word is not restricted in its application only to the *ghanīma* obtained in war. As Ibn Manẓūr says: '*Al-ghunm* is the obtaining of a thing without [having had to] toil [for it].'[80] The Qur'an also brings in this word when describing the blessings of Paradise:

*With God are plenteous spoils ...* (Sūra al-Nisā', IV: 94)

In principle, *ghanīma* should be seen in contrast with *gharāma* (indemnity). When someone is forced to pay an indemnity or reparation in the form of a sum of money, this will be called a *gharāma*; if one receives the profit thereof, it will be called a *ghanīma*.

Therefore, there is no reason for restricting the import of this verse to the spoils of war alone, nor can one make such a restriction simply on account of the verse being revealed after the Battle of Badr. The law of the *khums* applies universally to profits made, and is not confined to the circumstances in which the verse was revealed.

Secondly, certain narrations make it clear that the Prophet made the *khums* tax obligatory in respect of all types of profit. A group from the tribe of ʿAbd al-Qays came to the Prophet and said: 'Between us and you there is the forbidding barrier of the polytheists, and it is only during the sacred months that we are able to come close to you. Make clear to us some orders which, if acted upon, will lead us to Paradise, orders that we can invite others to act on also.' The Prophet said: 'I give you the order of *imān* (faith),' then he proceeded to explain *īmān*: 'To bear witness that there is no god but God, to establish prayer, to give the poor-due, and to give one-fifth of your profits (*maghnam*).'[81] It is obvious that the meaning of *maghnam* in this hadith does not pertain to spoils of war, for the tribe in question lived in a place from which they could not easily make contact with the Prophet since, out of fear of the polytheists, they could not reach Medina, except during the sacred months. Such persons as these, surrounded as they were by the polytheists, did not have the power to fight them, and thus could not have given one-fifth of the spoils of war resulting therefrom.

Also, there are narrations related of the Imams of the *ahl al-bayt* that show very explicitly the necessity of paying a tax of one-fifth on all profits, such that there is no room for ambiguity on this issue.[82]

These are some branches of *fiqh* in relation to which the Shiʿa have a particular perspective and mode of application. Of course, the points over which the Shiʿa differ with other schools are not limited to those which we have mentioned. For example, there are also differences of opinion on such matters as legacy and inheritance.[83] But, in addition to taking into account the universal principles and rules that are held in common by the Shiʿa and the Sunnis, a close comparative analysis of *fiqh*, with special emphasis upon the lofty and verified perspectives of the family of the Revelation [that is, the *ahl al-bayt*], can help to reduce the gap between the Shiʿa and the Sunnis.

## Article 149

### The Shiʿi Contribution to Islamic Civilization

The civilization of Islam owes its success to the ceaseless efforts of the Muslim *umma*. Many different peoples all over the world were fused into one community by the power of faith and belief, and exerted every effort in the cause of the lofty ideals of Islam. As a result, a glorious civilization was established, one to which human society will forever be indebted.

The Shiʿa played an effective part in the establishment of this brilliant civilization. It suffices to turn the pages of the books on

Islamic civilization and learning to see the degree to which the names of great Shiʿi luminaries shine forth. In literature and the literary sciences, for example, the foundations were laid by Imam ʿAlī, and then developed by his disciple, Abū'l-Aswad Duʾalī, after whom there came other Shiʿi personalities, mostly living in Iraq, such as: Māzanī (d.248/862), Ibn Sukayt (d.244/858), Abū Isḥāq Naḥwy (a companion of Imam Kāẓim), Khalīl b. Aḥmad Farāhī, author of the book *al-ʿAyn* (d.170/786), Ibn Durayd, author of *al-Jumhura* (d.321/933), Ṣāḥib b. ʿAbbād, author of *al-Muḥīṭ* (d.386/996)—these and hundreds of other Shiʿi writers, who were the veritable repositories for their times of the literary sciences of philology, grammar, etymology, poetry and prosody.

In the science of Qurʾanic exegesis (*tafsīr*), the first commentators after the Holy Prophet were Imam ʿAlī, the Imams of the *ahl al-bayt* and ʿAbd Allāh b. ʿAbbās (d.68/686), and then their disciples. And throughout the course of fourteen centuries they have written hundreds of commentaries on the Qurʾan from different angles. We can see the detailed history of this science, as it was developed by the Shiʿi exegetes, in the introduction of *al-Tibyān* by Shaykh Ṭūsī.

In the science of Hadith, we note that the Shiʿa preceded all other groups in Islam. During the period when the first caliphs prohibited the writing down of hadiths, the Shiʿa were already recording the Sunna of the Prophet both by way of writing and through their discourses. In this connection we ought to mention ʿAbd Allāh b. Abī Rāfiʿ, Rabīʿa b. Samīʿ, ʿAlī b. Abī Rāfiʿ, companions of Imam ʿAlī, and then the many individuals among the disciples of Imam Sajjād (ʿAlī b. al-Ḥusayn), Imam Bāqir and Imam Ṣādiq. The expansion of the science of Hadith in the period of Imam Ṣādiq reached such a point that Ḥasan b. ʿAlī al-Washshāʾ said: 'I saw nine hundred *muḥaddiths* in the mosque of Kufa, all of them recounting thus: "Jaʿfar b. Muḥammad [al-Ṣādiq] reported ..."'[84]

In the domain of *fiqh*, the most outstanding *mujtahids* were trained in the school of the Imams of the *ahl al-bayt*: Abān b. Taghallub (d.141/758), Zarāra b. Aʿyīn (d.150/767), Muḥammad b. Muslim (d.150/767), Ṣafwān b. Yaḥyā Bijillī, author of thirty books (d.210/825); and hundreds of other highly capable and learned scholars, such as Shaykh Mufīd, Sayyid Murtaḍā, Shaykh Ṭūsī, Ibn Idrīs, Muḥaqqiq al-Ḥillī, ʿAllāma Ḥillī, who have all left behind precious works as testimony to their knowledge and learning.

It was not only in such domains of knowledge that the Shiʿa contributed in such a dedicated way; they have also made worthy and profound contributions to other branches of knowledge, such as history, biography, science, poetry and literature. It would not be possible to name all of these figures in a book such as this.

What has been mentioned so far pertains to the transmitted (*naqlī*) sciences; but in the intellectual (*ʿaqlī*) sciences, such as theology and philosophy also, the Shiʿa excel, given the great value placed on the role of the intellect in Shiʿism. Assisted by the inspired sayings of Imam ʿAlī and his inerrant progeny, the Shiʿa have exerted themselves intellectually to the utmost in the endeavour to clarify Islamic beliefs. The Islamic world has been graced with Shiʿi theologians of the most distinguished calibre and philosophers of the highest rank; and Shiʿi theological perspectives have produced one of the most brilliant schools of theology in Islam, which, in addition to making use of the primary sources of the Qurʾan and Sunna, has also taken full advantage of the intellect and human wisdom.

One of the foundations of a scientific civilization is knowledge of the natural world and its laws; and in the time of Imam Ṣādiq, one of his disciples by the name of Jābir b. Ḥayyān attained such a degree of knowledge in the sciences of nature that he is today regarded as the founding father of the science of chemistry. And in the science of geography, Aḥmad b. Abī Yaʿqūb, known as al-Yaʿqūbī (d.290/901) was the first 'geographer', who travelled throughout the length and breadth of the Islamic world and wrote the book *al-Baladān*.

These diverse efforts by so many learned members of the Shiʿi community have continued from the very first Islamic century through to our own times; so much so that today there are a great number of seminaries, colleges and universities that have been established all over the world that continue to serve the cause of knowledge and learning for the good of all mankind.

What we have said here has been but a brief allusion to the part played by Shiʿism in the cultivation of Islamic science and civilization; to gain a more complete picture, the reader should refer to the many books on this subject.[85]

### Article 150

**A Plea for Muslim Unity**

The Imami Shiʿa do not regard differences in juristic details as undermining Islamic brotherhood or as precluding the solidarity of the Muslims as a unified community. They believe that by engaging in scholarly debate, in a calm atmosphere, many of the intellectual and jurisprudential differences and difficulties can be resolved. In principle, human society is characterized by the fact that there will always be differences of opinion. Closing the door of intellectual debate and enquiry to the intelligentsia causes the swift demise of knowledge and learning, for it cannot but erode intellectual thought and reflection. Our great predecessors, in all ages, tried always to illuminate and assimilate the eternal and unchanging truths through intellectual and religious debate; and, as regards action, they attempted always to uphold and enhance the unity, the solidarity and the integrity of the Muslim *umma.*

# Notes

## Translator's Foreword

1. The Arabic commentary is entitled *Mafāhīm al-Qur'ān* (Qom, 1413/1992); and the Persian commentary, *Manshūr-i jāvīd-i Qur'ān* (Qom, 1984–99). His biography of the Prophet has been translated into English under the title, *The Message—The Holy Prophet of Allāh* (Tehran, n.d) and his biography of Imam ʿAlī, *Furūgh-i vilāyat* (Tehran, 1378 Sh./ 1999) is currently being translated into English.

2. Shiʿism was the officially adopted creed of the Safavids who established their rule over Iran in 907/1501; the large-scale adoption of Shiʿism by the hitherto predominantly Sunni population of the country dates from this time. See R.M. Savory, *Iran under the Safavids* (London, 1980) and S.H. Nasr, 'Religion in Safavid Persia', *Iranian Studies*, 7 (1974), pp. 271–86.

3. See the following articles by S.H. Nasr on this important confluence of different streams of thought in the world of Iranian Shiʿism: 'Spiritual Movements, Philosophy and Theology in the Safavid Period', in *The Cambridge History of Iran*, vol. 6, *The Timurid and Safavid Periods*, ed. P. Jackson and L. Lockhart (Cambridge, 1986), pp. 656–97; 'The School of Iṣpahān', in M.M. Sharif, ed., *A History of Muslim Philosophy* (Wiesbaden, 1966), vol. 2, pp. 904–32; 'The Metaphysics of Ṣadr al-Dīn Shīrāzī and Islamic Philosophy in Qajar Iran', in C.E. Bosworth and C. Hillenbrand, eds, *Qajar Iran* (Edinburgh, 1983), pp. 177–98. See also H. Dabashi, 'Mīr Dāmād and the Founding of the School of Iṣfahān', in S.H. Nasr

and O. Leaman, eds, *History of Islamic Philosophy* (London, 1996), vol. 1, pp. 597–634.

4. A few examples of specific in-depth studies may be usefully referred to here:

a) As regards the philosophical and mystical aspects of Shiʿism, we have the excellent studies by H. Corbin, especially his magisterial work *En Islam iranien* (Paris, 1971–72), 4 vols, the first of which is devoted entirely to exploring these aspects of the Twelver Shiʿi tradition in general; and M.A. Amir-Moezzi, *The Divine Guide in Early Shiʿism: The Sources of Esotericism in Islam*, trans. D. Streight (Albany, N.Y., 1994).

b) On the plane of popular piety, the work by Mahmoud Ayoub, *Redemptive Suffering in Islam* (The Hague, 1978) is a revealing study of a central dimension of Shiʿi devotional life, the commemoration of the martyrdom of the grandson of the Prophet, the third Imam, Ḥusayn b. ʿAlī.

c) On Shiʿi messianic ideals, A.A. Sachedina's *Islamic Messianism: The Idea of the Mahdi in Twelver Shiʿism* (New York, 1981) is a useful, if somewhat controversial, theoretical complement to the historical work by Jassim Hussain on the same theme, *The Occultation of the Twelfth Imam* (London, 1982).

d) Etan Kohlberg's *Belief and Law in Imāmī Shīʿism* (Aldershot, 1991) offers a very useful overview of doctrinal and legal themes, many of which figure in the present book.

e) In terms of history, S.H.M. Jafri's *The Origins and Early Development of Shiʿa Islam* (Beirut, 1979) gives a good overview of both the doctrinal and historical roots of the tradition.

f) Farhad Daftary's comprehensive study, *The Ismāʿīlīs: Their History and Doctrines* (Cambridge, 1990), makes a major contribution to the contemporary understanding of the Ismāʿīlī branch of Shiʿism.

g) *The Fatimids and their Traditions of Learning* by Heinz Halm (London, 1997) offers an illuminating insight into the rich intellectual traditions inaugurated by the Fatimid dynasty in Egypt, including such abiding scholarly institutions as the al-Azhar in Cairo.

5. See the concise but informative *Shiism* by Heinz Halm (Edinburgh, 1991). The two anthologies of original texts selected from Shiʿi traditions of discourse, together with contemporary scholarly articles on these traditions, compiled and edited by S.H. Nasr, H. Dabashi and S.V.R. Nasr, are also extremely valuable contributions: *Shiʿism: Doctrines, Thought and*

*Spirituality* (Albany, N.Y., 1988) and *Expectations of the Millennium: Shiʿism in History* (Albany, N.Y., 1989).

6. The books published in recent years by the Muhammadi Trust in London go some way towards filling this lacuna in Western languages; see for example the translation of the classic Shiʿi text (often referred to below in the current work), *Kitāb al-irshād: The Book of Guidance*, by Shaykh Mufīd, trans. I.K.A. Howard (London, 1981); M.R. al-Muzaffar, *The Faith of Shiʿa Islam* (London, 1983); and *A Manual of Islamic Beliefs and Practices* (in 2 vols.), trans. and ed. K. Sadiq and A.M. Naqvi (London 1990, 1992). Also important in this connection is ʿAllāmah S.M.Ḥ. Ṭabāṭabā'ī's *Shiʿite Islam.* trans. and ed. S.H. Nasr (Albany, N.Y., 1975). As regards the Ismāʿīlī tradition, a similar role is being played by The Institute of Ismaili Studies in London, among whose publications the following three works should be noted: Nāṣir Khusraw, *Knowledge and Liberation*, a new edition and English translation of *Gushāyish wa Rahāyish*, by F.M. Hunzai (London, 1998); Naṣīr al-Dīn Ṭūsī, *Contemplation and Action*, a new edition and English translation of *Sayr wa Sulūk*, by S.J. Badakhchani (London, 1998), and A.R. Lalani, *Early Shiʿi Thought: The Teachings of Imam Muḥammad al-Bāqir* (London, 2000).

7. This seminal figure of the 7th/13th century will be frequently referred to in the present book.

8. See in this connection the important recent work, offering a fresh interpretation of the earliest sources on the subject, by W. Madelung, *The Succession to Muḥammad: A Study of the Early Caliphate* (Cambridge, 1997).

9. See Daftary, *The Ismāʿīlīs*, pp. 32–90, 580–93, for a good account of the process by which these groups crystallized.

10. We can discount, for our present purposes, the Kaysāniyya, those who believed that the fourth Imam, after Ḥusayn b. ʿAlī, was another son of ʿAlī b. Abī Ṭālib, namely, Muḥammad b. al-Ḥanafiyya, whose mother was not Fāṭima, and who was therefore not a descendant of the Prophet. The movement was soon absorbed within the developing Shiʿi tradition, but it remains important because of its connection with the earliest expression of certain key Shiʿi themes, such as messianism and occultation. See Halm, *Shiism*, pp. 16–20, for a concise account of this movement.

11. See for more details the article 'al-Zaidīya' by R. Strothmann in *Encyclopaedia of Islam*, 1st ed., vol. 4, pp. 1196–8, and R.B. Serjeant, 'The

Zaydīs', in A.J. Arberry, ed., *Religion in the Middle East* (Cambridge, 1969), vol. 2, pp. 285–301.

12. We are referring here to the larger of the two principal branches within the Ismāʿīlī community, the Nizārīs; for details on the smaller branch, the Mustaʿlī Ṭayyibīs (for whom the Imam is in concealment (*satr*), and who are consequently led by a *dāʿī muṭlaq*, or 'supreme summoner'), see Daftary, *The Ismāʿīlīs*, ch. 5.

13. Translator's note: The term *ahl al-bayt* ('People of the Household') signifies, in the first place, the five persons deemed to belong to the Prophet's household during his own life, namely, himself, his daughter Fāṭima, his cousin and son-in-law, ʿAlī, and their two sons, Ḥasan and Ḥusayn; in the second place, the Imams descended from them. It also designates the school of thought associated with Shiʿism. See Article 92 below where the author discusses the term in relation to the key Qurʾanic verse (Sūra al-Aḥzāb, XXXIII:33) in which the term is mentioned.

**Chapter One: The Worldview of Islam**

1. In Islamic narrations, such persons are referred to as *muḥaddath* ('those who have been addressed'); this will be explained below. [Translator's note: see also the explanation of this term in the article 'The Term "*Muḥaddath*" in Twelver Shīʿism', in Kohlberg, *Belief and Law*, V, pp. 39–47.]

2. The purification of the soul from all sin and defilement gives rise to certain kinds of inspiration, some of which can also be regarded as means of knowledge.

3. The sending forth of Messengers, the specifying of their inheritors, the revival of the dead—all of these are manifestations of divine activity.

4. 'Truly God possesses two evidences which He has imposed upon mankind: an outward evidence and an inward evidence. The outward one comprises the Messengers, the Prophets and the Imams; and the inward one is the intellect.' al-Kulaynī, *al-Uṣūl min al-kāfī* (Beirut, 1401/1980), vol. 1, p. 16.

5. See also, in this connection, Sūra al-Baqara, II: 102 and 249, and Sūra Āl ʿImrān, III: 49 and 166; for further information, see the books of Qurʾanic commentary and theology, such as ʿAllāma Ṭabāṭabāʾī, *al-Mīzān* (Beirut, 1393/1973), vol. 1, p. 72.

6. *Nahj al-balāgha*, compiled by al-Sharīf al-Raḍī (Qom, 1395/1975), Saying no. 190.

7. Shaykh Ṣadūq, *Kitāb al-tawḥīd* (Qom, 1398/1978), ch. 53, hadith no. 9.

8 Aḥmad b. Ḥanbal, *Musnad* (Cairo, n.d.), vol. 2, p. 54; Muḥammad al-Bukhārī, *Ṣaḥīḥ* (Cairo, 1378/1957–58) vol. 2, *Kitāb al-jumʿa*, ch. 11, hadith no. 2, p. 284.

9 Translator's note: At this point, we are translating the term *qaḍā' wa qadar* as 'divine predestination', as the phrase has this meaning in Persian, even though in the original Arabic the two words have different connotations, *qaḍā'* pertaining to the divine decree, and *qadar* to the 'measuring out' of what is decreed. This distinction will be brought out below, when the author deals more fully with the whole issue of predestination, see Article 48ff.

10. *Nahj al-balāgha*, Letter no. 38.

11. Ḥurr al-ʿĀmilī, *Wasā'il al-Shīʿa* (Beirut, 1403/1982), vol. 11, ch.12, p. 424.

12. Ibid., ch. 4, p. 407.

13. Ibid.

**Chapter Two: General Beliefs**

1. Shaykh Ṣadūq, *Kitāb al-tawḥīd*, ch. 3, hadith no. 3.

2. Translator's note: The Sūra al-Ikhlāṣ, CXII:1–4, reads: *'Say: He is God, the One. God, the eternally Besought of all. He begets not, nor was begotten. And there is none like unto Him.'*

3. Ṣadr al-Dīn al-Shīrāzī, *al-Asfār al-arbaʿa* (Beirut, 1402/1981), vol. 6, p. 135.

4. Cited by Shaykh Ṣadūq in *Kitāb al-tawḥīd*, ch. 11, hadith no. 1.

5. *Nahj al-balāgha*, sermon 1. Some erroneously refer to this point of view by the term *muʿaṭṭila* [a theological term referring to those who strip God of all attributes and qualities], whereas in fact this term applies to one who denies that the positive [divine] attributes pertain to the Essence of God; and from this point of view, one is compelled to empty, as it were, and thus deprive the Essence of God of all ontological attributes and perfections. This erroneous position has nothing to do with the conception of the oneness of the attributes with the Essence; rather, this conception of identity, even while affirming the attribution

to God of positive qualities, is also utterly devoid of the errors of several early thinkers who held that the attributes were additional to the Essence.

6. We shall return to the subject of human freedom in the discussion on divine justice (*ʿadl*).

7. Translator's note: The author seems to be implying the following idea, or principle of theodicy: since God is both absolute reality and infinite goodness, all that stems from Him cannot but be both real and good; evil is grasped in this light as a transient and thus relatively unreal phenomenon, one which acquires its appearance of reality only from its capacity to negate reality/goodness: that which negates reality can thus be grasped as 'unreal', hence the statement, 'evil does not really enter into existence'.

8. See Sūra al-Anʿām, VI:76–78.

9. See Sūra Yūnus, X:18, and Sūra al-Furqān, XXV:55.

10. See, among others, Sūra al-Baqara, II:21; Sūra Ibrāhīm, XIV:30; Sūra Saba', XXXIV:33; Sūra al-Zumar, XXXIX:8; Sūra Fuṣṣilat, XII:9.

11. Translator's note: The Arabic here is '*fa'l-mudabbirāti amran*'. The reference, according to most interpretations, is to the angels.

12. Translator's note: The author is referring here to the late medieval Christian practice of selling 'indulgences', one of the key issues provoking Martin Luther's protests against the Church, and thus an important element in the Protestant Reformation.

13. Translator's note: This distinction may also be viewed in terms of cataphatic (positive) and apophatic (negative) theology. One should not confuse the author's distinction between *jamāl* and *jalāl* with another commonly encountered form which this distinction takes, that is, the divine attributes of wrath, rigour and power on the one hand, subsumed under *jalāl*; and the attributes of mercy, gentleness and love on the other, subsumed under the category of *jamāl*.

14. Translator's note: One might also mention in this connection Sūra Fuṣṣilat, XLI:53: *We shall show them Our signs on the horizons and in their souls until it becomes clear to them that He is the Truth.*

15. Shaykh Ṣadūq, *Kitāb al-tawḥīd*, ch. 10, hadith no. 9.

16. Ibid., ch. 9, hadith no. 15.

17. Ibid., ch. 9, hadith no. 9.

18. al-Kulaynī, *al-Uṣūl min al-kāfī*, vol. 1, p. 109.

19. *Nahj al-balāgha*, Sermon no. 184.

20. Shaykh Ṣadūq, *Kitāb al-tawḥīd*, ch. 30, hadith no. 2.

21. *Nahj al-balāgha*, Sermon no. 179.

22. Translator's note: In Islamic religious sciences, *naqlī* knowledge, that is, knowledge transmitted by tradition, is contrasted with *ʿaqlī* knowledge, that knowledge to which the intellect has direct access.

23. See in this regard also Sūra al-Raʿd, XIII, 2; al-Sajda, XXXII, 4; al-Aʿrāf, VII, 54.

24. Shaykh Ṣadūq, *Kitāb al-tawḥīd* (ch. 61, hadith no.13, footnote 1).

25. Translator's note: The term *ʿadliyya* refers to both the Shiʿi and the Muʿtazili schools which stress justice as one of their key theological principles.

26. Translator's note: The author is alluding here to classical Ashʿarite theology, according to which: That is just which God does, and it is just because He does it.

27. The following explanation by the sage Naṣīr al-Dīn Ṭūsī, in his *Tajrīd al-iʿtiqād* (Sidon, 1353/1934), concerns this intellectual proof: 'If the means of proving good and evil were restricted to those means provided by religious rulings alone, the good and evil of acts would, in a general manner, cease to have any meaning, since they could be proved neither by intellectual nor by religious means.' (Maqṣad 3, faṣl 3, masʾala 1) Translator's note: This can be commented upon as follows: religious rulings on what is good or evil are in accordance with the principles of good and evil; and these principles in turn are discernible by the intellect. If the intellect were intrinsically incapable of this discernment, then the principles of good and evil become meaningless, being unprovable either by the intellect or religion: an act commanded by God would then be 'good' not because it is an expression of the universal principle of goodness, but only because it has been commanded by God.

28. Translator's note: The question dialectically posed to himself by the author is intended to probe the implications of the principle of the intelligibility of good and evil: if God's actions were to be evaluated in terms of the said principle, by being, as it were, 'accountable' to a higher principle—one that is posited by the human intellect—would it not be tantamount to subordinating God to man? The author's response is intended to show that the question is ill-posed, since the supposition that God could perform an evil act is grasped as an impossibility by the intellect: it is an innate function of the intellect to discern the infinite wisdom and, thus, the unimpeachable goodness of God, from whom all principles—spiritual, intellectual and moral—are derived.

29. Translator's note: 'Proof' here translates the Arabic *ḥujja*, which has the combined meanings of proof, evidence and argument; in other words, the totality of the self-evident truth of the divine message, against which no sane or rational person can have a counter-argument or an excuse for failing to submit thereto.

30. *Nahj al-balāgha*, saying no. 287.

31. Shaykh Ṣadūq, *Kitāb al-tawḥīd*, ch. 60, hadith no. 28; *Nahj al-balāgha*, Saying no. 88.

32. Aḥmad b. Zakarīya b. Fāris, *Muqāyis al-lugha* (Cairo, n.d.), vol. 5, pp. 63, 93. See also Rāghib al-Iṣfahānī, *al-Mufridāt fī gharīb al-Qur'ān* (Cairo, 1324/1906), on the two terms *qaḍā'* and *qadar*.

33. al-Kulaynī, *al-Uṣūl min al-kāfī*, vol. 1, p. 158.

34. al-Majlisī, *Biḥār al-anwār* (Beirut, 1403/1982), vol. 5, p. 96.

35. Shaykh Ṣadūq, *Kitāb al-tawḥīd*, ch. 59, hadith no. 8.

36. *Nahj al-balāgha*, Sermon no. 143.

37. One who followed this procedure was Qaysar, the Roman Emperor. See al-Ṭabarī's *Ta'rīkh al-rusul wa'l-mulūk* (Beirut, 1408/1987), vol. 3, p. 240, for the events of the sixth year after the Hijra.

38. Of course, divine revelation to the Prophet was not restricted to that brought about by the angel of revelation; there are other modes of revelation, as mentioned in Sūra al-Shuʿarā', XLII:51, and which was addressed in Article 38 above.

39. For a reference to this, see Rashīd Riḍā, *al-Waḥy al-Muḥammadī* (Beirut, 1406/1985), p. 66.

40. Translator's note: We would prefer to translate the Arabic term *ʿiṣma* as 'inerrancy' in contrast to what one increasingly finds as its translation, the word 'infallibility'. Neither English word, however, fully conveys the sense of this important concept. One needs to understand also its literal meaning, that of 'protection', implicitly, against sin and deviation; thus also 'impeccability' (from Latin: *im* = not, *peccare* = to sin). Because of the inadequacy of the English translations it is better to retain the Arabic both as regards this word and its derivative, *maʿṣūm*, the passive form, meaning one who has been rendered inerrant/impeccable by God; this being, as will be seen below, an attribute of the Prophets and, according to the Shiʿa, of the Imams of the *ahl al-bayt.*

41. Naṣīr al-Dīn Ṭusī, *Tajrīd al-iʿtiqād*, maqṣad 4, mas'ala 1.

42. The judgement of wisdom in this regard is clear. Therefore, some of the reports concerning the Prophet Job, relating to his undergoing

the trial of various repulsive diseases, are not only in direct contradiction with the decisive judgement of the intellect, but also stand in opposition to various sayings of the Imams. Imam Ṣādiq relates on the authority of his illustrious forefathers: 'The Prophet Job, throughout his illness, emitted no bad odour, nor did he become in any way ugly, nor did his body release any pus, blood or other substance such as might repel people. It is ever thus in the way of God for His Prophets and saints [never to be a source of repulsion for their people]. People distanced themselves from Job because of his poverty and his apparent weakness, but they were unaware of his lofty station in the divine proximity.' (Shaykh Ṣadūq, *al-Khiṣāl* (Qom, 1403/1982), vol. 1, hadith no. 107, p. 400). Naturally, any report that gives rise to an opposite view is unacceptable.

43. Sayyid Murtaḍā, *Tanzīh al-anbiyā'* (Tabriz, 1290/1873); Fakhr al-Dīn Rāzī, *'Iṣmat al-anbiyā'*, (Jeddah, 1407/1986); Sobhani, *Mafāhīm al-Qur'ān*, vol. 5 (section on the *'iṣma* of the Prophets).

44. al-Majlisī, *Biḥār al-anwār* (Beirut, 1403/1982) vol. 70, p. 22.

45. Imam 'Alī says, as regards such people: 'In relation to Heaven, such people are as those who have beheld it, and benefit from its graces; in relation to Hell, they are as those who have beheld it, and are undergoing its punishment.' *Nahj al-balāgha*, Sermon no. 193.

46. *Then she pointed to him. They said: How can we talk to one who is in the cradle, a young boy? He spoke: Lo! I am the slave of Allah. He hath given me the Scripture and hath appointed me a Prophet.* (Sūra Maryam, XIX:29)

47. Faḍl b. al-Ḥasan al-Ṭabarsī, *Majma' al-bayān* (Tehran, n.d.), vol. 5, p. 387.

48. See Sūra al-Naḥl, XVI:103.

49. al-Kulaynī, *al-Uṣūl min al-kāfī*, vol. 1, p. 59.

50. 'Abd al-Malik Ibn Hishām, *al-Sīra al-nabawiyya* (Beirut, n.d.) vol. 1, p. 209.

51. Ibn Hishām, *al-Sīra al-nabawiyya*, vol. 1, pp. 259–60.

52. In this connection, see the book by Muḥammad Ṣādiq Fakhr al-Islām, *Anīs al-a'lām fī nuṣrat al-islām* (Tehran, 1404/1983), where the references to the Prophet of Islam in the scriptures of the People of the Book have been collected.

53. Sūra Banī Isrā'īl, XVII:101.

54. Sūra Āl 'Imrān, III:49.

55. Sūra Banī Isrā'īl, XVII:1.

56. Sūra Āl 'Imrān, III:61.

57. Translator's note: The word *al-nās* can be translated either as 'mankind' or as 'people'.

58. The verses relating to finality are not restricted to what has been cited here; there are six other types of proof-text in the Qur'an on this point. See Ja'far Sobhani, *Mafāhīm al-Qur'ān,* vol. 3, pp. 130–9.

59. al-Bukhārī, *Ṣaḥīḥ,* vol. 3, pp. 54, 58; Muslim b. al-Ḥajjāj al-Qushayrī, *Ṣaḥīḥ* (Cairo, n.d.), vol. 2, p. 323 and vol. 4, pp. 1375, 1871; Shaykh Ṣadūq, *Amālī* (Beirut, 1400/1979) pp. 28, 47, 81; al-Majlisī, *Biḥār al-anwār,* vol. 37, pp. 254–89; Muḥammad b.'Īsā al-Tirmidhī, *Sunan* (Beirut, n.d.) vol. 2, p. 301; Ibn Hishām, *Sīra,* vol. 4, p. 162; Ibn Ḥanbal, *Musnad,* vol. 1, p. 174.

60. Translator's note: In the science of Hadith, *mutawātir* signifies the highest degree of authenticity that can be bestowed upon a saying of the Prophet, a saying which is confirmed by multiple chains of transmission.

61. Translator's note: *Ijtihād* literally means 'exertion'; in jurisprudence, it refers to the effort made by a jurist through his own reasoning to deduce an appropriate ruling from the primary sources of the Shari'a, where the ruling is not immediately and incontrovertibly evident from these sources. It is generally held that the 'door' of *ijtihād* was closed in the 4th/5th century AH for the Sunni schools, but the Shi'i school have always kept the 'door' open, as the author will go on to discuss below.

62. Gustav LeBon, *Tamaddun-i islāmī wa gharb,* Persian trans. of *Islamic Civilization and the West* (Tehran, 1376/1956), pp. 141–3.

63. *Nahj al-balāgha,* Sermon no. 3.

64. *Nahj al-balāgha,* Sermon no.171.

65. The following authorities can be referred to regarding this matter: 1) Faḍl b. Shādhān, (d. 260/873 AH; he lived in the time of the Imams), *Kitāb al-Īdāḥ,* p. 217; 2) Shaykh Ṣadūq (d. 381/991), *Kitāb al-i'tiqādāt,* p. 93; 3) Shaykh Mufīd (d. 413/1022), *Majmū'at al-rasā'il,* p. 266; 4) Shaykh Murtaḍā (d. 436/1044), *Jawāb al-masā'il al-tarabilsiyyāt;* 5) Shaykh Ṭūsī (d. 460/1067), *Kitāb al-tibyān,* vol. 1, p. 3; 6) Shaykh al-Ṭabarsī (d. 548/1153), *Majma' al-bayān* (see his introduction where he clearly stresses the absence of any possibility of alteration with regard to the Qur'an); 7) Sayyid b. Ṭāwūs (d. 664/1265), *Sa'd al-su'ūd,* p. 144 (where he says: 'The non-existence of alteration—such is the position of the Imāmiyya); 8) 'Allāma Ḥillī (d. 726/1325), *Ujūbat al-masā'il al-mihnā'iyya,* p. 121 (where he says: 'This is the truth: that no addition or

diminution has been effected in regard to the Qur'an, and I seek protection from God against speaking the word "alteration" (*taḥrīf*); for such an idea causes doubt to be cast on the miracle that was authentically transmitted to us by the Holy Prophet.').

66. See Aḥmad al-Najāshī, *Rijāl al-Najāshī* (Beirut, 1409/1988) vol. 1, no. 190, p. 211.

67. al-Najāshī, *Rijāl*, vol. 1, no. 689, p. 96.

68. Ayatollah Ruḥollāh Khumaynī, *Tahdhīb al-uṣūl* (Qom 1405/1984), vol. 2, p. 96.

69. *Qāf. By the Glorious Qur'ān* ... (Sūra Qāf, L:1); ... *This is indeed a noble Qur'an, in a hidden Book* (Sūra al-Wāqi'a, LVI:77–78); *Yā Sīn. By the wise Qur'an...* (Sūra Yā Sīn, XXXVI:1–2)

70. Jalāl al-Dīn al-Suyūṭī, *al-Itqān fī 'ulūm al-Qur'ān*, (Cairo, 1387/1967) vol. 11, p. 85.

71. al-Kulaynī, *al-Uṣūl min al-kāfī*, vol. 1, p. 241.

72. Muḥammad b. Ḥasan al-Ṣaffār, *Baṣā'ir al-darajāt* (Tehran, 1380/1960), p. 195.

73. Translator's note: See note 40 above for the meaning of *ma'ṣūm* and *'iṣma.*

74. Translator's note: It is important to recall, in the ensuing discussion, that the word *khalīfa* literally means 'successor', and is not just the title of the leaders of the Muslim community after the Prophet's death.

75. al-Ḥasan b. Mūsā al-Nawbakhtī, *Firaq al-Shī'a* (Beirut, 1405/1984), p. 17.

76. 'Alī b. Ismā'īl al-Ash'arī, *Maqālāt al-Islāmiyyīn* (Wiesbaden, 1980), vol. 1, p. 65.

77. 'Abd al-Karīm al-Shahrastānī, *al-Milal wa'l-niḥal* (Beirut, 1990), vol. 1, p. 131.

78. Translator's note: The author is referring here to, firstly, the idea that Shi'ism was born as a protest movement against the installation of Abū Bakr as the caliph, an event that occurred immediately after the death of the Prophet at the assembly hall called the Saqīfa of Banī Sa'āda; and secondly, to the idea that Shi'ism appeared only after the murder of the third Caliph, 'Uthmān, and the popular acclaim that swept 'Alī into power as the fourth Caliph. See Jafri, *Origins and Early Development of Shi'a Islam*, chapters 1–4 for extended discussion of the points being made here.

79. Jalāl al-Dīn al-Suyūṭī, *al-Durr al-manthūr* (Beirut, 1973), vol. 8, p.

589, as transmitted by Jābir b. ʿAbd Allāh, Ibn Saʿīd al-Khudrī, Ibn ʿAbbās and ʿAlī.

80. Ibn Sīnā, *al-Shifāʾ* (Qom, n.d.), article 10 of the *ilāhiyyāt*, chapter 5, p. 564.

81. Ibn Ḥanbal, *Musnad*, vol. 1, p. 159; al-Ṭabarī, *Taʾrīkh al-rusul waʾl-mulūk* (Beirut, 1408/1986–7), vol. 2, p. 406; al-Ṭabarī, *Jāmiʿ al-bayān* (Beirut, 1980), vol. 19, pp. 74–5 (commentary on Sūra al-Shuʿarāʾ, XXVI:214).

82. al-Bukhārī, *Ṣaḥīḥ*, vol. 6, p. 3 (edition of 1314/1895–6), in the section on the war of Tabuk; Muslim, *Ṣaḥīḥ*, vol. 7, p. 120, (chapter on the virtues of ʿAlī); Ibn Māja, *Sunan* (Beirut, 1975) vol. 1, p. 55, (chapter on the virtues of the companions); Ibn Ḥanbal, *Musnad*, vol. 1, pp. 173, 175, 177, 179, 182, 230; Ibn Hishām, *Sīra*, vol. 4, p. 163.

83. *'And We bestowed upon him of Our Mercy his brother Aaron, a Prophet.'* (Sūra Maryam, XIX:53).

84. *'And when Moses said to his brother Aaron: Take my place* (ukhlufnī) *among the people.'* (Sūra al-Aʿrāf, VII:142).

85. *'Appoint for me a minister* (wazīr) *from my folk.'* (Sūra Ṭā Hā, XX:29).

86. Recorded in Muḥammad b.ʿAbd Allāh al-Ḥākim al-Naysābūrī, *al-Mustadrak* (Beirut, n.d.), vol. 3, p. 351; Aḥmad b. Ḥijr, *al-Ṣawāʿiq al-muḥriqa* (Cairo, 1965) p. 91; Muḥammad al-Dhahabī, *Mīzān al-iʿtidāl* (Beirut, 1963), vol. 1, p. 224; Jalāl al-Dīn al-Suyūṭī, *Taʾrīkh al-khulafāʾ* (Cairo, 1964), p. 573, and *al-Khaṣāʾiṣ al-kubrā* (Hyderabad, 1319/1900), vol. 2, p. 266; Sulaymān b. Ibrāhīm al-Qandūzī, *Yanābīʿ al-muwadda* (Tehran, 1416/1995) p. 28; Muḥammad b. ʿAlī al-Shawkānī, *Fatḥ al-qadīr*, (Beirut, n.d.), p. 113; and other books.

87. This is to be understood according to the verse: *'By the stars they are guided'* (Sūra al-Naḥl, XVI:16)—the stars provide the light wherewith those at sea can navigate and find their way to the safety of the shore.

88. Ḥākim, *Mustadrak*, vol. 3, p. 149.

89. Muslim, *Ṣaḥīḥ*, vol. 7, p. 122; al-Tirmidhī, *Sunan*, vol. 2, p. 307; ʿAbd Allāh al-Dārimī, *Sunan* (Beirut, 1978), vol. 2, p. 432; Ibn Ḥanbal, *Musnad*, vol. 3, pp. 14, 17, 26, 59; vol. 4, pp. 366, 371; vol. 5, pp. 182, 189; Aḥmad b. Shuʿayb al-Nisāʾī, *Khaṣāʾiṣ al-imām ʿAlī* (Qom, 1983) p. 20; Ḥākim, *Mustadrak*, vol. 3, pp. 109, 148, 533; and other books. In this connection, one can also refer to treatises on this hadith in the publications of the *Dār al-taqrīb bayn al-madhāhib al-islāmiyya* (Office of

Reconciliation between the Legal Schools of Islam), under the imprint of *Mukhaymir.*

90. Scholars of Hadith and Qur'anic commentary have alluded to the descent of this verse after the end of the Prophet's final pilgrimage, on the day of Ghadīr. See al-Suyūṭī, *al-Durr al-manthūr,* vol. 2, p. 298; al-Shawkānī, *Fatḥ al-qadīr,* vol. 2, p. 57, 'Alī b. 'Īsā al-Arbalī, *Kashf al-ghima fī ma'rifat al-a'imma,* (Beirut, 1985), p. 94; al-Qandūzī, *Yanābī' al-muwadda,* p. 120; Rashīd Riḍā, *Tafsīr al-manār,* (Cairo, 1954), vol. 6, p. 463; and others.

91. Translator's note: The Arabic word here is *awlā,* which literally means 'closest' but in the present context it is, rather, the sense of 'claim upon' or 'right over' that the author wishes to stress. The Qur'an has the sentence, *'al-nabiyy awlā bi'l-mu'minīn min anfusihim'* (XXXIII:6), which can be translated as *'the Prophet is closer to* (or: *has a greater claim upon*) *the believers than their own selves.'*

92. Translator's note: *Mawlā* has a range of connotations, spiritual and temporal, over which much debate and dispute has taken place. The author goes into the question of the meaning of the term below. It is difficult to translate it by one word, since it combines the ideas of 'master' and 'protector' with those of 'nearest' and 'dearest'.

93. A group among the companions and the following generation understood this verse to relate to the event of Ghadīr, amongst them being: Abū Sa'īd al-Khudrī, Zayd b. Arqam, Jābir b. 'Abd Allāh al-Anṣārī, Abū Hurayra and Mujāhid al-Makkī. For the narrations of these individuals regarding the event in question, see 'Abd al-Ḥusayn al-Amīnī, *al-Ghadīr* (Beirut, 1387 /1967), vol.1, pp. 230–3, which gives relevant citations from *Kitāb al-wilāya* of Abū Ja'far al-Ṭabarī, *Kitāb al-manāqib* of Khaṭīb Khwārazmī, *Mā nuzila min al-qur'ān fī 'Alī* of Hāfiẓ Abū Nu'aym Iṣfahānī, and *al-Wilāya* of Abū Sa'īd al-Sijistānī; see also Khaṭīb al-Baghdādī, *Ta'rīkh Baghdād* (Beirut, n.d.); and al-Suyūṭī, *al-Durr al-manthūr,* vol. 2, p. 295, (for the narrations of Ibn 'Asākir al-Shāfi'ī).

94. Fakhr al-Dīn al-Rāzī says in his *al-Tafsīr al-kabīr* (Beirut, n.d.), vol. 3. p. 369, that after the descent of this verse, the Holy Prophet lived for not more than 81 or 82 days, and the verse was not subject to abrogation or any other kind of amendment. Therefore, this verse must have been revealed on the day of Ghadīr, which would have been the 18th of Dhī'l-Ḥijja, in the year of the Farewell Pilgrimage. Considering that, according

to the Sunnis, the Prophet passed away on the 12th of Rabīʿ al-Awwal, this would accord with the figure of 82 days precisely.

95. Ibn Hishām, *Sīra*, vol. 2, p. 422.

96. Translator's note: This term *ahl al-ḥall wa'l-ʿaqd* denotes those deemed to have some degree of authority in the community.

97. ʿAbd Allāh b. Muslim Dīnawarī, *al-Imāma wa'l-siyāsa* (Cairo, n.d.), vol. 1, p. 32.

98. Abū Nuʿaym al-Iṣfahānī, *Ḥilyat al-awliyā'* (Beirut, 1967), vol. 1, p. 44.

99. Rashīd Riḍā, *al-Waḥy al-Muḥammadī* (Beirut, 1406/1985), p. 212.

100. Jaʿfar Sobhani, *al-Ilāhiyyāt*, (Qom, 1417/1995) vol. 2, pp. 146–98.

101. See Sūra al-Mā'ida, v:6: '... *but He wills to purify you*'. This comes after mention of the ritual ablution.

102. Ḥākim, *Mustadrak*, vol. 2, p. 151; al-Suyūṭī, *al-Khaṣā'iṣ al-kubrā*, vol. 2, p. 266.

103. For all the narrations in this regard, see such Hadith compilations as *al-Uṣūl min al-kāfī*, *Kifāyat al-athar*, *Ithbāt al-hudā* and *Muntakhab al-athar*.

104. '*Lā yazālu'l-dīn manīʿan ilā ithnāʿashara khalīfa.*' [The other version reads:] '*Lā yazālu'l-dīn ʿazīzan ilā ithnāʿashara khalīfa.*'

105. Muslim, *Ṣaḥīḥ*, vol. 6, p. 3 (*Kitāb al-amāra*); Ibn Ḥanbal, *Musnad*, vol. 5, p. 86, 108; Ḥākim, *Mustadrak*, vol. 3, p. 18; and others.

106. There are slightly different reports as regards the dates of the births and deaths of the Imams, one version of which we have presented above; we know that in the majority of cases they met their death as martyrs, as has been recorded in historical accounts.

107. Translator's note: This is the name of an extremist Khārijite sect of the first century AH.

108. Ibn Ḥanbal, *Musnad*, vol. 1, p. 99, vol. 3, pp. 17, 70.

109. Translator's note: The author refers to Moses as a 'saint of God' (*waliyyu'Llāh*) since all Prophets are, by definition, saints, while not all saints are Prophets.

110. See Sūra al-Kahf, XVIII:71–82 [where the three apparently unjustified acts of al-Khiḍr are described and then shown to be beneficient in their outcome].

111. Shaykh Ṣadūq, *Kamāl al-dīn* (Qom, 1405/1983), ch. 45, hadith no. 4.

112. Shaykh Ṣadūq, *Kamāl al-dīn*, ch. 14, hadith nos 8, 9, 10.

113. al-Majlisī, *Biḥār al-anwār*, vol. 52, pp. 102–14.

114. Naṣīr al-Dīn Ṭūsī alludes to this point in his *Tajrīd al-iʿtiqād*: 'His being is a grace and his disposition is another grace; and his non-existence comes only from ourselves.' (Maqṣad 5, masʿala 1)

115. Shaykh Ṣadūq, *Tajrīd al-iʿtiqādāt*, ch. 17, p. 37.

116. Shaykh Mufīd, *Taṣḥīḥ al-iʿtiqād* (Tabriz, 1371/1950–1), pp. 45–6.

117. Naṣīr al-Dīn Ṭūsī, *Tajrīd al-iʿtiqād*, maqṣad 6, mas'ala 14.

118. See Aḥmad b. Ḥanbal, *al-Sunna*, (Beirut, 1405/1983); Abū'l-Ḥasan al-Ashʿarī, *al-Ibāna ʿan uṣūl al-diyāna* (Damascus, 1981); and Qāḍī ʿAbd al-Jabbār al-Muʿtazilī, *Sharḥ al-uṣūl al-khamsa* (Cairo, 1988).

119. It must be borne in mind that the spirit of man will be attached to a complete body at the Resurrection; there is here a clear incompatibility with the idea of reincarnation, which would have the spirit attach itself to a foetus.

120. See ʿAllāma Abū Manṣūr Ḥasan al-Ḥillī, *Kashf al-murād fī sharḥ tajrīd al-iʿtiqād* (Qom, 1413/1992), maqṣad 2, faṣl 4, mas'ala 8; and Ṣadr al-Dīn al-Shīrāzī, *al-Asfār al-arbaʿ*, vol. 9, p. 10.

121. See also Sūra al-Aʿrāf, VII:166: '*We said unto them: Be ye apes despised*'.

122. *We said unto them: Be ye apes, despised. And We made it an example to their own and to succeeding generations, and an admonition to the God-fearing.* (Sūra al-Baqara, II:65–66)

123. Masʿūd b. ʿUmar al-Taftāzānī, *Sharḥ al-maqāṣid* (Istanbul, 1305/1886), vol. 3, p. 337.

124. Allāma Ṭabāṭabā'ī, *al-Mīzān*, vol. 1, p. 209.

125. See Aḥmad Amīn Miṣrī, *Fajr al-Islām* (Beirut, 1969), p. 377.

126. Sūra Āl ʿImrān, III:49.

127. Sūra al-Baqara, II:259.

128. Therefore the verse '*It is but one shout, and behold them brought together before Us*' (Sūra Yā Sīn, XXXVI:53), is a clarification of the reality of the blowing of the trumpet referred to in verse 51 of the same Sūra, '*And the trumpet is blown and lo! from the graves they hie unto their Lord*'. This verse means that the second blast of the trumpet is a 'shout', after which all will suddenly be brought before God.

129. *There is not one of you but shall approach it. That is a fixed ordinance from thy Lord. Then We shall rescue those who kept from evil, and leave the evil-doers crouching there.* (Sūra Maryam, XIX:71–2)

130. 'Allāma Ṭabāṭabā'ī, *al-Mīzān*, vol. 13, pp. 191–2; Shaykh al-Ṭabarsī *Majma' al-bayān*, vol. 10, p. 549.

131. Shaykh Ṣadūq, *Man la yaḥḍuruhu'l-faqīh* (Tehran, 1390) vol. 3, p. 376.

132. Shaykh Ṣadūq, *al-Khiṣāl*, ch. 5; al-Bukhārī, *Ṣaḥīḥ*, vol. 1, p. 42; Ibn Ḥanbal, *Musnad*, vol. 1, p. 103.

133. Shaykh Mufīd, *Awā'il al-maqālāt fī'l-madhāhib wa'l-mukhtārāt* (Tabriz, 1371/1951), p. 54.

134. Muslim, *Ṣaḥīḥ*, vol. 3, p. 54.

135. Tirmidhī, *Ṣaḥīḥ*, vol. 4, p. 42.

136. *They said: O our father, ask forgiveness of our sins for us, for truly we were sinful. He said: I shall ask forgiveness for you of My Lord ...* (Sūra Yūsuf, XII:97–98)

137. 'Allāma al-Ḥillī, *Kashf al-murād*, maqṣad 6, mas'ala 7.

138. Translator's note: This is the literal meaning of *takfīr*, the verbal noun of the second form of the triliteral root k-f-r, *kaffara*, to 'cover over', in this context, the 'covering over' of sin, thus, expiation of sin by God; it is not to be confused with the other main meaning of the word *takfīr*, which is 'to judge someone a *kāfir*'. The Qur'anic use of *kaffara* is clear from the verse cited above from Sūra al-Nisā', IV:31.

139. al-Majlisī, *Biḥār al-anwār*, vol. 8, ch. 27, hadith no.1.

140. Shaykh Mufīd, *Awā'il al-maqālāt*, p. 141.

**Chapter Three: Faith, Disbelief and Other Issues**

1. al-Kulaynī, *al-Uṣūl min al-kāfī*, vol. 2, p. 33, hadith no. 2.

2. Shaykh Ṣadūq, *'Uyūn akhbār al-Riḍā* (Beirut, 1404/1983), vol. 1, p. 226.

3. al-Bukhārī, *Ṣaḥīḥ*, vol. 1, p. 16.

4. 'Alā' al-Dīn al-Hindī, *Kanz al-'ummāl* (Beirut, 1985), vol. 1, hadith no. 30.

5. al-Majlisī, *Biḥār al-anwār*, vol. 2, p. 263; Ibn Ḥanbal, *Musnad*, vol. 4, pp. 126–7.

6. al-Majlisī, *Biḥār al-anwār*, vol. 74, p. 202.

7. Ibn Ḥajar al-'Asqalānī, *Fatḥ al-bārī* (Beirut, 1402/1981), vol. 5, p. 156, vol. 17, p. 9.

8. Ibn Athīr, *Jāmi' al-uṣūl* (Beirut, 1980), vol. 1, p. 238. In article 131 we shall discuss briefly the question of cultivating love for the Holy Prophet and his family.

9. al-Ṭabarī, *Jāmiʿ al-bayān*, vol. 3, p. 153; al-Rāzī, *Tafsīr*, vol. 8, p. 113; ʿAbd Allāh al-Nasafī, *Tafsīr al-Nasafī* (Beirut, 1419/1998), vol. 1, p. 271; Maḥmūd Ālūsī, *Rūḥ al-maʿānī* (Beirut, n.d.), vol. 3, p. 121; Shaykh al-Ṭabarsī, *Majmaʿ al-bayān*, vol. 1, p. 430.

10. al-Rāzī, *Tafsīr*, vol. 8, p. 13.

11. Muḥammad Jamāl al-Dīn al-Qāsimī, *Maḥāsin al-taʾwīl* (Beirut, 1399/1979), vol. 4, p. 82.

12. See al-Ṭabarī, *Taʾrīkh*, vol. 7, pp. 195–206.

13. Rāghib al-Iṣfahānī in his *Mufridāt* (under the word '*wasala*', 'means') writes: 'A "means" brings about the achievement of a desired object; and the reality of the "means" for reaching God is to scrupulously follow His path, through knowledge and worship of Him, while observing the noble principles of the Law.'

14. See al-Bukhārī, *Ṣaḥīḥ*, vol. 5 (ch. on 'The killing of Abū Jahl'); and Ibn Hishām, *Sīra*, vol. 2, p. 292, among other sources.

15. Muslim, *Ṣaḥīḥ*, vol. 2 (ch. on 'What is said when entering the grave').

16. al-Bukhārī, *Ṣaḥīḥ*, vol. 2 (ch. on 'Funerals'), p. 17.

17. *Nahj al-balāgha*, Sermon no. 235.

18. al-Suyūṭī, *al-Durr al-manthūr*, vol. 3, p. 66.

19. al-Kulaynī, *al-Uṣūl min al-kāfī*, vol. 2, p. 470.

20. al-Bukhārī, *Ṣaḥīḥ*, vol. 4, p. 172.

21. Shaykh Ṣadūq, *Kitāb al-tawḥīd*, ch. 54; Shaykh Mufīd, *Taṣḥīḥ al-iʿtiqād*, p. 24; Muḥammad b. Ḥasan al-Ṭūsī, *ʿIddat al-uṣūl* (Qom, 1404/1983), vol. 2, p. 29; Muḥammad b. Ḥasan al-Ṭūsī, *Kitāb al-ghayba* (Najaf, 1385/1965), pp. 262–4. Translator's note: A useful discussion of this concept, especially insofar as the 'delay' or 'postponement' of the fulfilment of prophecies is concerned within Shiʿism, can also be found in Sachedina, *Islamic Messianism*, pp. 152–8.

22. See Sūra al-Baqara, II:55–56, for mention of the revival of a group amongst the People of Israel; verses 72–73 for the revival, by means of the cow of Moses, of those killed amongst the People of Israel; verse 243 for the death and revival of another group of people; verse 259 for the revival of Uzayr after one hundred years; and Sūra Āl ʿImrān, III: 49, for the miraculous revival of the dead by Jesus.

23. al-Majlisī, *Biḥār al-anwār*, vol. 53, p. 136. Translator's note: See Sachedina, *Islamic Messianism*, pp. 166–73, for further discussion of the doctrine of *rajʿa*.

24. See Sūra al-Tawba, ix: 100; Sūra al-Fatḥ, xlviii:18–29; Sūra al-Ḥashr, lix: 8–9.

25. Sūra Āl 'Imrān, iii:153–154; Sūra al-Aḥzāb, xxxiii:12; Sūra al-Tawba, ix:45–47.

26. Ibn Athīr, *Jāmi' al-uṣūl*, vol. 11, Book of Ḥawḍ, hadith no. 7972.

27. al-Bukhārī, *Ṣaḥīḥ*, vol. 5 (commentary on Sūra al-Nūr), pp. 118–19.

28. al-Hindī, *Kanz al-'ummāl*, vol. 1, hadith nos 70, 72; Ibn Athīr, *Jāmi' al-uṣūl*, vol. 1, p. 238.

29. Ibid.

30. Ḥāfiẓ Muḥammad b. Sulaymān al-Kūfī, *Manāqib al-Imām Amīr al-Mu'minīn* (Qom, 1412/1991), vol. 2, hadith no. 619, 700; al-Majlisī, *Biḥār al-anwār*, vol. 17, p. 13; Shaykh Ṣadūq, *'Ilal al-sharāyi'* (Beirut, 1966), ch. 117, hadith no. 3.

31. Ibid.

32. Cited by 'Abbās al-Qummī, *Safīnat al-biḥār* (Qom, 1416/1995), vol. 1, p. 199.

33. Ḥusayn b. Muḥammad Diyār Bakrī, *Ta'rīkh al-khamīs fī aḥwāl anfus nafīs* (Beirut, n.d.), vol. 1, p. 223.

34. Aḥmad b. Muḥammad al-Qastallānī, *al-Mawāhib al-laduniyya* (Beirut, 1412/1991), vol. 21, p. 27.

35. Sūra Yūsuf, xii:184.

36. Ibn Hishām, *Sīra*, vol. 1, p. 99.

37. Ibid. See also Aḥmad b. 'Alī al-Maqrīzī, *Imtā' al-asmā'* (Cairo, 1981), vol. 11, p. 164.

38. al-Suyūṭī, *al-Durr al-manthūr*, vol. 5, p. 203.

39. Translator's note: For the Qur'anic story regarding certain youths who were kept hidden, miraculously, by God in a cave, see Sūra al-Kahf (xviii: 9–26).

40. Ibn Māja, *Sunan*, vol. 1 (ch. on the visiting of graves), p. 113.

41. Muslim, *Ṣaḥīḥ*, vol. 3 (ch. on what is said when entering graveyards), p. 64.

42. Shaykh Mufīd, *Taṣḥīḥ al-i'tiqād*, p. 109.

43. al-Majlisī, *Biḥār al-anwār*, vol. 25, p. 364.

44. Ibid., p. 265.

45. Shaykh Ṣadūq, *Kitāb al-tawḥīd*, ch.1, hadith nos 21, 22, 23.

46. al-Majlisī, *Biḥār al-anwār*, vol. 18, p. 26.

47. al-Bukhārī, *Ṣaḥīḥ*, vol. 2, p. 149.

48. As regards the *muḥaddath* and the limits [of this possibility], see among other works, the book by al-Qastallānī, *Kitāb irshād al-sārī fī sharḥ ṣaḥīḥ al-Bukhārī*, vol. 6, p. 99.

49. Translator's note: See the article entitled *al-uṣūl al-arbaʿumiʾa* in Kohlberg, *Belief and Law*, VII, pp. 128–61.

50. Aḥmad b. ʿAlī al-Maqrīzī, *al-Mawāʿiẓ wa'l-iʿtibār bi dhikr al-khiṭaṭ wa'l-āthār* (Būlāq, 1270/1853), vol. 2, p. 344.

51. Translator's note: The word *farʿ* (pl. *furūʿ*), which literally means 'branch', in this context means 'detail', and is juxtaposed with *aṣl* (pl. *uṣūl*), which literally means 'root' and also signifies 'principle'.

52. Translator's note: The reading of *jarr* would have the word *arjulakum* read as *arjulikum*, that is, in the form of *majrūr*, the genitive case, with a *kasra* (an 'i') after the letter *lām*, indicating that it is governed by a preposition, in this case, the preposition *bi*, which governs *ru'ūsikum*, as in the construction *bi ruʾūsikum*; the reading of *nasb*, the ordinary reading of the verse, is to have the word *arjulakum* in the accusative case, *mansūb*, that is with a *fatḥa* (an 'a') after the *lām*.

53. Translator's note: The word *masjid*, commonly translated as 'mosque', literally means a place where one prostrates, being derived from the word *sajada*, to prostrate.

54. al-Bukhārī, *Ṣaḥīḥ*, vol. 1, p. 91, *Kitāb al-tayammum*, hadith no. 2.

55. Translator's note: The *tayammum* refers to the use of earth or a stone for purification in the ablution, when no water is available.

56. al-ʿĀmilī, *Wasāʾil al-Shīʿa*, vol. 3, ch.1, hadith no. 1, p. 591.

57. Ibn Ḥanbal, *Musnad*, vol. 3, p. 327; al-Bayhaqī, *Sunan*, vol. 1, p. 439.

58. al-Hindī, *Kanz al-ʿummāl*, vol. 7, p. 465, hadith no. 1981.

59. al-Bayhaqī, *Sunan*, vol. 2, p. 105.

60. Ibn Ḥanbal, *Musnad*, vol. 6, pp. 179, 309, 331, 377; vol. 2, pp. 192–7.

61. al-Bukhārī, *Ṣaḥīḥ*, vol. 1, p. 101; Muslim, *Ṣaḥīḥ*, vol. 1, p. 109.

62. The preferred time of the *ẓuhr* prayer is from the moment the sun begins to decline to the time that the shadow of an indicator of a sun-dial is as long as the indicator itself; the preferred time of the *ʿaṣr* prayer is until the shadow of the indicator is twice as long as the indicator.

63. al-ʿĀmilī, *Wasāʾil al-Shīʿa*, vol. 3, ch. 4, narration no. 1.

64. Ibid., vol. 3, ch. 4, narration no. 4.

65. Ibid., vol. 3, ch. 4, narration no. 6.

66. Muslim, *Ṣaḥīḥ*, vol. 2, p. 151, chapter, "On the joining together of the two prayers whilst at home".

67. See the commentary of Zarqānī on the *Muwaṭṭa'* of Imam Mālik on the joining together of the two prayers whilst at home and journeying, Muḥammad b. 'Abd al-Bāqī al-Zarqānī, *Sharḥ Zarqānī* (Cairo, n.d.), p. 294.

68. Translator's note: It is the principle of joining the two sets of prayers that is being stressed here; according to Shiʿi *fiqh*, it is preferable, if the two evening prayers are to be joined, that they be prayed at the time of *maghrib*, not *'ishā'*, although it is permissible to join them at the time of *'ishā'* also.

69. Translator's note: See Appendix II on temporary marriage written by S.H. Nasr in 'Allāma Ṭabāṭabā'ī's *Shiʿite Islam*.

70. 'Alā' al-Dīn al-Qūshajī, *Sharḥ tajrīd al-iʿtiqād* (Tabriz, 1307/1889), p. 464.

71. al-Bukhārī, *Ṣaḥīḥ*, vol. 6, p. 27, section on *Tafsīr*, the end of verse 196 of Sūra al-Baqara.

72. al-ʿĀmilī, *Wasā'il al-Shīʿa*, vol. 4, ch. 15, hadith no. 7.

73. al-Bayhaqī, *Sunan*, vol. 2, pp. 72, 73, 101, 102; Abū Dāwūd, *Sunan*, vol. 1, p. 196, hadith no. 730, 736; Tirmidhī, *Sunan*, vol. 2, p. 98.

74. al-ʿĀmilī, *Wasā'il al-Shīʿa*, 4, ch. 1, hadith no. 81.

75. al-ʿAsqalānī, *Fatḥ al-bārī*, vol. 2, p. 224; Bayhaqī, *Sunan*, vol. 2, p. 28.

76. Muḥammad b. Ḥasan al-Ṭūsī, *al-Khilāf* (Qom, 1416/1995), *Kitāb al-ṣalāt*, question no. 268.

77. Shaykh Ṣadūq, *al-Khiṣāl*, vol. 2, p. 152.

78. Shaykh Ṣadūq, *'Uyūn akhbār al-Riḍā*, vol. 2, p. 124.

79. al-Qastallānī, *Irshād al-sārī*, vol. 3, p. 226; Muḥammad b. Aḥmad Badr al-ʿAyn, *'Umdat al-qārī fī sharḥ ṣaḥīḥ al-Bukhārī* (Beirut, n.d), vol. 11, p. 126; Ibrāhīm b. Mūsā al-Shāṭibī, *al-Iʿtiṣām* (Beirut, 1996), vol. 2, p. 291.

80. See *Lisān al-ʿarab*, under the word *ghanam*; a similar meaning is given by Ibn Athīr in his *al-Nihāya*, and by al-Fīrūzābādī in his *Qāmūs al-lugha*. Translator's note: The books referred to here are classical Arabic lexicons.

81. al-Bukhārī, *Ṣaḥīḥ*, vol. 4, p. 250.

82. al-ʿĀmilī, *Wasā'il al-Shīʿa*, vol. 6, *Kitāb al-khums*, ch. 1.

83. There are certain differences between the two schools of

jurisprudence as regards the legal force of testamentary wills in which legacies are bequeathed to stipulated heirs. Also, *ʿawl* and *taʿṣīb* are disallowed in the rulings of Shiʿi *fiqh* and the difficulties attendant upon these two cases [which pertain to the amount of a legacy that is left over after the proportions stipulated by the Shariʿa have been allotted to their respective heirs] are resolved in a different way, as has been explained in the books of *fiqh*.

84. al-Najāshī, *Rijāl*, no. 79.

85. Ibn al-Nadīm, *al-Fihrist* (Cairo, n.d); al-Najāshī, *Rijāl*; Shaykh Muḥammad b. Ḥasan al-Ṭūsī, *al-Fihrist* (Najaf, 1380/1960); Āghā Buzurg Ṭihrānī, *al-Dharīʿa ilā taṣānīf al-Shīʿa* (Beirut, n.d.); Muḥsin Amīn, *Aʿyān al-Shīʿa* (Beirut, 1982); al-Shahrastānī, *al-Milal wa'l-niḥal*, Part 6.

# Glossary

*ʿadl*: justice; one of the foundational principles of Shiʿite theology, the others being Divine Unity, Prophecy, Imamate and the Hereafter.

*ʿadliyya*: a designation of those theologians who regard divine justice (*ʿadl*, q.v.) as a central theological perspective, normally taken as a reference to the Shiʿi and Muʿtazili schools.

*ahl al bayt*: 'the folk of the household [of the Prophet]', the precise members of which are defined in different ways. In Shiʿism referring, principally, to the Prophet and his immediate family, that is ʿAlī, Fāṭima, Ḥasan and Ḥusayn, (occasionally including Salmān al-Fārisī), and extending to all the Imams. It is one of the designations of the Shiʿi school of thought. In Sunnism, the term refers, in addition to the immediate members of the Prophet's family, to his wives also. See Qur'an, XXXIII: 33, for the verse in which the term occurs and over the referents to which there is disagreement between the two schools.

*ʿaqlī*: intellectual; referring, in the traditional classification of Islamic knowledge, to those sciences that are directly accessible by the intellect, as opposed to those which are of a revealed nature and are transmitted by tradition, termed *naqlī* (q.v.).

*ashrāṭ al-sāʿa*: 'the portents of the hour', signs of the imminence of the final Judgement.

*ʿāshūrā'*: the tenth day of the month of Muḥarram, during which the martyrdom of the Prophet's grandson Ḥusayn and seventy-two of his close relations and companions at Karbala in the year 61/680 is commemorated.

*awlawiyya*: precedence.

*awliyā'*: (s. *walī*) literally 'friends', implying 'friends of God', thus saints; also refers in Shiʿism more specifically to the Imams.

*badā'*: a complex theological doctrine whereby a certain alterability is attributed to the manifestation of divine decrees, this being held to explain apparent changes in one's destiny.

*barzakh*: the intermediary domain, 'barrier', or 'isthmus' between this world and the domain of Heaven and Hell.

*bidʿa*: literally, innovation; in terms of the Shariʿa any unprecedented action to which religious sanction is wrongly attributed.

*biʿtha*: the prophetic mission.

*dhāt*: essence; in Islamic theology, the Essence of God, as opposed to the *ṣifāt*, qualities.

*duʿā'*: petitionary prayer; personal supplication.

*faqīh*: jurisprudent.

*fiqh*: Islamic jurisprudence; divided into *uṣūl* (q.v.), 'principles' and *furūʿ* (q.v.), 'details'.

*fiṭra*: the original, primordial, normative nature of the human state, as fashioned by God as *al-Fāṭir*, 'The Originator', this being one of the divine names.

*furūʿ*: literally, 'branches' (s. *farʿ*); pertaining to the applications, subdivisions, details, of primary principles, *uṣūl* (q.v.) in the domain of jurisprudence (*fiqh*, q.v.).

*ghayba*: a state of occultation or hiddenness; in Shiʿism, the state in which the Twelfth Imam subsists until his re-appearance in the outer world to re- establish true Islam and justice worldwide as the awaited Mahdi (q.v.).

*ghulūw*: exaggeration, extremism; a term used by both Sunnis and Shiʿis to refer to those excesses of glorification of the Imams which entailed, for a group of Shiʿis (*ghulāt*, s. *ghālī*), the transgression of certain basic Islamic norms and principles.

*ḥādith*: originated in time (as opposed to *qadīm*, eternal).

*ḥarām*: 'prohibited', one of the five categories of Islamic law, pertaining to actions, the others being *wājib* (obligatory), *mustaḥabb* (recommended), *mubāḥ* (indifferent) and *makrūh* (discouraged).

*ḥikmat*: traditional Islamic philosophy or theosophy.

*ḥujja*: proof, argument, self-evidence; in Shiʿi theology, a term used to refer to the Imam, the 'proof' of God on earth.

*ijtihād*: literally, exertion; the practice of applying one's reason directly to the principles of jurisprudence (*uṣūl,* q.v.); one qualified to perform such a function being termed a *mujtahid* (q.v.).

*al-ilāhiyyāt bi-maʿnā'l-ʿāmm*: theology in the general sense; comprising such principles as the nature of being, definitions of substance and accidents, etc.

*al-ilāhiyyāt bi-maʿnā'l-khāṣṣ*: theology in the specific sense; comprising such principles as the divine attributes, prophecy, eschatology, etc.

*imāma*: the principle of religious leadership devolving in Shiʿism upon a religious authority deemed to be divinely appointed (and not humanly selected), the authority being designated an Imam.

*īmān*: faith.

*ʿiṣma*: inerrancy, a quality attributed to Prophets, and in Shiʿism also to the Imāms and to Fāṭima, daughter of the Prophet. The root meaning is protection, one having the quality of *ʿiṣma* being called *maʿṣūm* (q.v.), 'protected' by God from the commission of sin and gross error.

*jabr*: absolute predeterminism or divine compulsion, a doctrine that negates the reality of man's free will in respect of action.

*jalāl*: majesty; in Shiʿi theology, a term denoting certain divine attributes, those which negate all imperfection or deficiency in regard to God and are therefore also called *salbī,* 'negative', attributes.

*jamāl*: beauty; in Shiʿi theology referring to those attributes and qualities of the divine nature that are positively affirmed as such and are therefore called *thubūtī,* 'positive' attributes.

*karāma*: a 'charism', miraculous act, performed by someone other than a Prophet; a miracle performed by a Prophet is referred to as a *muʿjiza* (q.v.).

*khāliqiyya*: creatorship, the quality pertaining to one who creates.

*kufr*: disbelief, one who disbelieves being a *kāfir.*

*maʿād*: literally the 'place of return'; the domain of the Hereafter.

*madhhab*: school of jurisprudence.

*Mahdī*: literally the 'guided one'; the awaited restorer of Islam and justice worldwide; in Shiʿism identified with the Twelfth Imam, currently in occultation (*ghayba,* q.v.).

*makrūh*: 'discouraged', one of the five categories of Islamic law, pertaining to actions, the others being *wājib* (obligatory), *mustaḥabb* (recommended), *mubāḥ* (indifferent), *ḥarām* (prohibited).

*maskh*: the transformation of the outer bodily form of a given human soul, not to be confused with *tanāsukh* (q.v.), 'reincarnation'.

*maʿṣūm*: one who is 'protected' by God from the commission of sin and gross error. In Shiʿism, this quality is attributed to the Prophets and the *ahl al-bayt*; traditionally, reference is made to the fourteen *maʿsūmīn*—the Prophet, his daughter Fāṭima, and the twelve Imams.

*mawlā*: a term which combines the following meanings: master, protector, nearest, dearest.

*muʿaṭṭila*: a negative designation of those theologians who strip or negate all attributes from the divine nature. Mostly applied to the Baghdadi school of Muʿtazilism.

*mubāḥ*: 'indifferent', one of the five categories of Islamic law, pertaining to actions, the others being *wājib* (obligatory), *mustaḥabb* (recommended), *ḥarām* (prohibited) and *makrūh* (discouraged).

*muḥaddath*: one to whom divine speech has been addressed; in Shiʿism, referring not just to the Prophets but also to the Imams and certain saints.

*muʿjiza*: a miracle, by a Prophet, the literal meaning of the word being 'that which weakens', i.e. that which weakens disbelief in God and the Prophet.

*mujtahid*: an authority in jurisprudence, one deemed capable of exercising *ijtihād* (q.v.), independent reasoning, to particular issues in order to arrive at juristic rulings based on the principles (*uṣūl*) (q.v.) of jurisprudence.

*mumkin al-wujūd*: a specifically Peripatetic philosophical term referring to a possible or contingent being, in contrast to *wājib al-wujūd* (q.v.) necessary being, that is, God.

*mustaḥabb*: 'recommended', one of the five categories of Islamic law, pertaining to actions, the others being *mubāḥ* (indifferent) and *makrūh* (discouraged), *ḥarām* (prohibited) and *wājib* (obligatory).

*mutʿa*: temporary marriage; permissible in Shiʿi jurisprudence, prohibited in Sunni jurisprudence.

*mutawātir*: in the science of hadith classification this term refers to a saying of the Prophet (and, in Shʿism, to a saying of any of the Imams), to which the highest degree of authenticity (*tawātur*, q.v.) is attributed, a saying confirmed by multiple chains of transmission.

*muwaḥḥid*: one who professes *tawḥīd* (q.v.), affirms the oneness of God.

*naqlī*: transmitted; referring, in the traditional classification of Islamic knowledge, to those sciences of a revealed nature transmitted by tradition, in contrast to those designated *ʿaqlī* (q.v.) which are directly accessible by the intellect.

*naṣṣ*: text or authoritative proof-text; also meaning the explicit designation by the Prophet of his successor, or by the Imam of his successor.

*nubuwwa*: prophecy.

*qaḍāʾ wa qadar*: the term refers to divine pre-destination, the meaning of the first word being related to the divine decree, and that of the second, to the 'measure' or 'portion' or 'lot' that is decreed.

*rajʿa*: 'return'; in Shiʿism, a doctrine which holds that certain individuals will reappear on earth before the Resurrection.

*shirk*: polytheism or associationism, the attribution of partners (*sharīk*, pl. *shurakāʾ*) with God, either as objects of worship or as sources of creation and governance.

*tafwīḍ*: the doctrine according to which man has absolute liberty in respect of his actions.

*taḥrīf*: alteration, of a revealed text.

*tanāsukh*: reincarnation, transmigration of souls, the attachment of the same soul to successive bodies, to be distinguished from *maskh* (q.v.), 'transformation'.

*tanzīh*: conceiving of God's utter incomparability or transcendence; in contrast with *tashbīh* (q.v.), 'making similar'.

*taqiyya*: concealment or dissimulation of one's true beliefs in circumstances where life, honour, or property would be endangered if they were revealed.

*taqlīd*: 'imitation'; the following of authoritative guidance, principally in the domain of jurisprudence.

*tashbīh*: 'making similar'; in Shiʿi theology, a mode of anthropomorphism by which God is regarded as similar to created things. To be contrasted with *tanzīh* (q.v.), pertaining to God's utter incomparability or transcendence.

*tawassul*: resort to intermediaries; principally the practice of petitionary prayer, addressed to God through a holy personage such as a Prophet or a saint.

*tawātur*: in the science of hadith classification refers to the highest degree of authenticity that can be given to a saying of the Prophet (and, in Shiʿism, to a saying of any of the Imams), such a saying being referred to as *mutawātir* (q.v.).

*tawḥīd*: literally 'making one': in theological terms, the affirmation of the oneness of God; in spiritual terms, the realization of the sole reality of God.

*uṣūl*: literally, 'roots' (s. *aṣl*); referring to primary principles, either of religion (*uṣūl al-dīn*), or of jurisprudence (*uṣūl al-fiqh*).

*wājib*: 'obligatory', one of the five categories of Islamic law, pertaining to actions, the others being *mubāḥ* (indifferent), *makrūh* (discouraged), *ḥarām* (prohibited), *wājib* (obligatory) and *mustaḥabb* (recommended).

*wājib al-wujūd*: a specifically Peripatetic philosophical term, referring to 'necessary being', that is, God; in contrast to *mumkin al-wujūd* (q.v.), 'possible being'.

*wasīla* (pl. *wasā'il*): intermediary means, such as natural causes, to which one has recourse for the sake of achieving given ends.

# Bibliography

(Note on dates: Where two sets of publication dates are given for a title, the first refers to the Hijra (lunar-based) calendar, and the second to the Common Era calendar; occasionally the solar-based (Shamsi) Hijra calendar, in use in Iran, is cited and is followed by the abbreviation 'Sh.')


'Abd al-Jabbār al-Mu'tazilī, Qāḍī. *Sharḥ al-uṣūl al-khamsa.* Cairo, 1988.

Ālūsī, Maḥmūd. *Rūḥ al-ma'ānī.* Beirut, n.d.

Amīn, Muḥsin. *A'yān al-Shī'a.* Beirut, 1982.

al-Amīnī, 'Abd al-Ḥusayn. *al-Ghadīr.* Beirut, 1387/1967.

Amir-Moezzi, M.A. *The Divine Guide in Early Shi'ism: The Sources of Esotericism in Islam,* trans. D. Streight. Albany, N.Y., 1994.

al-Arbalī, 'Alī b. 'Īsā. *Kashf al-ghima fī ma'rifat al-a'imma.* Beirut, 1985.

al-Ash'arī, Abu'l-Ḥasan 'Alī b. Ismā'īl. *al-Ibāna 'an uṣūl al-diyāna.* Damascus, 1981.

—— *Maqālāt al-Islāmiyyīn.* Wiesbaden, 1980.

Ayoub, Mahmoud. *Redemptive Suffering in Islam.* The Hague, 1978.

Badr al-'Ayn, Muḥammad b. Aḥmad. *'Umdat al-qārī fī sharḥ ṣaḥīḥ al-Bukhārī.* Beirut, n.d.

al-Baghdādī, Khaṭīb. *Ta'rīkh Baghdād.* Beirut, n.d.

al-Bukhārī, Muḥammad. *Ṣaḥīḥ.* Cairo, 1378/1957–8.

Corbin, Henry. *En Islam iranien.* Paris, 1971–2.

Dabashi, Hamid. 'Mīr Dāmād and the Founding of the School of Iṣfahān', in S.H. Nasr and O. Leaman, eds, *History of Islamic Philosophy.* London, 1996. Vol. 1, pp. 597–634.

Daftary, Farhad. *The Ismā'īlīs: Their History and Doctrines.* Cambridge, 1990.

al-Dārimī, 'Abd Allāh. *Sunan.* Beirut, 1978.

al-Dhahabī, Muḥammad. *Mīzān al-iʿtidāl.* Beirut, 1963.
Dīnawarī, ʿAbd Allāh b. Muslim. *al-Imāma wa'l-siyāsa.* Cairo, n.d.
Diyār Bakrī, Ḥusayn b. Muḥammad. *Ta'rīkh al-khamīs fī aḥwāl anfus nafīs.* Beirut, n.d.
Fakhr al-Islām, Muḥammad Ṣādiq. *Anīs al-aʿlām fī nuṣrat al-islām.* Tehran, 1404/1983.
Halm, Heinz. *The Fatimids and their Traditions of Learning.* London, 1997.
—— *Shiism,* tr. J. Watson. Edinburgh, 1991.
al-Ḥillī, ʿAllāma Abū Manṣūr Ḥasan. *Kashf al-murād fī sharḥ tajrīd al-iʿtiqād.* Qom, 1413/1992.
al-Hindī, ʿAlā' al-Dīn. *Kanz al-ʿummāl.* Beirut, 1985.
Ḥurr al-ʿĀmilī, Muḥammad b. al-Ḥasan. *Wasā'il al-Shīʿa.* Beirut, 1403/1982.
Hussain, Jassim. *The Occultation of the Twelfth Imam.* London, 1982.
Ibn Athīr, Mubārak b. Muḥammad. *Jāmiʿ al-uṣūl.* Beirut, 1980.
Ibn Fāris, Aḥmad b. Zakarīya. *Muqāyis al-lugha.* Cairo, n.d.
Ibn Ḥajar al-ʿAsqalānī. *Fatḥ al-bārī.* Beirut, 1402/1981.
Ibn Ḥanbal, Aḥmad. *Musnad.* Cairo, n.d.
—— *al-Sunna.* Beirut, 1405/1983.
Ibn Ḥijr, Aḥmad. *al-Ṣawāʿiq al-muḥriqa.* Cairo, 1965.
Ibn Hishām, ʿAbd al-Malik. *al-Sīra al-nabawiyya.* Beirut, n.d.
Ibn Māja. *Sunan.* Beirut, 1975.
Ibn al-Nadīm, Muḥammad b. Isḥāq. *al-Fihrist.* Cairo, n.d.
al-Iṣfahānī, Abū Nuʿaym. *Ḥilyat al-awliyā'.* Beirut, 1967.
al-Iṣfahānī, Rāghib. *al-Mufridāt fī gharīb al-Qur'ān.* Cairo, 1324/1906.
Jafri, S.H.M. *The Origins and Early Development of Shīʿa Islam.* London, 1979.
Khumaynī, Ayatollah Ruḥollāh. *Tahdhīb al-uṣūl.* Qom 1405/1984.
Kohlberg, Etan. *Belief and Law in Imāmī Shīʿism.* Aldershot, 1991.
al-Kūfī, Ḥāfiẓ Muḥammad b. Sulaymān. *Manāqib al-Imām amīr al-mu'minīn.* Qom, 1412/1991.
al-Kulaynī, Abū Jaʿfar Muḥammad. *al-Uṣūl min al-kāfī.* Beirut, 1401/1981.
Lalani, Arzina. *Early Shīʿī Thought: The Teachings of Imam Muḥammad al-Bāqir.* London, 2000.
LeBon, Gustav. *Tamaddun-i islāmī wa gharb,* Persian trans. of *Islamic Civilization and the West.* Tehran, 1376/1956.
Madelung, Wilferd. *The Succession to Muḥammad: A Study of the Early Caliphate.* Cambridge, 1997.
al-Majlisī, Muḥammad Bāqir. *Biḥār al-anwār.* Beirut, 1403/1983.

al-Maqrīzī, Aḥmad b. ʿAlī. *Imtāʿ al-asmāʿ*. Cairo, 1981.
—— *al-Mawāʿiẓ wa'l-iʿtibār bi dhikr al-khiṭaṭ wa'l-āthār*. Būlāq, 1270/1853.
Miṣrī, Aḥmad Amīn. *Fajr al-Islām*. Beirut, 1969.
Murtaḍā, Sayyid. *Tanzīh al-anbiyā'*. Tabriz, 1290/1873.
al-Muzaffar, M.R. *The Faith of Shiʿa Islam*. London, 1983.
al-Najāshī, Aḥmad. *Rijāl al-Najāshī*. Beirut, 1409/1988.
al-Nasafī, ʿAbd Allāh. *Tafsīr al-Nasafī*. Beirut, 1998.
Nāṣir Khusraw. *Knowledge and Liberation*, a new edition and English translation of *Gushāyish wa Rahāyish*, by F.M. Hunzai. London, 1998.
Nasr, Seyyed Hossein. 'Religion in Safavid Persia', *Iranian Studies*, 7 (1974), pp. 271–86.
—— 'Spiritual Movements, Philosophy and Theology in the Safavid Period', in *The Cambridge History of Iran*, vol. 6, *The Timurid and Safavid Periods*, ed. P. Jackson and L. Lockhart. Cambridge, 1986, pp. 656–97.
—— 'The School of Iṣpahān', in M.M. Sharif, ed., *A History of Muslim Philosophy*. Wiesbaden, 1966. vol. 2, pp. 904–32.
—— 'The Metaphysics of Ṣadr al-Dīn Shīrāzī and Islamic Philosophy in Qajar Iran', in C.E. Bosworth and C. Hillenbrand, ed., *Qajar Iran*. Edinburgh, 1983, pp. 177–98.
Nasr, S.H., H. Dabashi and S.V.R. Nasr. *Shiʿism: Doctrines, Thought and Spirituality* Albany, N.Y., 1988.
—— *Expectations of the Millennium: Shiʿism in History*. Albany, N.Y., 1989.
al-Nawbakhtī, al-Ḥasan b. Mūsā. *Firaq al-Shīʿa*. Beirut, 1405/1984.
al-Naysābūrī, Muḥammad b.ʿAbd Allāh al-Ḥākim. *al-Mustadrak*. Beirut, n.d.
al-Nisā'ī, Aḥmad b. Shuʿayb. *Khaṣā'iṣ al-Imām ʿAlī*. Qom, 1983.
al-Qandūzī, Sulaymān b. Ibrāhīm. *Yanābīʿ al-muwadda*. Tehran, 1416/1995.
al-Qāsimī, Muḥammad Jamāl al-Dīn. *Maḥāsin al-ta'wīl*. Beirut, 1979.
al-Qastallānī, Aḥmad b. Muḥammad. *al-Mawāhib al-laduniyya*. Beirut, 1991.
al-Qummī, ʿAbbās. *Safīnat al-biḥār*. Qom, 1416/1995.
al-Qūshajī, ʿAlā' al-Dīn. *Sharḥ tajrīd al-iʿtiqād*. Tabriz, 1307/1889.
al-Qushayrī, Muslim b. al-Ḥajjāj. *Ṣaḥīḥ*. Cairo, n.d.
al-Rāzī, Fakhr al-Dīn. *ʿIṣmat al-anbiyā'*. Jeddah, 1407/1986.
—— *al-Tafsīr al-kabīr*. Beirut, n.d.
Riḍā, Rashīd. *Tafsīr al-manār*. Cairo, 1954.

—— *al-Waḥy al-Muḥammadī.* Beirut, 1406/1985.
Sachedina, A.A. *Islamic Messianism: The Idea of the Mahdi in Twelver Shiʿism.* New York, 1981.
Sadiq, K. and A.M. Naqvi. *A Manual of Islamic Beliefs and Practices.* London 1990, 1992. 2 vols.
al-Ṣaffār, Muḥammad b. Ḥasan. *Baṣāʾir al-darajāt.* Tehran, 1380/1960.
Savory, R.M. *Iran under the Safavids.* London, 1980.
Serjeant, Robert B. 'The Zaydīs', in A. J. Arberry, ed., *Religion in the Middle East.* Cambridge, 1969. vol. 2, pp. 285–301.
al-Shahrastānī, ʿAbd al-Karīm. *Kitāb al-Milal waʾl-niḥal.* Beirut, 1990.
al-Sharīf al-Raḍī, Muḥammad b. al-Ḥusayn. *Nahj al-balāgha.* Qom, 1395/1975.
al-Shawkānī, Muḥammad b. ʿAlī. *Fatḥ al-qadīr.* Beirut, n.d.
Shaykh Mufīd, Abū ʿAbd Allāh Muḥammad. *Taṣḥīḥ al-iʿtiqād.* Tabriz, 1371/1951.
—— *Kitāb al-Irshād: The Book of Guidance into the Lives of the Twelve Imams,* trans. I.K.A. Howard. London, 1981.
—— *Awāʾil al-maqālāt fiʾl-madhāhib waʾl-mukhtārāt.* Tabriz, 1371/1951.
Shaykh Ṣadūq (Ibn Babawayh), Abū Jaʿfar al-Qummī. *ʿIlal al-sharāyiʿ.* Beirut, 1966.
—— *Man la yaḥḍuruhuʾl-faqīh.* Tehran, 1390/1970.
—— *Kitāb al-tawḥīd.* Qom, 1398/1978.
—— *Amālī.* Beirut, 1400/1979.
—— *al-Khiṣāl.* Qom, 1403/1982.
—— *ʿUyūn akhbār al-Riḍā.* Beirut, 1404/1983.
—— *Kamāl al-dīn.* Qom, 1405/1983.
al-Shīrāzī, Ṣadr al-Dīn. *al-Asfār al-arbaʿ.* Beirut, 1402/1981.
Sobhani, Ayatollah Jaʿfar. *Mafāhīm al-Qurʾān.* Qom, 1413/1992.
—— *al-Ilāhiyyāt.* Qom, 1417/1996.
—— *Furūgh-i vilāyat.* Tehran, 1378 Sh./1999.
—— *Manshūr-i jāvīd-i Qurʾān.* Qom, 1984–99.
—— *The Message—The Holy Prophet of Allāh.* Tehran, n.d.
Strothmann, Rudolf. 'al-Zaidīya' in *Encyclopedia of Islam* (1st edition), vol. 4, pp. 1196–8.
al-Suyūṭī, Jalāl al-Dīn. *Taʾrīkh al-khulafāʾ.* Cairo, 1384/1964.
—— *al-Itqān fī ʿulūm al-Qurʾān.* Cairo, 1387/1967.
—— *al-Durr al-manthūr.* Beirut, 1973.
—— *al-Khaṣāʾiṣ al-kubrā.* Hyderabad, 1319/1901.

al-Ṭabarī, Abū Ja'far Muḥammad. *Jami' al-bayān*. Beirut, 1980.
—— *Ta'rīkh al-rusul wa'l-mulūk*. Beirut, 1408/1986.
al-Ṭabarsī, Faḍl b. al-Ḥasan. *Majma' al-bayān*. Tehran, n.d.
Ṭabāṭabā'ī, 'Allāma Muḥammad Ḥusayn. *al-Mīzān*. Beirut, 1393/1973.
—— *Shi'ite Islam*, trans. and ed. S.H. Nasr. Albany, N.Y., 1975.
al-Taftāzānī, Mas'ūd b. 'Umar. *Sharḥ al-maqāṣid*. Istanbul, 1305/1887.
Ṭihrānī, Āghā Buzurg. *al-Dharī'a ilā taṣānīf al-Shī'a*. Beirut, n.d.
al-Tirmidhī, Muḥammad b.'Īsā. *Sunan*. Beirut, n.d.
Ṭūsī, Naṣīr al-Dīn. *Contemplation and Action*, a new edition and English translation of *Sayr wa Sulūk* by S.J. Badakhchani. London, 1998.
—— *Tajrīd al-i'tiqād*. Sidon, 1353/1934.
al-Ṭūsī, Shaykh Muḥammad b. Ḥasan. *al-Fihrist*. Najaf, 1380/1960.
—— *Kitāb al-ghayba*. Najaf, 1385/1965.
—— *'Iddat al-uṣūl*. Qom, 1404/1983.
—— *al-Khilāf*. Qom, 1416/1995.
al-Zarqānī, Muḥammad b. 'Abd al-Bāqī. *Sharḥ Zarqānī*. Cairo, n.d.

# Index